'Ciaran is the rarest thing: a writer of heart and clarity, who has spent thousands of hours absorbing the rules, codes and heartbreaks of life in some of London's most vulnerable communities . . . I read everything that Ciaran writes because it feels necessary to understand the city that I live in'

Sam Knight, *New Yorker* staff writer

'A potent mix of personal anecdote, social history and politics . . . the result is trenchant, page-turning and sometimes challenging reading, but also a blueprint for positive change'

Caroline Sanderson, *The Bookseller*, 'Editor's Choice'

'A crucial contribution and a compelling read. Thapar combines captivating narratives with a sophisticated understanding of the policy landscape – a must-read book for anyone interested in, or working to improve, the safety and well-being of children and young people'

Keir Irwin-Rogers, Lecturer in Criminology,
The Open University; lead criminologist to
the Youth Violence Commission

'*Cut Short* is at once a compelling memoir, a biting critique of Britain's hideous inequality, and a beautiful tribute to the remarkable strength and spark of London's youth – and those who work with them. Weaving together reflective autobiography, expert interviews and the stories of young people he works with, Ciaran Thapar paints a portrait of London's greatest assets and deepest injustices. Everyone – from teenagers to government ministers – can learn a lot about contemporary Britain from *Cut Short*'

Luke Billingham, youth and community worker,
co-author of the Youth Violence Commission Final Report

Cut Short

'Honest, authentic and raw, this book confronts our deepest assumptions about violence, and lays down a transformative path to peace'

David Lammy MP

'A devastating and beautifully drawn tribute to the young boys that the media turns into statistics of knife crime. In telling their stories, Ciaran Thapar brings to the page their dreams, their imaginations and their hearts'

Candice Carty-Williams, author of *Queenie*

'Ciaran's work is informed by lived experience at the frontline of social change. It takes a sensitive and respectful look at the truths less often told'

George the Poet

'An incredibly important look at the plight of Britain's youth, delivered with clarity, honesty and an open heart. Brilliantly, compellingly written, this lays out the impact of cuts to youth services over the last decade and the effect it's had on young people. Looking at issues like gentrification, education, policing, race/class and opportunity, this presents a sobering look at what it means to be young and live in the city in Britain today. As a former youth worker who witnessed these cuts myself, I'm grateful to Ciaran for this honest and compelling book'

Nikesh Shukla, editor of *The Good Immigrant* and author of *Brown Baby*

'Angry, impassioned, informed, accurate – the story behind the cutting short of public health and young lives'

Danny Dorling, author of *Inequality and the 1%*

'Gripping and dramatic yet also poignant and reflective, *Cut Short* is essential for our times. Deftly weaving together stories of youth brilliance and youth violence, academy schools, gentrification, cops and cutting-edge rap music, what jumps off the page most of all is Thapar's empathy, and his ability to capture the hopes and fears of his mostly young interviewees – if you want to truly understand London in the 2020s, there is no better place to start'

Dan Hancox, author of *Inner City Pressure*

'*Cut Short*'s superpower is Ciaran's unique experiences in seeing, week by week, session by session, how youth work and trained mentoring can turn, not just a young person, but a whole community around. His insights of every layer of the system, from prisons to youth centres to committee rooms at Westminster allow him to lay out a framework for a real solution. I came away from this book enraged, enlightened and with a sense of urgency to do something'

Annie Mac, DJ

'No bullshit, no filter, just facts from the trenches of the most neglected in society, and the power of music, mentorship and education to change lives. Everyone must read this'

Toddla T, DJ

'This book strongly gives a voice to the voiceless . . . essential reading'
Kenny Allstar, DJ

'Big up Ciaran x10 on the new book. Ciaran was basically there from where we really started to take off and it's good to see him doing big things and always tryna encourage and give back to the youth 'cause they need that'

Skengdo, rapper

'Shout out Ciaran on the new book, everyone go cop that and take in the gems – real life issues being addressed. It's important to know that even though the book's called *Cut Short* your life don't have to be cut short, as long as you're breathing you got opportunities if you just focus and stay consistent'

AM, rapper

Cut Short

Youth Violence, Loss and Hope in the City

CIARAN THAPAR

VIKING

an imprint of

PENGUIN BOOKS

The events described in this book are based on the life, experiences and recollections of the author. Confidentiality and the privacy and safety of others have been taken very seriously. Many of the names and identifying features have been changed; many of the stories told are not based on any one specific individual. Any similarities are purely coincidental.

VIKING

UK | USA | Canada | Ireland | Australia
India | New Zealand | South Africa

Viking is part of the Penguin Random House group of companies
whose addresses can be found at global.penguinrandomhouse.com.

Penguin
Random House
UK

First published 2021
001

Copyright © Ciaran Thapar, 2021

The moral right of the author has been asserted

Set in 12/14.75 pt Bembo Book MT Std
Typeset by Jouve (UK), Milton Keynes
Printed and bound in Great Britain by Clays Ltd, Elcograf S.p.A.

The authorized representative in the EEA is Penguin Random House Ireland,
Morrison Chambers, 32 Nassau Street, Dublin D02 YH68

A CIP catalogue record for this book is available from the British Library

ISBN: 978-0-241-43498-7

Follow us on LinkedIn: https://www.linkedin.com/company/penguin-connect/

www.greenpenguin.co.uk

MIX
Paper from
responsible sources
FSC
www.fsc.org   FSC® C018179

Penguin Random House is committed to a
sustainable future for our business, our readers
and our planet. This book is made from Forest
Stewardship Council® certified paper.

In loving memory of Michael Anthony Jonas
Earth's Blessing: 20 October 2000
Heaven's Gain: 2 November 2017

'I spit these stories for the lost souls that got froze
in time. The good youts that never got home . . .
I do it for my boys that never got no food for thought
and got fed time.'

– Jesse James Solomon

Contents

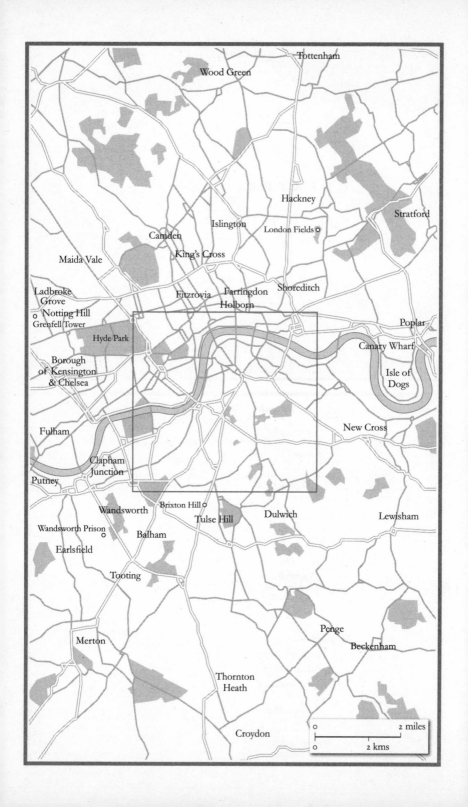

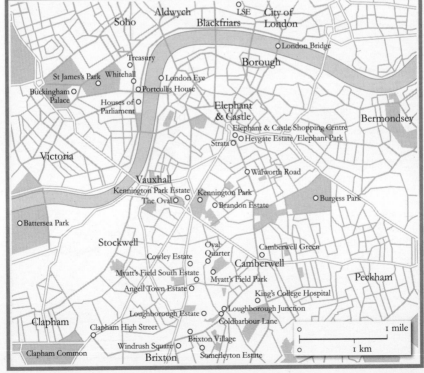

Prologue

The Nine Night: July 2018

A teenage boy sprints through the front door of Jacob Sawyer Community Centre, darting into the foyer. Seeking a hiding place, his momentum carries him to the far side of the main room, where he dives beneath a defunct pool table.

The atmosphere is buzzing. People have gathered for a Nine Night: a Caribbean funeral wake on the ninth night after a death, a chance for friends and relatives to say their goodbyes in binding catharsis. Dancing, storytelling, singing, feasting and praying are commonplace. Tonight, people are remembering an elderly woman who lived a stone's throw from the centre's front door. The Nine Night has drawn a crowd.

Sat on the table in the main room is a framed, smiley photograph of the fallen, next to a cross and some tea lights. Reggae music plays from an old sound system. Some guests – children, grandchildren, friends, young and old – stand recounting fond memories and whispering short prayers; others queue up at a foldaway table to write messages in a book of condolences. In the kitchen, pots of Jamaican dishes like stew chicken and rice-and-peas sit on the counter. A circle of older men sits outside in the small garden, under the night sky, beside painted wooden pots filled with growing vegetables planted by local teenagers. They play dominoes while smoking, holding cups of white rum and bottles of Dragon Stout.

A few seconds after the boy's entrance, with people beginning to stir, wondering who has burst the night's ritualistic bubble, another boy enters the building. He heads through the foyer, stopping on reaching the main room. He is dressed in black tracksuit bottoms, a black-and-green Deliveroo jacket and a black moped helmet, its tinted visor clicked shut. From the look of his slight frame, he can't be much older than sixteen or seventeen. He has a sawn-off shotgun. He holds the weapon awkwardly. His hands are bony, their bareness the only evidence of his dark skin.

Conversations stop. Like an audience at the theatre watching the arrival of a new character on stage, everyone turns in unison to face the intruder. The door to the men's toilet bursts open and slams shut as someone dives inside to take refuge. Elders glare, angry at this ultimate violation. The boy wrapped in shadows beneath the pool table remains hidden from view, his life spared by the power of his community.

Two Days Earlier

Tony arrived at the Jacob Sawyer Community Centre at 10 a.m., wearing jeans and a light-blue polo shirt. At five foot nine inches, having recently turned fifty-one, he was well-built, filled out with a combination of natural strength and desk-bound middle age. His grade-1 hair was cut neatly, with clean, straight lines around its edges, faded to his bare skin on the sides. As Managing Director, he was responsible for the day-to-day running of the centre, which had served local young people for the best part of half a century.

Tony had seen on the BBC ten o'clock news that there had been a murder nearby. A seventeen-year-old boy had been stabbed and left on a road in Camberwell. Still alive, he was found by a member of the public and taken to King's College Hospital a few hundred metres away. He died in the night.

Tony turned on his computer and opened his emails. The

morning sun peered over the distant housing blocks and into the office windows, lighting up his keyboard. At 11 a.m. he received a phone call from a police inspector. Because of the blood trail left along the backstreets, the police believed the murdered boy was stabbed somewhere near the community centre before being carried to his death on the back of a moped. An investigation was underway. The inspector requested a meeting with Tony to get hold of the centre's CCTV footage. Tony mentioned that Nike had been filming an advert out on the astroturf the day before and the inspector said he'd need to contact them for footage they'd captured. He wanted to speak to Tony about how they could keep the local community as safe as possible. They both knew this murder was not a stand-alone event. It would have roots in the past, and further ramifications in the future.

The rest of the morning was quiet. Tony took calls from concerned members of the community. Other staff members sat at their desks completing paperwork and talking to one another, speculating about what might have happened. The gardener came. A few young men, regulars at the centre, passed by to greet Tony through the windows from outside in the car park. They didn't stay for long, before walking up the road to leave, glancing over their shoulders self-consciously as they went.

The inspector arrived with two police officers in the late afternoon. They sat opposite Tony on chairs in the classroom at the side of the building. On the purple walls next to them were stencilled, in green, the words 'Respect', 'Loyalty' and 'Time'. Because the victim of the murder was from Kennington, roughly two kilometres north of the centre, they agreed that a retaliation was likely, and that the centre should therefore stay open as a place for young people to feel safe. At the end of their meeting Tony showed the officers out into the car park, where they got into their car and pulled away. Gravel crunched under tyres, then silence fell.

Tony hadn't eaten yet, so his stomach growled. He pulled out a cigarette from its pack, wiping his forehead with his handkerchief and closing his eyes.

On the other side of Jacob Sawyer was a mechanic's, where the scrape and hammer of metal would occasionally rip through the hum of local life. On the far side of that stood brick railway arches. A low chug echoed, signalling the approach of an overground train. At rush hour, full carriages would trundle by every few minutes, taking people from the leafy southern suburbs to and from the city centre. The train moved lethargically, as if slowed down by muggy heat. Tired, sluggish commuters were returning to their homes, leaning against one another and the doors and the windows in tight formation, tutting, cursing in their minds' racket, sweating.

Tony took long tokes on the cigarette tucked between curled fingers. His eyes focused on a faded bouquet of flowers leant against the black metal fence across the road. A tattered red T-shirt had been wrapped around the railings nearby to commemorate another son – brother, nephew, grandson, friend, aspiring footballer – murdered years before. Glancing up the road, Tony saw the SOCO team, scene-of-crime officers, removing the red-and-white tape from between two lamp posts. They'd closed the road to wipe blood samples from the tarmac.

Tony's mind was jumping from concern to concern. His stomach growled again and he thought about walking to get a patty. He needed to sort this month's payroll, ensure the safety of his young people, prevent local parents from panicking and maintain the easily tarnished reputation of the centre. He wondered who was responsible for the murder, taking another long drag on his cigarette.

A white BMW drove past, playing the new anthem of popular

Harlesden rapper Nines, 'I See You Shining'. Over the summer, the song's title had become a subtle catchphrase for London's teenagers to uplift one another in conversation. The driver nodded at Tony through his open window. Tony feigned a smile, taking the final draw of his cigarette. The car sped off, slowing for the road bump. The buzz of a fly in his ear caused Tony to swat it away, then he heard a small child crying in a pram and the furious mother yelling, 'Be quiet!'

Tony threw his cigarette to the floor, stubbing it out with the bottom of his black Nikes. He grabbed his phone to start making some calls.

The Next Day

In the late afternoon Carl picked up his younger brother from a football tournament taking place on the astroturf pitch out the back of Jacob Sawyer. Sometimes he didn't like his brother hanging out at Sawyer. It was a safe place for him to use the recording studio, get fed and see his friends. But right now the centre felt different to normal Friday nights. Everyone was on edge because of the murder earlier in the week.

Carl was wearing black tapered tracksuit bottoms and a black T-shirt. His hair was longer than usual, forming a thick Afro. His friends arrived at Jacob Sawyer and sat with him on the pink chairs in the main room. Their group talked about what they could do later that night because it was the birthday of one of their friends.

When football finished, the centre closed for the night. As Carl and the other boys were leaving, Tony told them all to be careful over the weekend. Carl left with his brother, announcing to his friends that he'd come back in a couple of hours. The pair walked north to go home, where they ate a plate of food that their mum had prepared, before Carl went back out on his moped to meet the others. It was getting dark.

When Carl arrived, he parked his moped. One of his friends held his phone up high to record the group in a selfie video on Snapchat. Carl was leaning against a brick wall. In the corner of his eye he saw two more of his friends approaching through the driveway. They were walking quickly, glancing backwards over their shoulders. Then they started sprinting.

'OI, IT'S PAIGONS! IT'S PAIGONS!' one yelled.

Two mopeds carrying two passengers each, all of them wearing helmets and Deliveroo jackets, like an army in uniform, mounted the kerb. They entered the car park, their engines buzzing loudly.

Carl saw that one of the passengers was cocking a gun. He ran with everyone else in the opposite direction. A gunshot fired behind him. A bullet whizzed past Carl's ear, smashing into the block wall, shattering a brick. As he passed his parked moped, its lights flashed and its alarm started ringing.

Carl's heart thumped loud and fast in his ears. He could hear the footsteps of the others running away and the intruders giving chase. He darted round a hedge and sprinted towards the alleyway that led into the estate. He hopped over the metal bars and his trainers hit the concrete hard on the other side. He stumbled and almost fell. Another gunshot sounded from behind him. Carl thought about his other friends who weren't so fast. He thought about his mum and his brother. He thought he might be about to die.

Carl was sprinting – nobody could catch him – but he felt like he was floating. He weaved through the estate's warren, round the grass area with the swings and pull-up bars, and then past the music studio. When he arrived at the football cage, he stopped. He bent over, panting and speechless. His T-shirt was damp with sweat, but he was safe. Why did the person chasing him only have two bullets? Carl was lucky that he didn't have more.

He walked home, thanking God that he was still alive. He took out his phone from his tracksuit pocket and called one of his friends.

'This road ting is long, fam! I nearly just got burst!' Carl explained. His friend at the other end of the line, who lived in one of the Loughborough blocks, replied that he'd heard the gunshots.

When Carl hung up the call there was a notification showing on his screen. He'd received a Snapchat message. It showed them all hanging out, ending with the loud bang of the first gunshot.

Later that night, Carl kept checking Snapchat every few minutes to figure out where his opps were. One of his friends had gone back to where the gun was fired and captured another video. It showed a bullet shell resting on the floor of the block stairwell.

The Nine Night

'Rah!' the faceless intruder blurts out. Thirty, forty pairs of eyes stare back at him. His helmet wobbles as he looks left, then right, as the cackle of an idle moped engine cuts into the room from outside. He holds the shotgun in his sweaty hands. He starts to walk backwards, turns round and comes face-to-face with Andre, a security guard standing in the foyer. Andre moves forward to tackle him, but another guard grabs Andre before he gets too close.

The intruder bursts out of the front door. Andre walks over and peers out. The boy's trainers thud on the concrete before he jumps on to one of two mopeds, both carrying other masked riders. Andre grabs his phone and writes down the details of the moped, including its registration number.

White moped. Black helmet. Black and green jacket.

The mopeds speed off, revving their engines as they go, flying over the speed bump. Andre watches their red rear lights zoom off into the night.

It has taken roughly ten seconds from the moment the first boy hiding under the pool table ran into the community centre seeking refuge until the exit of the intruder. The same reggae song plays from the sound system in the main room. The same tea-light flames sway on the table.

Andre walks briskly into the staff office to ring an alarm to alert the police. In the main hall, whispers return to normal conversations. A few people hover by the pool table trying to comfort the boy underneath it, who remains knotted into a foetal position.

Andre heads outside. After a couple of minutes a police car with its sirens off turns into the road and whizzes towards where the men are standing.

'Which way?' the driver asks through the window.

Andre points north. The police car speeds off, slowing for the road bump.

Seventeen minutes later, during which time the stroke of midnight passes, an officer arrives at the centre in his car with a police dog. Andre is confused as to why there is a dog present. He tells the officer what happened. The policeman calls for backup, taking out his notepad to record the details.

Twenty-five minutes later, another police car arrives. Andre explains what happened again. Two of the officers walk inside and help to coax the boy out into the open from under the pool table. Looking like he has seen a ghost, the young man walks with the police silently through the foyer and out into the car park, where one officer opens the back door of their car for him to get in.

Some guests say their goodbyes and leave. But for others, the Nine Night cannot end. Family members and friends begin their remembrance again.

A little laughter, peace and prayer return to Jacob Sawyer.

Introduction: Cold Season

The British summer of 2018 was the hottest since records began. A heatwave between June and August brought temperatures peaking at 36 degrees Celsius during the last week of July – around the time of the Nine Night at Jacob Sawyer Community Centre. Most Londoners embraced the warmth after the dreary hibernation of winter. Yet it is understood by some that the summer is to be feared as much as celebrated. Not everyone can enjoy craft beer in a private garden, recline on deckchairs at a suburban picnic or ramble towards a pub lunch in the country-side. In the English capital city, once the seat of global imperial power, a citizen's capacity to enjoy the brighter months is a function of their socio-economic positioning; their freedom to act, move, spend money and think beyond daily subsistence.

School holidays turn hot pavements, beige patches of grass and rusty playgrounds into idle hangout spots. During the extended daylight hours, to thrive, or even plainly survive, young people must navigate the fickle moral code of the roads for longer, dodging the unpredictable moving parts of inner-city life. Parties and block barbecues are filled with laughter, and interrupted by arguments and punches. Speakers vibrate, dances break out, fizzy drinks wash down boxes of fast food. Skunk weed is smoked, something harder is sold. Knives are drawn. Screams yell: 'Leave him!'

The wariest don't attend the function. Some know to stay in, or away, restricting themselves to solo endeavours: playing video games or going to the BMX track to ride alone or flicking through Snapchat feeds and YouTube channels from the comfort of their single bed. These individuals have learnt about the risks they need not take; that stepping outside, showing their faces, migrating from one part of the city to another, can amount to a roll of the dice. It's not always worth it; a gamble whose odds are stacked up against them, adhered together by forces that are entirely out of their control: economics, trauma, greed, humidity. Thinly veiled chaos. Society's stratification-by-design, mapped over the same neat pavings that some people in a faraway land once believed were lined with gold; stretched across shrinking, privatized floor space; digitized in live streams and the Cloud; made visible in the red of bloodstained concrete.

For hormonal, competitive teenagers trying to make their mark, thick, sweaty heat raises tempers and the prospect of confrontation. Agendas collide, like atoms above a Bunsen burner. In the summertime, those who in wintry months are more likely to stay indoors – sheltered from the wet, leaf-pressed kerb, warmed by a radiator behind net curtains, held in detention after school, scratching graffiti into a wooden desk, protected beneath the tattered fabric of a hand-me-down puffer jacket – spill out into the public arena.

Monitoring youth violence becomes a heightened challenge. Adults tasked with maintaining order find it harder to predict, prevent or respond. You might say, in cruel logic, that if ethics were measured by temperature, summer is the cold season.

There was a peak in knife violence in the United Kingdom roughly a decade before 2018. The number of hospital admissions for knife assaults nationwide reached an all-time high, just short of 5,000, in 2007. The number of knife-related homicides reached its highest level ever, 272, in the same year, before incrementally falling, alongside the number of knife offences, to a low of 186 in 2015.

These statistics alone merely reveal the sharp tip of a deep iceberg. But in doing so, they signal something true about the wavering force of social trends over time in the darkest shadows of the metropolis. For centuries, violence among young people has taken place in London and other major cities like Liverpool and Glasgow, where poverty's victims must love and hate in close quarters. But in the few years leading up to 2015, it ceased to be a major public concern and was widely understood to have fallen, and to be falling. Soon, however, these downward slopes of shallow progress reached a valley basin. They started to creep upwards again. The tides turned.

Main indicators of year-on-year knife violence rose for the first time in a decade between 2015 and 2016. Across 2017, which became the worst year for deaths of children and teenagers since 2009 – 39 minors were killed by a knife across the UK, 20 in the capital city – it became accepted that youth violence was a social problem worth paying more urgent collective attention to again. Journalist-turned-academic Gary Younge and the *Guardian* newspaper launched 'Beyond the Blade', a year-long campaign to monitor, analyse and further the discourse about so-called 'knife crime'. A startled awareness had been bubbling away already in the least visible but most informed spaces: youth charities, social inclusion teams, hospital trauma units and hollowed-out police intelligence offices – those feeling the impact of government spending cuts. Coverage focusing on violence started to pop up on television screens, social media timelines and the front pages of newspapers. A cocktail of necessary concern, shaken with a self-fulfilling prophecy of panic, served over an icy public willingness to put yet another austerity-driven Conservative party into government, intoxicated wider society.

Three murders took place in the capital city across the last few hours of 2017 and the earliest hours of 2018. Londoners woke up to their New Year's Day mornings with yet more reports of tragedy in the news. It contradicted the sense of healthy renewal that gym membership deals, paper diaries with unsullied pages and Veganuary were otherwise instilling. By early April 2018, 47 people nationwide had been killed, most of them with a knife. With questionable validity, headlines reported that London's murder rate had temporarily surpassed that of New York, allowing President Donald Trump to take rhetorical jabs at London Mayor Sadiq Khan about his city's apparent insecurity.

Violence had not let up in the cold. But by the hotter months of 2018, as hot as any before them, people like myself, close to young people because of my community volunteering and relationships forged as a youth worker, felt a predictive tremor suggesting summer was going to deliver more tragedy. I was told to 'wait for the summer' or that 'the worst of the summer isn't here yet'. Teachers, parents, pastors, police and youth workers worried. In light of events happening in my part of town, it felt to me like they were right to.

I moved into Brixton, in south London, in 2015, after which my life consisted of working with, socializing among and writing about people who call London their home. Having felt the magnetic tug of the inner city for as long as I can remember while growing up among the sterile, grey Heathrow suburbs in the capital's west, I immersed myself in my new environment. Meanwhile, my dual career practices of youth work and writing developed organically: taking and giving, pulling and pushing, learning and teaching.

Education and youth work became a way to act on my beliefs about social justice. It let me draw from the privileges with which I was born and put them to a greater purpose. Both of my parents grew up in traditional working-class settings: my mum in a Church of England, White British, small-town household; my dad in an immigrant, Hindu Punjabi one in west London. So while my sisters and I were always lucky enough to enjoy childhoods free from financial and emotional stress, we were explicitly taught values – an automatic compassion for the circumstances of others, an appreciation for public services and an openness to diverse local community life – that my mum and dad had derived from their respective experiences as children growing up in the 1960s and 1970s. These values now underline my personal politics, the social impact I've sought to achieve in the pages of this book and, by extension, the purpose, voice and style of my writing.

As a respected GP, my dad served tens of thousands of local people while I was growing up. I have memories of being with him as a child, cycling along the river, or playing cricket in the park, or sitting down at a table at a pub with my two sisters and my mum, when a member of the public might interrupt us to thank him for helping them or someone close to them: their mother with her hip pains, their child with a chest infection, their partner with depression. 'My parents say to thank your dad for helping out my gran,' a student at my school once said. 'Your old man is the reason I'm still here talking to you,' an elderly man once told me while I painted the rooms at my dad's surgery over one summer holiday break.

I saw from a young age how people viewed their doctor as an integral cog in the mechanics of local life. To witness this admirable trait in a parent's professional identity – my mum is a school nurse, my grandmother was a school nurse and my great-grandfather was an English teacher – was to understand that to function and be valued in society you don't get on with things in isolation. You help out. You apply whatever capability you have to ensure others can benefit from the stable base of your own life. And through doing this, you don't just give, you learn, too – you gain, flourish and connect with people so that everyone is better off.

Youth work is also just fun; a role in which I can have autonomy to be myself, leverage my lasting interest in youth culture and solve problems creatively. In central London, I soon realized, I could do this under the comforting patchwork quilt of multicultural life that I crave as someone who grew up in a biracial household.

Simultaneously, writing became my way of making sense of the world; a means of untangling webs of injustice and bottling moments of inspiration. Fitting words together as sensitively and accurately as possible, like they were pieces of a complex puzzle, helped me to analyse my interactions and surroundings. This habit developed into a writing career by accident. I wouldn't have been able to dare try to write for a living without the privileges of my upbringing. I took risks with my career because I could afford to. I know that not everyone is so lucky, and this knowledge has made me take seriously the responsibility of earning from my words.

By combining my access to otherwise silenced voices via work in different public sector institutions with my determination to write stories, I found a natural synergy. I aimed to raise awareness about social issues, hold powerful people to account and engage audiences in my hopeful, if sometimes naive, visions of progress. Whether writing about music culture, austerity or youth violence, in my journalism I tried to provide an otherwise inaccessible platform for the hidden perspectives of people in my education and community work. This aim has brought this book into your hands. I maintained my writing while being fully aware that, as an outsider, I have had to earn, rather than assume, the right to represent the stories of others. I knew from the start that if I was going to write about the experiences of the young and impoverished, for example – those belonging to communities who have suffered from neglect and demonization for generations, into which I'd only recently become embedded – my intentions would need to be laid bare. I needed to be vulnerable and open, my commitment to moral argument unwavering and long-term.

I didn't want to be the type of journalist who parachutes in and out of people's lives. In fact, believing myself to be a youth worker first and social activist second, I have been reluctant to regard myself as a journalist, per se, at all. Those of us working to challenge the status quo and break down inequalities between groups of people have the power and responsibility to steer the stories being told. As advertising, brands and capital investment control what or who is written about in the media, and therefore what we collectively care about, it is increasingly difficult to produce truly impactful written work on a large scale. Something has to give, or drastically change.

I have long thought that it must be possible to commit to providing a thorough front-line service – volunteering, mentoring, teaching, caseworking, caring, fixing, giving – while also communicating the wholesome realities, failures and successes of that service in contemporary media discourse. This is a common struggle that charitable entities face: offsetting the need to expend energy achieving human impact with the need to expend energy telling the wider world about said impact – so you can celebrate its worth, and then do more of it. But both sides of this see-saw must be honoured at once.

I have written as transparently as possible with whoever might be implicated in my work: teenagers I've mentored, educators I've befriended, community leaders I've been schooled by. I have sat, talked and listened to hundreds of people. I have poured thousands of hours into forging dialogues with those whose lives feature in these pages to ensure, as best I can, that they are not only content for me to represent them, but that they actually feel better off for it. Writing responsibly is much more than just the practice of putting pen to paper: it is about conducting oneself in the most humane and effective way to disrupt regimes of stuffy privilege and power, before any ink has been drawn.

I have not always got things right. I am always learning. I have identified some of my mistakes in this book. But, in essence, articulating myself to a wide audience has become my best search for a universal language, and what you are reading is my purest attempt at relaying my findings.

Since I started writing journalism I've had a mantra. If a Black British teenage boy or girl in Brixton enjoys reading my words as much as my white grandmother in Hampshire, I know, on some level, that I am on the right track. Writing about my experiences and how they intertwine with those I have grown with over the last half-decade has become my way of creating common ground between socially disparate people. My pen is my vehicle for elevating the impact of my youth work, driving incremental change – one conversation, one article, one theme, one chapter at a time.

In the summer of 2018, having recently left my job as a youth worker in London prisons to become a freelancer, I had more daylight hours to kill than ever before. I spent it scraping together writing commissions and ad hoc bits of youth work to pay for my rent and living costs. But with more time to myself, away from full-time employment, I read lots and travelled across the city. My sense of geography evolved daily with things I learnt and saw.

This transition occurred in three ways. It was physical, in terms of the buildings, tarmac and infrastructure around me. It was social, in terms of my unique positioning in relation to nearby people's habits and behaviours, because of my social life as a twenty-something with plenty of friends living nearby, and my established youth work career in south London. And it was political, in terms of the top-down decisions being made by politicians I was paying attention to in the news, and the bottom-up, community-based initiatives working to make change on the ground, to which I'd become privy over the years.

Questions swirled in my mind. What does it mean to be a Londoner? What binds residents of our capital together? What separates us and makes us invisible to one another? How might I make sense of the distinct universes and characters spread across my life?

I'd tumbled down the complex thematic rabbit hole of thinking about serious youth violence because of one event in particular. A seventeen-year-old young man called Michael Anthony Jonas – the older half-brother of Jhemar Jonas, who I have mentored since before the start of my youth work career – was murdered in November 2017. Trying to see the world through the eyes of a grieving younger sibling and his family motivated me to dedicate my life to uncovering learnings that might be extracted from such an ordeal.

I've travelled to various parts of the capital to work with young people – from mansion-laden Maida Vale in the west to the forgotten, post-industrial corners of the Isle of Dogs in the east – but immediately south of the river has always felt most like home.

From my front door I could walk south, past Angell Town housing estate, where many boys who I'd got to know as a community volunteer lived, and whose paths I'd jog through to get to the pull-up bars. I could head further south, down the busy high street and up Brixton Hill, where I first started mentoring Jhemar in January 2015.

I could work my way south-west towards Clapham, Balham and Tooting, where I'd go to get my closest fix of decent Indian, Pakistani, Afghan or Sri Lankan food when I missed my dad's home cooking to an unbearable degree. Or I could veer further west, through Battersea Park, Wandsworth and Putney, the leafy sanctuary of the city that peers outwards towards suburbs like Kingston-upon-Thames and Hampton Court, where I spent much of my early life.

I could head north, cutting between Vauxhall, Kennington Park, its flower garden, the tall brutalist towers of the Brandon Estate and the Oval cricket ground – to which I attached fond, intense childhood memories of supporting both sides when England played against India. From there I could keep going, past Elephant & Castle, and end up at Willow Academy. A state secondary school where I met the second of my most esteemed mentees, Demetri Addison, as well as hundreds of other inspiring young people, Willow rested between ageing housing estates and monochrome luxury flat towers, stuck in the flux of gentrification.

I could walk east between the Cowley Estate, the glistening new blocks and green park of Oval Quarter, the old low-rise buildings of Myatt's Fields South Estate and the enclosure of Myatt's Fields Park. By going this way I'd end up in Camberwell, where friends of mine lived as legal guardians of a huge, abandoned care home overlooking the Green, an arrangement which had come about as an adaptive response to the city's housing crisis.

Most importantly, however, by heading east, but dropping just south of Camberwell, north of Brixton, I'd end up in the residential hinterland of Loughborough Junction. It was here that I'd first lived for eighteen months as a newcomer to Brixton, and where Jacob Sawyer Community Centre lay – the nucleus around which young life orbited. By July 2018 I'd visited to volunteer, learn and work every week for almost three years.

It was at Jacob Sawyer where I spoke to Tony – the boss, my mentor – about the pressure he felt trying to spin the plates of community life in the days following the murder.

It was at Jacob Sawyer where I'd met Carl, seventeen at the time – the third of my core mentees – whose life had flashed before his eyes when a bullet grazed his ear and hit the brick wall of his friends' housing block.

It was at Jacob Sawyer that I sat with Andre, a burly security guard, who told me how the faceless intruder at the Nine Night had the air of a child, 'not a gunman'.

On the evening following the murder in July 2018, while Tony talked with police officers at Jacob Sawyer, armed police wearing bulletproof vests surrounded a group of teenage boys filming a music video in London Fields, north-east London. A helicopter circled overhead.

'Turn around and face the fence!' one officer yelled. A female member of the public ran over and shouted at the police to stop harassing the boys as the propellers of the helicopter pumped high above. The police later said they had received reports of a firearm at the video shoot. After searching everyone, they found nothing. The resulting music video, Balistik's 'Who's Next' by videographer PacmanTV, which features footage of the raid, would garner millions of views on YouTube.

The incident demonstrated how a moral panic about UK drill music had by the summer spiralled out of control. Politicians, police and journalists were using it as a scapegoat for violence. And this was happening in front of an all-consuming political backdrop. In June 2016, more than 30 million people across Britain voted in a referendum deciding whether the country would remain in the European Union. The UK-wide (marginal) 48 per cent vote for 'Remain' was significantly lower than London's average of 60 per cent. Only four of London's thirty-three boroughs voted 'Leave'. In my local boroughs of Lambeth and Southwark, the 'Remain' vote shares were 78.6 per cent and 72.8 per cent respectively. This disparity with the rest of the nation made many Londoners, especially young Londoners, feel they were citizens of a separate country, existing in a bubble, in contrast to the more Eurosceptic countrymen and women.

Teenagers I would speak to from immigrant families who had

settled in the UK over recent generations from all over the world, including European countries like France, Portugal, Poland and Spain, would express confusion. Because of Brexit, the mould of a national division had been set. It gave added weight to the perception that societal ties were becoming frayed by austerity, which had been draining public services of life since the start of the decade.

By July 2018, public attention had become split: between obsessing over Brexit's limbo state on the one hand and, on the other, chasing shallower distractions like the men's football World Cup, reality television show *Love Island* or even the inflatable of US President Donald Trump wearing a diaper that was suspended in central London to greet him on his first state visit to the UK. It was easy, smartphone in hand, to dissociate from any immediate and proximate crisis – not least monstrous existential issues like climate change, which in the heatwave of the moment was making itself known on the exposed skin of anyone who stepped outside.

The severity of London's youth violence epidemic felt more and more visceral every day, yet the narrative of sunny celebration persisted. On weekdays, office workers across the city flocked in parks and squares for extended lunch breaks and Prosecco-splashed evening socials. The raised female vocals of sugary, late-1990s UK garage anthems blared from speakers out of open bar fronts and car windows, showering pavements in upbeat nostalgia. The bunting in pub gardens stayed up. Meaty smoke from hog roasts, outdoor burger grills and huts serving fusion concepts like 'paneer chips' filled the air. Tourists queued to take selfies next to Buckingham Palace and Downing Street.

All the while, police and ambulance sirens echoed. News media teams caught cabs from one end of the city to the other to report on stabbing after stabbing. Mothers and community leaders appeared on television calling for the bloodshed to end.

On their journeys to and from work, overheated commuters read headlines about murder taking place in some of the most gentrified parts of the city. But no level of sadness or intense collective despair could compete with the euphoria of a great British summer.

Four days before a teenage boy walked into Jacob Sawyer Community Centre with a shotgun, the country's politicians broke up for recess. Parliament's canteens closed, deep cleans of the building's carpets and oak panelling began, and the corridors echoed with the footsteps of research aides collecting papers. Meanwhile, children continued to be murdered by other children. With British life cast under the seasonal spell of holiday tradition, what might have been labelled as a national emergency under other circumstances – if all lives were truly equal – would have to wait.

In the months leading up to July 2018, Lucy Knell-Taylor, a youth worker for Redthread, based at King's College Hospital, noticed teenagers talking about guns and knives more than usual. To her, it seemed like there had been a sudden increase in the availability of weapons.

'One girl told me how she saw someone get pistol-whipped at a party. Others were regularly talking about seeing guns,' Knell-Taylor said. 'I remember feeling a growing sense of doom.' She had worked at the hospital for several years. In her day-to-day practice, she would undertake extensive safety planning with every young person who passed through the hospital, including exploring their risk to and from others, establishing safe contact people and figuring out their route home. She'd sat with young men from Brixton to figure out a way for them to get back to the refuge of Jacob Sawyer.

At the end of July, Knell-Taylor had multiple people from Kennington on her caseload. For a lot of the boys during the

summer, she concluded that it wasn't safe for them to travel
home from hospital, or to come back to see her using public
transport. When there was no other alternative mode of transport available, she would book cabs for them. On occasion, with
young people for whom there were concerns about exploitation
or coercive control, she would decide on 'safe words' to ensure
that she was never inadvertently increasing their risk while
communicating over the phone. During this time, some of her
young people were assessed as being particularly high risk, and
therefore required daily check-ins.

'My work phone was ringing constantly with various young
people, their mums, their girlfriends, calling to express their
fear about what would happen next.' She advised some to stay
inside, others to stay with family outside of London. All were
given bullet-pointed 'how to stay safe' plans sent to them by
text or WhatsApp. 'We had long chats about how what had
happened might affect the trajectory of our work. Immediate
safety became absolutely paramount. Some of them were really
stressed out and anxious, others were on retaliation, which
meant I spent a lot of time essentially talking them down.' On
the Thursday and Friday of that week, she was continuously
calling her young contacts. 'All of my young people survived.
But they were scared and telling me that the roads were mad.'

The murder in Camberwell took place as part of a messy territorial feud between local young men in south London. To call
it a 'postcode war', a term for the overwhelming concept of geographically defined urban violence, is in some ways useful. It
captures the extreme hyperlocality and occasionally definitive
borders of the territories involved. But the term is also mislead-
ing because it implies that patches of land are firmly and
timelessly drawn, like postcodes are, as if demarcating a peren-
nial distinction between battling areas. This is far from true.
Street rivalries and their terms are forever changing.

Postcodes, or anything written on a page or map, had something to do with it, but not everything. The laws of the land were defined by birthplace, personal association, organic, unpredictable swings in allegiance and plots that condensed with protectionism after every act of betrayal. Beefs vary for those at the centre of them, who've often grown up together, attending the same handful of schools, playing in the same football teams and inviting one another to the same birthday parties. Little about these wars, indeed any war, is clear or set in stone. The line between victim and perpetrator is thin.

By 2018, a portion of young men living around the northern half of Brixton had feuded with those from Kennington to the north. Others had done the same with those from Tulse Hill and Brixton Hill to the south, or Stockwell to the west. Some rivalries were inherited from generations of the past. Some were sparked or repurposed to suit a more reckless digital age. In July and August 2018, the complex iterations of this grand web of impending violence – one of thousands like it taking place across the capital at any time, such as between Tottenham and Wood Green in the far north, Forest Gate and Beckton in the east, and Ladbroke Grove and Shepherd's Bush in the west – reached another explosive peak.

Carl and his friends were targeted by a group of gun-wielding attackers in July 2018 because of where they were standing. Most likely, it was also because their faces were 'bait', or easily recognizable, as a result of their social media presence. Images and videos showing memes, taunts, fights and brags circulated every day over Snapchat and Instagram and within WhatsApp groups, away from the prying eyes of adults, for the most part of the 2010s. Such technological advances were having a huge but vague impact on community relations across British cities and on the level of social anxiety among teenagers, let alone adults spending our time increasingly glued to our phones.

I therefore felt that to ignore or deny social media as a fundamental component of youthful consciousness would be to fail as an educator. Moved by my interest in London's music scene, I chose the new, deep, dark UK drill universe as a linked focus of study. I paid attention to the way masked artists would develop personal brands, concede to committing crimes in their lyrics, seek to delegitimize each other's content or performatively goad one another in a battle of hypothetical violence. I tried to explore these subjects in youth groups and mentoring workshops as a way of connecting with young people, helping them make safer, more reflective decisions. In my mind, understanding drill music means understanding what life is like for trendsetting young people – and therefore our city's future.

My work in schools gave me another perspective on how the British education system was succeeding and failing. The main place I gained this perspective from was Willow Academy in Elephant & Castle. On the one hand, I saw some young people overcome the trappings of intergenerational poverty, injecting their energy into achieving top A-level results and eventually reaching university. On the other hand, I saw some become overwhelmed by their environment, and the school's inability to intercept their path to societal rejection.

On the Monday following the Nine Night, Tony met again with police officers. They were still investigating the murder, while struggling to deal with the volume and intensity of further uprisings. They asked Tony to close the community centre because they feared that the building might become the target of attacks; the castle beyond the moat. It was normally a safe haven, providing security, stability and shelter for young members. Now, so the risk-averse logic of the police went, it could put people in danger by association.

I'd met adults, young and old, who'd spent their adolescent years at Jacob Sawyer. They learnt to box. They were given advice about how to respond calmly while being stopped and searched by police. They might have had fond memories of watching films like *E. T.* there on a Friday night. They were fed when there was no food in the fridge at home. I saw older boys standing outside the front of the building with the slit windows to the office open so they could charge their phones from the socket inside and use the Wi-Fi. I saw jovial and serious fist fights. I heard uncontrollable laughter and played games of table tennis and saw poetry recitals. I spent hundreds of hours sitting and chatting with Tony and other staff members. I facilitated group discussion workshops with boys of all ages and characters. I spoke to teenagers dealing with pressures and traumas that I didn't know existed in British society until I stepped out of my comfort zone to start confronting them. I'd come to realize how complex and important, if imperfect, the community centre's role had been over the years.

Jacob Sawyer sat near Coldharbour Lane, south London's historic major artery, which connects Brixton to Camberwell. Alongside providing a genuine source of belonging for me, its location, character, reputation and sensitive, long-standing history captured many of the insidious injustices that plague the wealthy capital. It was a youth service, home, base and kitchen. It was a protectorate and vulnerable target, sitting on liminal land. In some ways, its staff and young people were hidden from and rejected by the regenerative cycles of modern London life. Yet it managed to stay relevant and alive. The community centre was a relic of Brixton in an earlier time, but also the most crystallized symbol of a society struggling to cope with all the messy, ballooning trends of the twenty-first century.

In August of 2018 I had no idea of the obstacles that still lay ahead, but I wondered how London had found itself in this state. Would it last for ever? When does inner-city pressure let up? How did we get here, and where would 'here' lead to?

The big metal gates of Jacob Sawyer were padlocked shut.

This book grapples with London's epidemic of serious youth violence (SYV), while highlighting causes and uncovering solutions. In telling this story, my first aim is to make an argument that in contemporary Britain the state is failing young people, and this is one core reason why youth violence occurs. The second aim is to provide a blueprint for how we might overcome challenges and move forward.

In Chapters 1–3, I will rewind the clock to introduce Jhemar, Tony, Carl and Demetri, as their lives first intertwined with my own throughout 2015. I will introduce the small stretch of south London, between Brixton and Elephant & Castle, where most of my youth work and community volunteering has taken place since.

Chapters 4–12 will follow my career, research and the lives of the four main characters from 2015 to 2020. Each chapter will focus on events through a different lens: policing, education, social media, gentrification, 'knife crime', British politics, criminal justice, youth services and public health. Each chapter lens has been chosen so that I and the other voices featured can speak from as much direct, first-hand experience and knowledge as possible. These lenses have not been chosen at the expense, or without consideration, of all others. For example, clearly parenting, early-years support and mental health services are other fundamental, necessary lenses for understanding and preventing intergenerational social disadvantage and serious youth violence. But because these have not featured as tenets of my youth work and research, they will not be considered as stand-alone themes in this book. Furthermore, regarding parenting, I believe that we as a society ought to be constructing a strong safety net made up of services that can intervene effectively when a young person's household circumstances fail them. This book therefore seeks to make this case, motivated by a fundamental faith in the power of collective action and a compassionate welfare state; a belief in the public sphere over the private. 'It takes a village to raise a child,' the saying goes. So how can we make sure the village, its inhabitants and institutions are prepared to raise its children?

Given that an overwhelming majority of offenders and victims of SYV in London are male (77 per cent and 75 per cent, respectively) – which is an extension of male over-representation in school exclusions (more than three times the rate of females) and the criminal justice system (men make up roughly 95 per cent of the prison population) – the book will focus on the male experience. This also reflects the identities of the main characters and the targeted leaning of my social and educational engagement work, which I have consistently tried to design and deliver as a gendered response to at-risk boys and young men in south London.

By starting with the formative months of my volunteering work at Jacob Sawyer Community Centre, Chapter 4 explores how the London Metropolitan Police has failed to serve multicultural city life, and shows how this failure affects particular young people and community members on the ground.

By drawing on my mentoring work at Willow Academy, Chapter 5 assesses the successes and failures of the British state education system and attempts of 'City Academies' to engage with teenagers most at risk of exclusion.

Chapter 6 comes to terms with how the tightening grip of social media technology, and resulting forms of youth culture, shape the experiences of being a young person in sometimes empowering, sometimes dangerous ways.

By taking Elephant & Castle and Brixton as examples,

Chapter 7 captures how gentrification has served to displace poor communities, disempower young lives and mask lagging social problems in the name of profit and regeneration.

Chapter 8 draws a distinction between the media-generated discourse of 'knife crime' and the tragic reality of youth violence as it is experienced and felt by young people.

Via trips to and from the Houses of Parliament, Chapter 9 shows why the British political system is detached and ill-equipped to deal with the nexus of social problems that lead to violent crime, and makes a case for placing young people's voices at the heart of advocacy and policy.

Through profiling the harsh regime of a prison wing and tracking the criminalization of Black British music culture, Chapter 10 considers how poor young people become trapped in an excessively punitive and non-rehabilitative criminal justice system.

Returning to Jacob Sawyer Community Centre, Chapter 11 argues for the importance of youth services in areas of high social deprivation, and against their decimation under austerity.

Chapter 12 highlights how some of the most powerful solutions for treating the epidemic of serious youth violence grow out of trauma-informed community mobilization, as part of what might usefully be understood as a 'public health approach'.

The Conclusion will take stock of the challenges presented across the book, see how the four main characters have fared against them, and thus point towards solutions.

I wrote most of *Cut Short* during the Covid-19 crisis of 2020. The Epilogue will therefore show how its themes and analyses are applicable to a world in pandemic.

1. If You Ruled the World

Jhemar

Jhemar was playing PlayStation 3 with his half-brother, Michael. Michael was two years older than Jhemar. Jhemar would often spend the weekend at Michael's mum's house in Penge, south-east London. They were in Michael's bedroom; Jhemar was lying on his front on the floor and Michael was sitting on the single bed. They faced a television screen next to the open window, which looked out on to the road and dull marble sky. The walls were painted light blue, the ceiling white.

The only game the brothers played was *Grand Theft Auto 5*. They would steal different cars and race them around the virtual map. If the car was worth keeping, they took it back to their virtual garage to store it for the next time they played. Jhemar and Michael both loved cars and other types of transport, just like their dad, Michael Senior, a bus driver. Jhemar wanted to be a pilot when he grew up. He and Michael were excited to turn seventeen and drive real cars. Jhemar often had visions of visiting the dealership so that Michael could buy his first car.

They were driving an Obey 9F, a virtual car made to look like an Audi R8. Michael was in control, speeding around the city. He paused the game to go to the toilet, handing Jhemar the controller. Jhemar floored the accelerator, pressing hard against the R2 button. His heart started beating faster. His eyes widened. On screen, the car sped down the main highway, weaving through traffic. Jhemar could see the sparkly sea to one side and tall buildings standing along the other. After a few minutes he slowed down and started doing donuts in the middle of the road. Smoke rose from the tarmac and Jhemar grinned.

Suddenly a truck smashed into the rear left-hand side of the car. It was thrown across the road and became dented. The bumper had fallen off. One yellow star appeared in the right-hand corner of the screen. The police were on their way.

Jhemar gasped. He didn't have enough money to go to the custom shop to repair the car so he tried to find another one of the same model. He heard the click of the toilet light being turned off and Michael's footsteps approaching across the landing. He climbed into the nearest car he could see and started driving it down the highway. A police car began tailing him with its sirens on.

Michael sat back down on the bed, looked at the screen and frowned.

'Where's the Audi?' he asked.

'I'm not even sure,' Jhemar replied. He didn't dare look up at his brother. Sensing Jhemar was hiding something, Michael got him in a headlock.

'Where's the Audi!?' Michael asked again, wrestling Jhemar to the floor.

'I'm sorry!' Jhemar yelled, laughing and wincing in painful defeat.

Michael softened and smiled. Justice was served, so he let Jhemar go and put his hands on his little brother's shoulders, announcing a penalty: Jhemar couldn't play until after lunch. Jhemar hung his head in shame, frustrated with himself. He lay down on his front and placed his elbows on the floor, cupping his chin with his two hands.

After lunch they decided to go to buy chocolate and drinks. They walked towards the main road then approached the convenience shop. The entrance bell clinked as they went through the door and the man napping behind the counter shook his head to wake up. He peered over his nose, like a meerkat on lookout, keeping a close eye on the boys. Jhemar was going through a phase of buying strawberry-flavoured things. He chose a can of strawberry KA and Michael got black grape flavour KA, then they chose a chocolate bar each. Michael paid and thanked the man behind the counter when he gave him change. The boys left the shop, unwrapping their chocolate bars.

Three older boys were walking towards Michael and Jhemar. They had their hoods up. Jhemar felt the hair on his arms stand on end.

'Where you from?' one of the boys asked the brothers.

Neither Jhemar nor Michael said anything.

'Where you from, cuz?' another one of the boys asked, stepping forward.

Jhemar tightened his fist slightly to get ready. His heart started beating faster.

'We just went to the shop,' Michael replied, holding his ground.

Jhemar's feet were glued to the spot. He became dizzy with thoughts. Were they going to fight? He felt safe in Michael's company, but Jhemar didn't want Michael to do anything. He wanted to go home and play PlayStation again. If Michael swung for one of the boys, the boys would have to swing back. Jhemar would have to help and who knew what might happen.

Then Jhemar saw it. One of the boys pulled out the handle of a small knife from his pocket, showing its blade, whose metal caught the reflection of the sun. Jhemar's heart beat even faster. The can of drink felt slippery in his sweaty hand. He sensed Michael tensing beside him and so he tensed his own fist harder.

It was a stalemate. The boy put his knife back in his pocket. Jhemar blinked and took a deep breath and the three boys went on their way. Jhemar could see Michael was relieved, even though he was trying not to show it. Jhemar was relieved, too.

His heartbeat slowed and they began to walk home, sipping their drinks and eating their chocolate bars.

'Let's find another Audi,' Michael said. Jhemar grinned, nodding with enthusiasm.

The first time I met Jhemar Jonas, in January 2015, he was twelve years old. He had just started his second term of Year 8 at a Lambeth secondary school. We met on the first floor of an education centre at the top of Brixton Hill: the southernmost end of Brixton. When we shook hands he was wearing a puffer jacket over the top of his navy-blue school blazer and, beneath that, a jumper of the same colour, covering a light-blue shirt. His tie was carefully knotted into a half-Windsor and his top button fastened. He exuded excitement, cheek and confidence.

The charity which owned the building was called Into-University. They had bases across the United Kingdom in areas of high socio-economic disadvantage, where there is low progression into higher education among young people. Each centre was run by a team of staff who worked long hours, with children participating in programmes throughout the year. The charity organized a student mentoring scheme, connecting undergraduate and postgraduate students at London universities to children and teenagers across the capital. While completing my master's degree in political theory at the London School of Economics, in Holborn, five kilometres north of Brixton, I signed up to be a student mentor. I'd been chosen as Jhemar's.

Jhemar, who lived near central Brixton with his family, had been visiting the IntoUniversity centre on a weekly basis for three years. During the school holidays he would go on trips to London universities like Brunel or Roehampton.

On each visit to the Brixton Hill centre, Jhemar would work on his school subjects and homework with a member of staff. Because he was always so keen to write rap lyrics about his day, the staff team offered him a deal: he could write lyrics after he'd done his schoolwork.

'I'll always remember Jhemar's rap that he performed at King's College. The chorus went: "Ecology, ology, better than biology, and technology, any other ology." It was a science focus week in Year 6 during the holidays. There was a ceremony and all the kids dressed up in hats and gowns like they were graduating,' says Ben Kahn, a youth worker who worked with Jhemar during his early years at IntoUniversity. 'Jhemar had the gift of the gab. He had more energy than anyone else in his class, and it was exhausting, to be honest. He would be talking all the time, shouting out stuff, but it was always in a positive way. He was never bringing anyone else down. If you take a step back, I suppose he was a driving force behind the energy of the room.'

Kahn had initially engaged Jhemar and his friends by running outreach sessions at his Brixton primary school. Soon, Jhemar started turning up at the IntoUniversity centre with his friends. He would later come with his younger brother, Jerome. 'They were a handful but they were also amazing and dynamic. Jhemar was always one you'd look forward to seeing. He would stroll into the staff office and tell you about his week. It was like he wanted to bless everyone; to make sure all the adults knew he had arrived in the building. He was talkative but respectful. There were never any tensions with him, like there might be with other kids. Jhemar obviously had to face all the challenges in life that come with being a Black boy growing up in Brixton. But I think having the safe space that his parents created for him at home was an aspirational driver for him to create another safe space at IntoUniversity; he had the foundations to explore and grow. To this day, I've never met another young person as pro-active as Jhemar. There is no school holiday when him and Jerome are not busy. I think his parents understand the value of getting the boys out of that mentality of doing nothing in the holidays. They've learnt to make good use of their spare time. They are constantly trying new things out of their comfort zone, which means they learn so much.'

When he started secondary school, Jhemar was asked if he wanted a mentor. Initially, he was sceptical. 'I didn't really like the idea of meeting with some random person I didn't know, and who didn't know me,' he later told me. But he trusted the staff. They told him that having a mentor would help him, so he agreed. Before our first meeting, Jhemar was nervous but excited. One thing that surprised him was that I wasn't Black. He knew London was a multicultural city, but he hadn't been exposed to many white or Asian adults, apart from the mostly white teachers at his school.

'At first, because of the way you looked and spoke, I thought you were a bit posh. I thought I needed to speak properly to you, to watch my words. But I wanted to be myself, too, so I went in and out of slang,' he explained.

We took seats at a desk. It was a Wednesday, shortly after school finishing time, and outside it was freezing cold. A window before us looked out on to a darkening, empty car park. Inside, a pile of folders was stacked at one end of the desk beside me; Blu-Tacked to the walls were colourful laminated posters alongside photographs of children posing on trips. Leftover Christmas tinsel hung from the ceiling and swayed in the heat rising from radiators. Two other pairs sat together at their own desks. We were instructed to identify an aim we could work towards with our mentees and told to think about different areas: social (interacting with others), personal (character strengths and weaknesses) and academic (study skills and school subjects).

'I wanna get better at dissecting words, 'cause English is looking a bit peak right now,' Jhemar said. He was humbly conceding what he saw as his weakness at school. Jhemar hated English because he was always being asked to read pieces of text that bored him, so he got impatient in lessons. He got into trouble for talking to other people or messing around with his stationery. He would drive his ruler around his desk, pretending he was steering a bus, like his dad did in real life. 'I know every bus route in and out of Brixton!' he would tell me with pride. The only time he liked English was when it was creative writing because he could write raps and empty his mind of its busy, restless thoughts. Jhemar often wrote lyrics in the back of his exercise books. He pulled out a book from his bag to show me some of his scribbles. I mentioned that I liked music, too, especially hip-hop and grime. He cackled with laughter, happy to sense some immediate alignment in our interests.

'No way, don't lie!'

I suggested that he write our names on the front of the orange exercise book we'd been given to document our work together. He spelt my name wrong, with a 'K' instead of a 'C'. I corrected him and he apologized.

'What shall we call the book?' I asked.

'The Book of . . .' He squinted in concentration, tapping an index finger on his chin. The light bulb in his mind flicked on. 'The Book of Wisdom?' he posed. I smiled and nodded. He wrote it neatly below our names:

Jhemar and Ciaran.
The Book of Wisdom.
Mentoring. January 2015.

He opened the book to the front page to write down our aim. 'Ciaran is going to help me . . .' he muttered slowly as his hand moved across the fresh lined paper, before pausing.

'Do you know how long I've been waiting for a mentor?' he asked me, looking up.

I shrugged my shoulders and shook my head.

'For, like . . . a year!' Jhemar continued, his voice going up into a high pitch. He held out his palms and spread his fingers wide, like he was about to catch a beach ball. Then he tilted his head down over the desk.

'Ciaran is going to help me get better at dissecting words,' he wrote.

He was scribing something that would come to define our meetings for years to come.

Across 2015, Jhemar and I made progress filling in the pages of 'The Book of Wisdom'. We met every fortnight. By August, when Jhemar was enjoying his summer holiday – he would spend long hours playing PlayStation with his older brother, Michael, in Penge – our interactions acted as a welcome break from writing my dissertation. They were a dose of realism and comedy to balance out my long, abstract hours spent in the library.

At the start of every meeting, Jhemar would burst into excitable updates: the success of his school assembly performance; his new lyrics; his family holiday to Jamaica. He would explain how his mum had cooked the best curry goat he'd ever tasted the previous evening. He spoke whatever came to his mind. He was automatically fearless. He was beginning to trust me.

Every other Wednesday evening I printed off a piece of writing on the computers at the library before catching the 59 bus from Aldwych to Brixton Hill. I tried to plan the dissection of each resource so that both Jhemar and I could personally connect with it. We read poems like 'The British' by Benjamin Zephaniah and 'Half-Caste' by John Agard to discuss multiculturalism and identity. Jhemar was surprised that I self-identified as 'mixed race' because he had only heard people who were half Black, not half Asian, use the term before.

I became familiar with Jhemar's tendency to blurt out

observations about whichever topic I presented him with. He was often unable to contain his excitement. He would habitually interrupt me while I was speaking or jump from one thought to the next while explaining himself, so that his expressions sometimes remained incomplete. I tried to find a suitable balance in my response: commending him on his enthusiasm, while recommending that he might be more effective as a communicator if he slowed down, listened more and gathered his thoughts. In search of a solution, we read extracts from the Lebanese poet Kahlil Gibran's early-twentieth-century work *The Prophet*. I noted to Jhemar that Gibran, like many poets, used few words but still achieved a great amount of creative meaning in his descriptions and moral preaching. One page proved especially pertinent.

> For thought is a bird of space, that in a cage of words may indeed unfold its wings but cannot fly.

After reading it, Jhemar drew a diagram in 'The Book of Wisdom' of a birdcage, constructed of words linked together, with thought bubbles trapped inside it.

We also listened to verses by British MCs like UK hip-hop legends Klashnekoff and Jehst, and grime originators Dizzee Rascal, Kano and Devlin. We dissected lyrics that described the grey monotony of British life, the cold, dreary weather, the headspace of a teenage boy growing up on a housing estate and the failure of the welfare state to look after the most vulnerable people in society. We focused on metaphor using Tupac Shakur's poem 'The Rose That Grew From Concrete'. On the page, Jhemar wrote: 'Concrete is the system that is put in place. It is hard to crack.' He announced that he wanted to write his own version as homework. At our next meeting he returned with a series of lines written in four stanzas on a fresh page:

Starting from the bottom
Tryna get to the top
Never ever gonna stop
Until you get to that spot

Did you hear about the rose from a crack in the concrete
Growing into something beautiful and started so weak
Couldn't ask for help
Couldn't even speak

Noone was there to help
Tryna fend for yourself
Noone cared about your future
They all worried bout their self

You kept on pushing
Movin right on
From little scraps
Built into an icon

We turned to the work of other American rap greats like Common, Mos Def and J. Cole. We looked at how Nas paints a portrait of a utopian world in his famed 1996 single 'If I Ruled the World (Imagine That)'. In his verses, he imagines stopping police harassment, getting rid of the need for government welfare support, freeing political prisoners and a life of carefree riches for all. He imagines liberating school curricula from the biases of history, extinguishing jealousy and ending racial inequality in America. By dissecting the song's contents, Jhemar was able to identify language skills such as simile and colour – Nas describing himself as wise like an old owl – and internal rhyme, as he raps about feeling the wind breeze in the West Indies. I used the song to introduce him to the concept of a 'thought experiment' – a hypothetical scenario used in philosophy that is imagined to test one's intuitions – by picturing a world with himself in charge, just like Nas did. It was a chance to combine the terms I was learning about in my study of political theory at university with our mutual appreciation for music. Jhemar answered questions I threw at him. What does a world with him in charge look like? How does it differ to the version of reality we experience already? What rules would there be, and why?

'Give justice and equality to all,' wrote Jhemar in red felt-tip at the top of the page, next to words like 'KABOOM!' and 'alliteration!' in celebration of Nas's lyrical dexterity. He wrote 'Black excellence' next to Lauryn Hill's soulful chorus.

'You've got to imagine thought experiments to learn about the best of life,' he wrote at the bottom of the page, underlining it twice.

2.   We're From Different Ancient Tribes

Tony and Carl

'It's going to take time,' said Tony. He looked me up and down, showing on his hardened face signs of the calculation taking place in his mind: a mix of judgement and curiosity about who I was and what we wanted. 'The boys here are gonna think you're feds.'

I first met Tony in the foyer of Jacob Sawyer Community Centre in September 2015 after I'd buzzed the white button at the front door with my flatmate Rory Bradshaw – a friend from university. Tony was wearing a checked shirt tucked into some jeans, and black shoes. I guessed he was roughly fifty.

He introduced himself as Managing Director and walked us through into the main hall, which contained a sofa, chairs, pool table, table tennis table and suspended television screen with an Xbox plugged in. A half-open shutter separated the kitchen on the far side of the room and a small gym housed some weights, punchbag and dip bars. We entered the staff office, where Tony told Rory and me to take a seat on two deep-cushion chairs. The room was cramped, with two desks each supporting a computer and scattered piles of paper.

I explained that we had just moved into a flat on the other side of the nearby community park. Tony chuckled, explaining that during the so-called 'second summer of love' between 1988 and 1989, as acid house music and ecstasy spread while the rave scene took shape across the UK, he went to parties held in a warehouse on our road. He would also go on trips out to nearby cities like Oxford, following secret, telephoned instructions to find plots of land outside the M25's ring to attend parties in the middle of fields and abandoned buildings. Back then, Tony said, raving was for all races and creeds – groups of young Black people from the inner city, like him, as well as middle-class white people from the suburbs. 'You know what they say about the summer of love though, don't you? If you can remember it, you weren't there!' he finished, chuckling and groaning with brief glee. His broad frame bounced on his office chair and his eyes slanted in happy reminiscence. Seconds later his face had returned to firm seriousness.

It was my first introduction to Tony's turn of phrase; his willingness to divulge memories from his wild youth before returning to professional conversation. This neat balance was a perfected fusion which made his words easy to remember, his stories feel dynamic, colourful and true. He spoke in a weathered, gravelly voice and authoritative local accent, a blend of slang-laden punchlines and intellectual observations, weaving together threads of social commentary about the extremes of life for people in Brixton with divergences into bouts of laddish comedy.

Tony had worked in the local community for three decades and had lived in south London his whole life. He asked where we'd grown up. Rory was originally from Oxford and had moved into London to complete his PGCE as a Geography teacher. On discovering that I was half Punjabi, Tony said his sister-in-law was a Sikh, and that he loved her food, which made me feel at ease. Then he asked what brought us to the door of Jacob Sawyer.

'We'd like to start volunteering,' I told him, assuming that such an offer could only receive an affirmative reply. But it was more complicated than that.

'I see,' Tony replied, nodding with raised eyebrows. He shot a wary glance at another staff member sitting at the other desk, who smiled without looking up from his computer screen. I fidgeted in my seat, looking nervously between Tony and Rory to cut through the abrupt silence. I wondered whether I'd said something offensive.

I hadn't. But at first, as he would later reveal to me, Tony had mixed feelings about Rory and me.

On the one hand, his trusting, optimistic side was happy we'd knocked on his door. The young people who spent time at Jacob Sawyer were used to a certain type of adult male working there – Black, older, more experienced. Maybe they had several decades under their belt as a youth worker. Maybe they'd grown up nearby. But Tony believed that, on top of having access to familiar faces, young people need exposing to other horizons too. By welcoming newcomers like us, he suspected that fresh opportunities might be possible for Jacob Sawyer. Similarly, he felt that people arriving to live in Brixton in large numbers, as gentrification proceeded to restitch the fabric of the town, needed to gain a connection to people who already lived there. Tony reasoned that our enthusiasm might be naive – we would struggle to engage with some of the more distrusting of Jacob Sawyer's young people – but he considered that we might add diversity to the centre's membership.

On the other hand, Tony was sceptical. We looked like undercover policemen. He reasoned that his boys – who were even more vigilant than him – would think we were, too. And if it turned out that we were undercovers, what would people in the community think? Even if we weren't, he didn't want to let us in thinking we could save the world.

Why did we walk into his centre? Why did we want to volunteer? Were we doing this just because it was a fad? Would we leave when things got difficult? Our conversation quickly evolved into an impromptu job interview.

I found it intimidating. It pushed me out of my comfort zone. Nonetheless, it began my and Rory's journey at Jacob Sawyer, and a dialogue between Tony and me that has never stopped.

★

Henceforth, our visits to Jacob Sawyer always unfolded in two stages. First, we checked in with Tony. He would tell us about Brixton's history, demographic make-up and social character. He schooled us about how the area was changing, for better and for worse.

Lambeth is one of the most densely populated boroughs in the country. It has an average of 12,020 residents per square km, more than twice the average population density of London. Coldharbour ward, the administrative division in which Jacob Sawyer sits, has long been the poorest ward in Lambeth, and therefore one of the poorest in London. It has the highest proportion of social rented households – 60 per cent as opposed to 22 per cent of private rented and 16 per cent owner occupation – and the highest unemployment rate in the borough; the highest proportion of dependent children in non-working households; and the highest proportion of those with no adults in employment with dependent children. Coldharbour also has the highest proportion of residents hailing from ethnic minorities in the borough, the highest number of Black Caribbean residents and the highest number of Black African residents. This goes some way to explaining why, over the years, Brixton as a whole has become synonymous across the world with Black British identity and culture.

Tony brought these statistics to life. He was sometimes hilarious, sometimes intimidating, but always interesting and absolute with his advice. Sitting with him was like visiting an eccentric university professor during office hours. Tony's lectures, however, were not laced with academic jargon or literary reference. He wasn't hypothesizing on what might be possible in an alternate ideal universe or making assumptions about inequality and justice. He was talking in real terms about the impact of social division and family breakdown. He painted a hardened but sympathetic picture of alienation among young people. He recounted stories of local violence and tragedy. He explained the trap of the criminal justice system; the conveyor belt to prison that can exist once a child is permanently excluded from their secondary school. He told me that 'for some boys, picking up a knife before leaving home is normal, like tying up your shoelaces'. He reminisced about when he was a drug-and-alcohol worker and football coach. At twenty-two years old, as a chef in the Queen's catering service at Buckingham Palace, at the end of a working day Tony would bring home salmon and meat on aluminium plates for his family at his mum's house. He'd always served his community. I found him deeply inspiring.

The second half of our evening visits would be spent in the rest of the building, talking to young people. As Rory and I tried to embed ourselves as familiar faces, Tony's prediction was, of course, correct: we were treated with mistrust and suspected of being police.

'Are you an undie?' or 'I don't talk to feds!' were consistent replies.

It therefore took both Rory and I a few months to prove our loyalty to the habit of visiting every week, without fail. I've since either volunteered for, worked at or advocated on behalf of Jacob Sawyer for over half a decade.

Various activities, workshops and services – therapy, support for families, sports coaching – were available for frequenters of Jacob Sawyer throughout the weekdays. Young men would meet with their caseworker or counsellor on quiet afternoons. Mothers would come to see Tony in tearful concern about their sons. Different organizations or practitioners would hold sessions in the evenings on a range of topics: stop-and-search awareness lessons, arts and crafts, Black history lectures or film nights. Different visiting food charities encouraging healthy eating or meal budgeting would set up shop in the kitchen. Football coaching and impromptu games of five-a-side took place on the astroturf out the back for different age groups almost every weekday evening. During my initial months at Jacob Sawyer, the place was rammed: an intensity that would not last for ever. Over the years of my visits, attendance would rise and fall with the times.

Visitors were mostly male, although small groups of girls and young women would pass through as part of a designated group run by one of the female youth workers. Anecdotally speaking, the young people I interacted with were almost exclusively Black British and mixed race*, and from what I could tell from my conversations over the years, mostly from Caribbean origins, alongside West Africans (Nigerian, Ghanaian) and East Africans (Somalian, Ugandan). A few Latin Americans from the growing influx of Colombians and Ecuadorians in south London passed through, too. To this day, from a total of hundreds, I can name on one hand the number of white teenagers I have met within the centre's walls – British, European or otherwise. Rory was often the only white person in the building. I have never met a fellow British Asian person there.

Young visitors were diverse in age range. Eleven- or twelve-year-old boys would bounce in for the first time since their age permitted them entry. Eighteen-year-olds would stop by: those who had recently started their undergraduate degrees at university; those taking their A levels or pursuing an apprenticeship; or others who simply had nowhere else to spend their evenings.

---

* Henceforth, when I refer generally to 'Black' people and communities, and do not specify otherwise, I mean to include those who are of mixed-race (white and Black) heritage, too. This is in the same way that when I refer to 'British/South Asian' people and communities, I consider myself, as a mixed-race (white and Asian) man, to fall under this broad descriptor. This is because these terms are typically used to group those who do not belong to the majority White British group. It is important to note that there is a vast spectrum of experiences within each of these terms, but unpacking each and every one is beyond the scope of this book.

They would socialize with their friends, sit playing FIFA on the ageing games console or use the weights equipment in the gym area. There was also a whole older stream of young men in their twenties who had been frequenting Jacob Sawyer for many years: from those working jobs in customer service or construction to those who had never had a job; young fathers; aspiring rappers; upbeat, budding youth workers; gang members who were in and out of prison, and others who sought sturdy counsel from staff.

Then there were middle-of-the-road teenagers: not quite kids any more, but not quite adults, either. Some seemed intimidated by the centre's natural hierarchy and the looming presence of elders. Others would compete for attention with boisterousness, one-upmanship and comedy. Others had clearly learnt, by nature or force, about keeping themselves to themselves, their hoods zipped up and their faces held like stone sculptures, their eyes scanning the room in silent surveillance of unfamiliar faces. Their age group was split between those dressed in their own clothes and those in the uniforms of various local secondary schools, including that of the local pupil referral unit ('PRU'), where young people were sent after being permanently excluded from mainstream education.

When I first approached one group of friends, they were standing around the table-tennis table. Among awkward scoffs and stern glances, one young man stepped forward to shake my hand without hesitation.

'Nice to meet you, I'm Carl,' he said respectfully, his face absent of suspicion. He said he was fourteen. I would later find out that he was half Jamaican, half Kenyan; his dad Caribbean, his mum East African. Carl's friends greeted me, too. A couple of them introduced themselves; others remained hunched to the side in blank shyness. I asked if I could play table tennis. Carl nodded, handing me a bat, and hopped over to the table.

★

On 5 August 2015 a charity based near Jacob Sawyer called Keeping Kids Company (or more commonly 'Kids Company') was forced to shut down following the launch of a police investigation into allegations of physical and sexual abuse. It had been running out of a building off Coldharbour Lane since 1996 and held a fond significance in the hearts of local families and minds of sector leaders, nationwide. It was regarded as one of the most successful charities in the capital. The organization was known to have benefited from the support of several prime ministers, including Gordon Brown and David Cameron, receiving a total of over £42 million of public money, as well as backing from celebrities like Coldplay and J. K. Rowling. Its closure became the talk of the town: nursery school teachers, parents and teenagers alike discussed it with regret. The organization had long provided a safe space for children and vulnerable adults across Camberwell and Brixton to spend time with staff, receive help on issues ranging from their mental health to housing, and get fed. It had become known as a necessary if imperfect model of community support. But to others who were more critical – a position that would, in the end unjustly, dominate media discourse for years to come – by 2015 it had ballooned into an apparent safeguarding nightmare and political scandal.

Kids Company's demise permeated national news to an extent that reflected its unmatched profile in the public imagination on the one hand and the distorting tendencies of the British media on the other, who, forever seeking a juicy story, habitually over-prey on the perceived corruption or inefficacy of the charity sector. In February 2016 – one month after the Met dropped their abuse investigation – the BBC produced a deep-dive documentary into its final months and spent time with founder Camila Batmanghelidjh as she persisted in serving local young people despite the chaos unfolding around her. The fate of Kids Company was emblematic of the desperate state of social and youth services halfway through the 2010s: a nexus of cynical political point scoring, bureaucratic negligence, lack of PR control and rapidly expanding social need among the public. Even with unprecedented government backing, the charity appeared to have become stretched by the complexities of life for young people and their families in south London, while trying to plug the widening support gaps being hollowed out by austerity.

A House of Commons report published in 2016 condemned the lack of scrutiny placed upon the organization over the years, which it claimed had contributed to its unsustainability. It blamed the unquestioned support it had received from senior government ministers, the lack of experience held by its trustees and the mismanagement of its finances. It also acknowledged that the charity had provided vital support to many local people since its inception, stressing that the shadiness of its closure should not take away from the hard work of its committed employees and the importance of its mission: providing vulnerable young people with personalized care and compassion.

Years later, however, after a long and exhausting legal battle, Batmanghelidjh and Kids Company's former trustees would be exonerated from claims of their mismanagement of the service. The *Guardian* reported in February 2021 that the court acknowledged that while the charity had faced financial difficulty, 'its board had taken steps to ensure it had a plan to manage the challenges it faced, and the charity might have survived had it not been brought down by unsubstantiated allegations of sexual abuse'. The judge presiding over the case, Mrs Justice Falk, concluded that there had been no dishonesty, bad faith, personal gain or inappropriate expenditure. She praised Batmanghelidjh for her dedication shown to vulnerable young people over the years, as well as her founding of an organization that 'until 2014 was widely regarded as a highly successful one, doing what senior members of the government rightly described as incredible work'.

Falk added: 'It would be unfortunate if the events in the focus of this decision were allowed to eclipse those achievements.'

Hindsight therefore makes it all the more tragic that a few months after Kids Company's closure, in the same weeks that Rory and I began volunteering at Jacob Sawyer, keys to its front gate and building were handed over to a private company who rented rooms to legal guardians for cheap rates under short-term tenancy contracts, in what is known as a 'guardianship' scheme. The dark common room remained, full of old, piled-up furniture, its walls still decorated with colourful, childish murals, its filthy floor littered with rat droppings and syringes from squatting drug addicts who had settled in the interim period. What was once a source of community security became an eerie tombstone of the public sector's market failure; a crushed victim of the unforgiving media machine's fist at a time in which the British government was deliberately creating a culture of small-state survivalism and ruthless competition. Local people were disappointed and outraged. Some penned banners and stood outside in the autumn wind chanting at the loss of another lifeline.

'Kids Company was a really good resource, and like so many things, they messed it up. Even we used to go there as children! So to find out that it was closed down due to negligence was heartbreaking for everyone,' said Amanda Elie, a local mother who grew up in Loughborough Junction with her twin sister, Miranda. I first met the Elie sisters at Jacob Sawyer in December 2015. Rory and I had been paying our final visit of the year. Friday nights were always the busiest, before the centre became a private hire space for local churches, community groups, birthday parties and funeral wakes at the weekend. On arrival, we were encouraged to take a seat in the main room, before Tony explained there were going to be some poetry performances in memory of a young man called Jerrell who used to visit the centre.

Jerrell was Amanda Elie's son (Miranda's nephew). He'd

been run over by a car in the weeks following the closure of Kids Company, days before Rory and I picked up the keys to our flat. The Elie sisters talked fondly of Jerrell as placid, kind and popular among young people in Brixton. They fight to this day to uphold his legacy and inject positivity into their community.

'Jerrell was so disappointed when it happened,' Amanda recalled, referring to the closure of Kids Company. 'I remember him saying: "What are we gonna do now? I suppose we've got Jacob Sawyer, but that's it," and I think that's what a lot of the young people felt, like now they had nowhere else but Sawyer to go to.' Considering that, in 2017, Coldharbour was the only Lambeth ward with over 4,000 people aged under twenty, from a total population of over 17,000, having only one surviving youth centre in the whole area underserves those young people.

At the poetry event chairs were set up facing the front wall. I saw Carl and his friends taking their seats at the back; Miranda and Amanda were standing at the front with their sister Debbie. The crowd of mostly young people took a few seconds to moderate its volume. Staff and a couple of other visiting adults stood to the side. The three sisters introduced themselves tearfully, explaining their relation to Jerrell. They urged everyone in the room to take the time to reflect on what had happened to him. The atmosphere was thick with contemplation, interspersed with whispers. I'd heard people, especially Tony, referring to Jerrell's passing a few times. But the way the centre's young visitors had turned out now, on a cold Friday night in the lead-up to Christmas, signalled an unspoken need for catharsis: an opportunity for those closest to Jerrell to vocalize their pain and share the burden of their loss in a public forum.

'Brixton was dark, like a curse was put over the city, if you wanna go that deep,' Miranda said when, years later, I asked what drove the sisters to organize the poetry event. 'We were already feeling it that year. You could sense something was coming. Something wasn't right. The young people who died around this area were all connected, you know? They knew each other. Jerrell went to at least three or four funerals of boys he knew who were stabbed here, stabbed there. It was grim.'

After seeing how many hundreds of local young people had turned up to Jerrell's Nine Night, which was held at Jacob Sawyer, and then his funeral at a nearby church, the sisters spoke to Tony about turning their planned poetry event into a memorial. 'We were trying to think: what good can we get out of this horrible moment? It gave us the push and motivation. Something tragic happens, but you've really gotta take the good with the bad. That's why I think people say things like "blessings in disguise" and "divine intervention", because you can't have someone's death in vain. Of course it's hard, and you've got to stick together as a family, but you've also gotta take something positive, too. Jerrell wouldn't want us to be moping around. If he saw us like that he'd probably roll his eyes and take himself off to Jacob Sawyer!' Miranda continued, laughing in fond memory. 'Losing him inspired us to do more things for the community.' The sisters have since run regular poetry workshops to help local young people deal with trauma.

On the night of our first meeting, Miranda performed some improvised spoken word, part-prayer, part-story, pieced together from her memories of Jerrell. She invited others to stand up and share if they wanted to. Several young people's heads swivelled as they looked around to see who was going to go first. After a moment of hesitation a girl stood up and walked to the front holding two pages of A4 paper covered in scribbled handwriting. People clapped and she smiled nervously, before sharing her message to Jerrell. 'It was such a powerful moment. She spoke all about what was happening in the area, telling people to wake up. It was touching to see,' Amanda recalled.

Another boy stood up to do a short rap about the pressures of local life, including one line, which stuck with me, about the frustration of having a father in prison. He received claps of support from the rest of the room. Afterwards, Miranda, Amanda and Debbie thanked everyone for attending. The smell of food cooking in the kitchen started wafting into the room. The young people stacked their chairs away and queued up to receive their dinner on paper plates.

Leaving Jacob Sawyer after saying our goodbyes, Rory and I turned right to head home. I zipped up my winter coat to fight the festive cold that frosted the streets with a damp glimmer. I glanced across the road at the worn flowers still tied to the black railings on the floor, lying beside a red T-shirt. Tony had pointed out of the staff window to explain they had been left there in memory of a teenage boy who was stabbed to death in 2012. Like Jerrell, he too had been a much-loved member of the local community; a talented footballer and popular school student, taken before his time. Every time I have visited the centre since, the flowers have remained, a relic of immovable loss.

3. There Will Be Consequences

Demetri

Demetri had been back at school for one week and already the teachers were getting on to him. Every lesson started with the same lecture about the big four letters: 'GCSE'. He was in Year 11 now, top of the school. He'd messed around in Year 10. He'd answered back to teachers. He'd bent the rules where he could get away with it. Now he was ready to take things more seriously.

It was a Monday evening at 9.30 p.m. and Demetri had finished eating dinner – leftover chicken, potatoes and vegetables from the weekend roast. He'd finished his homework and spent time on Snapchat. He belonged to a few WhatsApp groups that popped off every evening with people sharing photographs, videos and music. Music was coming from his phone speaker – 'Salute' by Brixton crew 150. He preferred 150 to 67. '*You cross me, there will be consequences,*' went the American voice at the start.

He was playing *Grand Theft Auto 5* when suddenly he heard sirens coming from outside his bedroom. He put the PlayStation 4 controller down and stood up to look out of the window.

Filling his view was Strata SE1: the skyscraper that everyone living south of the river recognized because of the three wind turbines at its head that peered over the city. Demetri could see the ramp where people drove their cars down to enter the private car park. He had watched the skyscraper grow from the ground up. They had started constructing it when he was in primary school, after knocking down the old block that was there before to start afresh. He'd seen the builders, scaffolding and cranes. When it was finished people started moving into the apartments, one lit window at a time. Still, so many of the floors remained dark and empty. Demetri wondered why. Could the people see him looking back at them? He'd never seen the wind turbines at the top of the building spin. Why were they there?

A police car turned the corner. Blue light refracted through the window and around Demetri's bedroom. An ambulance followed. Seconds later the noise of their sirens stopped, but Demetri could see the lights continuing to illuminate nearby buildings. He assumed that the police car and the ambulance must be somewhere close. He sat on his bed, picked up his controller and went back to playing PlayStation 4.

In the morning Demetri put his uniform and a hoodie on. He placed his school bag inside his Nike backpack. He ate cornflakes with brown sugar and milk in the front room and brushed his teeth. He left the front door with his earphones in and clicked his phone screen to play 'Salute' again while walking down the outer corridor of his block, which was draped with netting to stop people falling off. '*You cross me, there will be consequences.*' The indoor stairwell smelt like bubblegum. The cleaner must have just mopped the stairs with soapy water. Demetri left his block and headed towards where the sirens had stopped the night before.

He passed a crime scene, taped off. Police officers were crowded round, and members of the public stood watching them from their windows. Demetri had seen crime scenes like this before and learnt to mind his own business. He pulled his hood up over his head and kept walking, past the Chinese takeaway, crossing the busy Walworth Road. He headed down Heygate Street, past the huge, empty grounds on his left where the blocks of the Heygate Estate used to be. The flats had been empty for several years. They'd only been knocked down recently.

He reached the gates to Willow Academy and crossed the

playground, walking quickly, his head pivoting round in both directions to make sure there was no member of staff who might see his Nike bag.

He headed up the stairs to the Year 11 commons area by the canteen and walked over to his group of friends. A girl standing on the other side of the room suddenly screamed and ran towards the girls' toilet.

'Silence in the corridors, Year 11! Please make your way to registration quickly and quietly!' came the instruction of a teacher when the bell went.

'You hear what happened?' one of Demetri's friends asked him as they turned into their classroom.

Demetri shook his head.

A boy in the year above them had been murdered.

I started work at Willow Academy after the October half-term in 2015. Inspired by my experience mentoring Jhemar with Into-University and volunteering at Jacob Sawyer, I'd landed a job as a programme coordinator for The Access Project (TAP).

TAP worked with bright students from disadvantaged backgrounds to help them gain access to top universities. It trained graduates like myself as in-school education advisers, embedding them in state secondary schools where more than 30 per cent of students were eligible for free meals – a metric commonly used to denote the poverty line (a household income of under £16,000).

For two days per week I would be running the TAP programme at Willow. Over 40 per cent of the school's students were eligible for free meals, high above the 15 per cent national average. I would also work at two other schools: one in leafy Maida Vale, west London, and another on the hidden tip of the Isle of Dogs, a short walk south of Canary Wharf's domineering towers. Flitting between these parts of the city throughout my working

week, experiencing different school regimes, learning from teachers, young and old, and meeting London's teenagers – all races,
religions, languages and regional nuances – would prove to be a
crash course in educational progress and disadvantage.

During my training at TAP's head office in Farringdon, on
topics ranging from child safeguarding to the workings of the
British university ranking system, my new colleagues expressed
sympathy on hearing I'd been placed at Willow. 'Good luck,
you'll be fine!' exclaimed one. 'We haven't quite cracked it there
yet,' another conceded flatly. Like a number of schools that
employed the charity's support – roughly twenty spread across
London, in places such as Tottenham, Fulham and Plaistow, as
well as a handful in the Midlands – Willow was known as a challenging place to work.

On my first day I was accompanied across the tarmac playground and shown to my desk in a quiet common area in one of
the buildings. As I placed my bag down I heard some muffled
noise coming from the far corner of the room. I craned my head
round one of the bookshelves to find some sixth formers, a
group of four giggling boys dressed in suits, slumped on some
chairs. When they saw me they looked up for a moment, puz-
zled as to who I was, then resumed their whispered, excitable
bantering.

'Boys, I don't mind you sitting there during your free periods,
but you've got to be quieter than that! You're only supposed to
be here to get on with your work!' came a female voice from
elsewhere in the room.

'Yes, miss!' muttered the students.

I hadn't noticed at first, but a few metres away from my own
desk stood another, piled high with folders. Sheets of highlighted paper were Blu-Tacked neatly all over the wall. Plastic
drawers contained colourful pamphlets about work experience
and various local sixth-form colleges.

A smartly dressed female member of staff sat in an office chair. She was peering past me with glaring eyes at the four boys. Then she relaxed and stood up to shake my hand, switching into a welcoming, maternal tone.

'Hello, love, nice to meet you. I'm Monica,' she beamed. 'Are you the new Access Project person?'

During my first weeks with TAP I met various teachers at my new places of work. But at Willow I was largely left to my own devices. It felt like teachers mostly saw my presence as an irritation; a distraction away from their heaving workload. Given how rigorous the school day seemed, I could hardly blame them.

By wandering around the school and getting into conversations with staff members, I learnt about lesson timetabling and lunch provision. Using a list of names from TAP's Salesforce computer software, a matrix of data about the charity's contacts and beneficiaries, I started finding students listed as on my TAP programme – those I would be working with as an adviser about higher education.

One afternoon I noticed a piece of paper bearing the portrait of a grinning boy tacked to a noticeboard with 'R.I.P' written above. I'd heard a reference to the recent tragic passing of a former student in an assembly and assumed the photograph must have been stuck on the wall to remember him, a makeshift shrine. A couple of sixth formers had explained to me that the student had been in their year when he was in the lower school. I talked to one teacher about it at lunch.

'There was an emergency staff briefing the morning it happened. Then I went up to my classroom before lessons started and just broke down crying,' he said. He explained he had taught the student before he'd been 'managed moved' in years prior – an agreement that takes place between two schools and parents so that a child can be exchanged from one school to another for a trial period, if not permanently, to avoid having to formally exclude them. 'I feel like the response from the staff body was muted, to be honest. People didn't know how to talk about it properly. We weren't being encouraged to have those conversations with the kids.'

I could not claim to know the intricacies involved in coordinating a school's response to the murder of a former student. But something didn't feel right. This teacher wasn't alone in his concern. As I adapted to the many practical tasks of my new job, the topic arose several times in conversation or passing comments.

'The morning after it happened, I found out on Snap before I got to school,' one female student I mentored on TAP explained. 'A couple of the boys who were close to him had sunken faces in lessons, and one of our teachers told them it was okay to not take part in the lesson. But in general it was all very hush-hush. I could see that some of the teachers were upset, but it was like they'd been told not to talk about it with us.'

Jacob Sawyer played a different role to that of a secondary school. It was much smaller, and by virtue of its space as a hub of youth work and community engagement – a more flexible set of practices than teaching a curriculum education – staff could approach things differently to teachers. As a consequence, adults and young people at Jacob Sawyer had talked openly and therapeutically about losing Jerrell. The contrast to Willow was palpable: here were two communities coming to terms with loss. Where one felt cold and corporate, the other felt warm and communicative; one was like a cold, stiff handshake, the other a caring hug. It added yet more value to the evolving impression of Jacob Sawyer in my mind, and the idea that people living and working in communities where violence is prevalent need safe and welcoming environments in which to talk about and process the traumatic events happening all around them. While I was excited by my new job at TAP, these formative moments provided anecdotal evidence of how academies' sterile onward march towards getting through the term undisturbed had the capacity to override the communal healing, and therefore well-being, of their students.

When she wasn't teaching humanities or taking phone calls, Monica would be there to show me the ropes. Having worked at Willow for nearly two decades, she was one of the few veterans who'd survived the transition from chaotic former years into the new academy era. She knew every nook and cranny; every technique for evading staff politics and getting on with her job. She enjoyed answering my questions, and she did so diplomatically. Because she knew every loophole to find stationery and get hold of snacks and milk for our teas – nuggets of information that she'd share with me, accompanied by a soft chuckle – she eventually gave us Dickensian nicknames: I was Oliver Twist, she was Fagin.

Monica became my guardian angel at Willow; an auntie to Tony's uncle. And aside from her timetabled job, she was constantly offering wraparound support to students. She communicated with their social workers or parents. She advised pupils on how to resolve any trouble they found themselves in. She helped them to complete application forms they were confused about. Helpless Year 11s applying to college, Year 10s signing up for work experience, Year 7s and 8s from her lessons who just wanted to stop by during their break time to say hello: every type of Willow student, boy or girl, big or small, came to consult Monica.

I began to notice older male students form regular queues at her desk. They might ask her for a character reference for a part-time job, or enquire about routes into construction or sports coaching, or request sheepishly to speak to her in private. At the end of her conversations, she introduced them to me. Their tentative, distrusting handshakes reminded me of boys at Jacob

Sawyer. Now, however, I was wearing a shirt and tie, not a T-shirt and jeans or tracksuit. I represented formal authority.

'This guy looks like an undie!' one boy muttered in jest, receiving a disapproving tut from Monica. When I bumped into the same student in an upstairs corridor later in the day he nodded at me, making the comment again to produce cackling laughter from his group of friends. I smiled, embracing the reality of this ongoing rite of passage. If I could have a pound coin for every time this would happen to me over the years, I would be a rich man.

Monica was basically running a youth service from her desk. Committed teachers like her were working overtime to ensure children who might not be getting that sort of extracurricular support from their parents were looked after. By the end of my first few weeks, she had quickly cemented a fundamental idea in my mind: that there were constant gaps that needed filling. They might not be visible to members of the public, nor recognized in computerized impact reporting, nor rewarded in raised wages. But as a state educator, you had a job description, and the curriculum, and the formal boxes to tick. And then, if you saw a way in, there was also an opportunity to go above and beyond to make progress. It made me start to think about how I might achieve my own version of this supplemental work – which I will explore in chapters 5 and 6.

My job for TAP was to enrol and mentor particular students who'd applied to be on the programme across Years 10 to 13 (fourteen to eighteen years old). I would help each student think about and apply to university. I was responsible for engaging with roughly fifty students in each of my schools; a minimum of ten in each year group. I held one-to-one check-ins and delivered group workshops about study skills and higher education. Each intervention would be responsive to the student's age, ability and academic interest. For example, engaging with a Year 13 student applying to study Physics or History at university looked very different to engaging with a Year 10 student who was unsure about what A levels or BTEC to choose.

I matched each student to a member of TAP's pool of volunteer professional tutors. This cohort included lawyers, bankers, advertisers, journalists and civil servants. Students would travel to their tutor's office on public transport to receive free, weekly, guided academic support in a GCSE or A-level subject of their choice. Some keen students took on two or three tutors. The tutorials served to improve their formal attainment in their subject and exposed them to their tutor's place of work.

Students attended tutorials at the Department for Education, the Treasury, JPMorgan and Save the Children; a Whitehall canteen, a meeting room on the twentieth floor of a skyscraper in Canary Wharf and an espresso bar in Soho. The exercise of commuting expanded their world views and expectations of what was possible. It normalized tight time-keeping. It granted them a sense of ownership and entitlement over spaces and interactions that were otherwise inaccessible. And via the tuition students were receiving, it helped them aspire to higher grades.

Students who were of highest priority to receive help from TAP were those who fitted the criteria: demonstrably academic, motivated to study at university, eligible for free school meals or 'pupil premium' funding, from a postcode where low numbers of young people have gone to university, the first person in their family to go to university or living in care. However, anyone could apply.

I gave assemblies to advertise the programme. I also spent break times handing out application forms to students, and one that returned from Year 11 caught my eye. It was signed 'Demetri A', and he stated that he wanted to study at university 'to understand why people carry knives'. His application was fearless and brutally honest. At the age of fifteen, he had perceived how academic study might help him to understand the more pressing angles of his social environment. I emailed him a time slot to come for an interview.

'Is it Mr Thapar?' Demetri asked as he nudged the door open after school later that week. 'I got your email,' he continued, holding my gaze with firm, unblinking eyes. He was confident but respectful as he walked with a bop over to my desk. His school uniform was neat and he wore white socks that clashed with his trousers. He took his seat, placing a Nike backpack on the floor beside him. He was short, five foot five, and slight, but had a naturally athletic build.

Demetri was in the same year as many of the boys I'd met who had come by to see Monica. But he had a different energy. Their visits to the library were typified by collective confusion. His visit was planted in individual certainty and determination.

'Why do you think studying at university will help you understand why people carry knives?' I asked.

'Cah,' he replied, 'I'm surrounded by other people like me. I've grown up around here, Elephant, just like they have. We've all gone through that phase of thinking we're a bad man. But still, I don't feel the need to carry a knife. So why do they?'

Years later, I would ask Demetri about what he was feeling during that time.

'When you tried to persuade me to apply to be on The Access Project, you were being bare persistent. I found it kinda annoying, still! Like, who is this guy!? But signing up brought loads of good things. It taught me that when you're unsure about whether to say yes or no to an opportunity, just do it, because you never know what might come.'

He noted that the recent murder of the student in the year above him had inspired him.

'That was so close to home. I wasn't that upset about it, but it literally happened near my yard. So it had been on my mind, even though, when you deep it, these stabbings are happening all over London, all the time. But everyone was talking about it. Some of the teachers were calm, but others were brushing it under the carpet. Everyone just tries to carry on like nothing has happened.'

4. Blue Light
Police

The crunch of a hatchback turning into the car park of Jacob Sawyer prompted Tony to look out of the window. His eyes tightened with concern as the car stopped and its doors burst open. Four young men hopped out. Tony stood up from his seat and a ring of keys jingled in his hands.

'Open the door!' yelled one of the arrivals through the slitted windows. Tony and another staff member rushed outside. A police car had sped into the car park behind the hatchback. Three officers got out – two male, one female, all white. One of the female officers called for backup on her radio. Seconds later another police car arrived, blocking the entrance. Three more officers jumped out, all male, all white. Then a police van turned on to the road and pulled up on to the pavement behind the second car. Its large sliding doors opened and out hopped six more officers – all male, all white – who moved in towards the building. A sea of uniforms approached in waves, drowning the quiet island of the community centre.

'I ain't got nothing!' one of the young men yelled.

'Don't touch me!' another protested.

Officers formed a cordon around the entrance to the car park. Two had walked towards the entrance of the centre to apprehend one young man who'd moved close to Tony. Tony placed himself steadily between the three of them.

'You've gotta calm down,' Tony said, holding the young man's triceps gently while he fidgeted in anger.

'Who are you?' one of the officers asked Tony in a northern

English accent, scrunching up his face. He pointed his finger so its tip was inches away from Tony's nose. 'Do you work here?'

Tony looked back without blinking. His expression was neutral, with weary eyes of moderated despair – a shield developed over decades.

'I run this place. Officer, is it necessary for this many of you to be here? There's four of them in one car,' said Tony. He spoke softly but authoritatively. It was a neat chess move. The policeman backed off, his excitement cooled by Tony's stoicism, and announced politely that he would need to search the young man. Tony nodded.

'Who's in charge here?' Tony asked, addressing the officers en masse. One of them who was standing near the hatchback nodded and walked over, introducing himself as the sergeant. He explained that they had followed the car from West Norwood.

'It's because it's four Black men in a new car, isn't it?' Tony gazed levelly at the sergeant.

'That's not why.' The sergeant shook his head. He looked well-accustomed to such accusations. 'This is an area with high gang activity.'

'All of this, it's too much. How is this a suitable response?' Tony pressed. The sergeant nodded, then persevered with formal procedure, a debrief to sterilize the situation. He explained that they'd checked and discovered that the car was registered to a woman's name – as it happened, one of the men's girlfriends. Tony explained that it was interactions like this that meant relationships between police and local people were so fraught. 'Do you realize what this sort of thing does to the community?' he asked. The sergeant nodded again in concession.

The officers searched the young men and opened the car's doors and boot, lifting up carpets and rummaging through the glove compartment, emptying its contents on to the passenger seat. The search yielded nothing.

The sergeant thanked everyone for their cooperation. The police officers got back into their vehicles and drove away. The road became quiet again. The young man with Tony breathed deeply, still recovering from the adrenaline rush of the confrontation. After a few minutes everyone went inside to find peace.

It was the first time I'd seen a clash between police and members of the public at such close quarters. In the few months prior, while hanging out at Jacob Sawyer, I'd heard many critical opinions about the police from young people. This was hardly surprising given the well-documented historic divisions between the Met and poor, multicultural communities across the capital city, and the history of racist policing in Brixton, specifically.

The Met face an extremely tough task of keeping people safe in a city as vast, busy and socially divided as London. What's more, Loughborough Junction has long been known for having high levels of crime, violent or otherwise. Between 2015 and 2016, Coldharbour ward had a rate of 189.95 crimes committed per 1,000 people, the second highest of the twenty-one wards in Lambeth; well above the borough average of 109.83, the city-wide average of 82.36 and the national average of 75. It made sense for the police to have a presence.

But I couldn't unsee what I'd witnessed.

My personal experience of police growing up was largely neutral. I've never been abused or subject to the law's heavy-handedness, only its moderate instruction. I've been stopped and searched twice in my life, both times as a teenager, and in circumstances that left me feeling uncomfortable but ultimately respected by the officers doing it. In other words, while I might have always felt some minor scepticism about the police, I had never seen or heard its institutional racism acted out within a Black British community first-hand. I had read about it in journalism and literature, and heard pained descriptions of it in hip-hop and grime lyrics, but I certainly hadn't witnessed it from such a front-row perch as the staff office of Jacob Sawyer. When I did, it was eye-opening.

Tony had told me lengthy stories about how policing in south London had evolved during his lifetime. He turned a teenager in the early 1980s, when public uprisings against incidents of racially motivated police brutality in areas with Black and Asian populations had punctured the social fabric of the capital. In 1979, thousands of people, the majority of whom belonged to immigrant families from the Indian subcontinent (including friends of my uncles), rioted in Southall, west London, where my dad grew up, after police killed Clement Blair Peach, an anti-racism activist. Peach had protested peacefully against a meeting held by the National Front, a far-right, fascist political party which would habitually attack Black and brown citizens.

Around this time a recession entrenched unemployment across the country. Unrest simmered between police and Brixton's Caribbean populace. To suppress the high levels of crime in Lambeth, the Met were granted powers to search anyone on the street they deemed suspicious – a methodological forefather to modern 'stop-and-search', which became known as the 'sus law'. It was quickly criticized as having been used disproportionately against Black people. Many violent incidents resulted from National Front activity, but plenty, too, stemmed from the negligence of and active discrimination enacted by the police, while they failed to come to terms with Britain's unequal, ethnically diversifying and restless population.

In her seminal 1973 book, *Society and the Policeman's Role*, sociologist Maureen Cain found that it was habitual for police officers in the UK to refer to Black people as 'pimps' and 'layabouts', and view them as 'different' and 'incomprehensible'. In a 1979 document called 'Police Against Black People', the Institute of Race Relations published extensive accounts of police malpractice taken from legal case files and records of community organizations. Reflecting on these institutional failures, Peter Fryer noted in his 1984 book, *Staying Power: The History of Black People in Britain*, that during this time 'criminal procedure was being used to harass [Black communities]'.

This context of police racism watered the fertile soil of widespread poverty and resentment in Thatcherite Britain to sow the seeds of mass outrage in multicultural areas. In January 1981, a fire killed thirteen Black teenagers at a house party in New Cross, south-east London, in a suspected racist attack that remains both unsolved to this day and active as a fatal symbol of the legal system's potential for institutional discrimination and failure to bring about justice for wronged communities of colour. Three months later, the first Brixton riot in April 1981 saw hundreds of people and police injured. Buildings and vehicles were torched. Two more Brixton riots followed: one in 1985, after the shooting of Cherry Groce by the police, which left her paralysed, while they forced entry to her home to look for her son, Michael; and another in 1995, after the death of twenty-six-year-old Wayne Douglas in police custody.

Tony remembered the 1981 riots because he managed to get a handed-down Adidas tracksuit from his elders' participation in the looting. 'Being Black in these kinds of areas back then meant that there was a different kind of police. The ones here were more vicious. It wasn't like out in Surrey, where if you bumped into a police officer on the train they might say hello, and ask how you are, and be polite. Here they would bully us, beat us up, spit at us, call us "n******" and "jungle bunnies". I saw my friends' parents being intimidated by these big, burly white guys in uniform. It wasn't every officer, but it was a lot of them. I always remembered the nice ones because they stopped you but they didn't treat you like shit. They cared about you and spoke to your parents properly. One officer greeted us every morning before school. I didn't hate the police. I just didn't like them.'

When Tony recalled vignettes of his upbringing, he relayed fond memories of his big family, fun social life and tight-knit south London community. But the dovetailing themes of violence, racism and policing were rarely far from mention. Police patrolled the streets in 1984 when he went to watch the West Indies cricket team famously dispatch England 5–0 in the Wisden Trophy at the Oval. On entering his late teens, Tony's group of friends called themselves the 'Small Axe Posse' after a Jamaican reggae sound system of the same name (a few of its members took this branding to a literal level by carrying small axes to defend themselves against National Front thugs). In his twenties, after Tony trained as a chef and later a drug-and-alcohol-abuse counsellor, he worked as a football coach for local teenagers in south London. This role included briefly coaching the late Stephen Lawrence shortly before he was killed in April 1993 by white racists in Eltham, south-east London. The failure to bring Lawrence's murderers to justice became perhaps the most public milestone in the lengthening history of institutional police racism. Tony attended Snoop Dogg's first UK concert, where, he said, 'every fed in the city was waiting outside when the show finished!' He drank in pubs with Irish gangsters. Young men of his generation became used to fighting to survive. But Tony was usually the voice of reason in his social group. He'd neutralize confrontations when others on his estate were up to no good. He gained a diplomat's reputation. Clashes with the police, however, were unavoidable.

'They used to call it "the mattress". They couldn't leave bruises on you, so instead they used to take you in a cell, roll you up in a mattress and kick you and hit you with truncheons and rolled-up magazines. When police came up and spoke to you, they might say: "I'm gonna nick you, you fucking Black cunt," and there would be nothing to stop them getting away with it. We were powerless. Stuff like that might still happen now occasionally, but it isn't as intense as it used to be. They can't get away with that sort of stuff because it'll get reported. Most of the time, anyway.'

Tony explained to me how some young men he'd once worked with had told him they'd been taken inside a police van and strip-searched while one officer started verbally abusing them about the size of their penises: 'I thought you were supposed to be hung like donkeys?' he'd allegedly said. The incident prompted a meeting between community leaders and senior police.

'Things still happen but in general they are better,' Tony continued. 'But then there have been changes that have made it harder for police to do their job. All the cuts. It used to be that you had your local police officer, the "bobby on the beat", and you knew them for years; they did proper community policing. They stopped you getting into trouble because they knew your siblings and your parents. But now you have young officers who are not from cities, shipped in from the army. They like to have a fight, maybe they're not used to talking to Black people. It makes it difficult to police an area like Brixton if you've got a force full of those types. And the other side of the coin is that I think a lot of officers want to get away from being seen as racist or corrupt all the time. I guess it's a bit like when someone sees a Black man and thinks he's a thief or a thug just because of stereotypes. For the Old Bill, one brush tarnishes all, but it shouldn't. The problem is that there has been so much corruption, it's hard for the good officers not to get dragged down with the rest of them.'

May 1980

Tony was thirteen. He attended secondary school in Clapham and was nearing the end of Year 8. The school day had finished and he spent time hanging out with his friends on Clapham

Common. On his way home he walked north up the high street. He always stopped at the pet shop, which had different fish and rabbits on display in the window. Tony wanted a pet to look after. He'd won a goldfish at the summer fair the year before but after keeping it in a purple Quality Street box overnight it had died.

He heard the sound of a vehicle pulling up behind him. A Black Maria police van was parking next to the pavement.

'What do we have here?' one of the officers asked after climbing out. 'What's your name, son?'

Tony froze. He'd been stopped by police before and they would say racist things to him. Once he and his friends had run away from some police on Brixton Road and the officers had called after them, shouting 'n******'. It reminded Tony of when he'd got his nose broken by some white boys who lived on the other side of Clapham Common, where all the National Front families lived. Some of the policemen were as bad as the boys. Tony only trusted one policeman because he was nice to him in the mornings before school.

'Like animals, do you?' the officer asked Tony. He used his left hand to usher Tony away from the window and make him face towards the wall with his legs apart. 'You're casing the place, aren't you?' he muttered in Tony's ear, patting him down.

'I'm not! I'm –'

'Your clothes. Off!' the officer interrupted. Tony froze, paralysed by humiliation. 'Did you hear what I said? Take your fucking clothes off!'

Tony removed his shoes, then undid his tie. He loosened and dropped his trousers. He undid his school shirt, then removed his white vest. He made a pile of clothes on the floor next to him. He stood in his white Y-fronts. He heard the footsteps of people walking by behind him, and buses and cars driving past.

'Leave the boy alone!' came a loud, wheezing male voice. An elderly white man with a walking stick had stopped nearby.

Tony noticed one of his older brother's friends standing across the road. When he noticed Tony looking at him he turned around quickly and walked in the other direction. Tony knew people would do anything to avoid dealing with the police, but he still felt betrayed. Tony's eyes filled with tears. His legs were shaking with the light breeze and despair.

'That's enough,' said one of the other policemen, standing in silence to the side. 'Pull them up.'

'You stay out of trouble,' the main officer muttered quietly. Tony grabbed his clothes and started pulling them on. The officers opened the van doors, climbed inside and drove off.

Tony wanted to disappear. He put on his shoes without doing them up and sprinted home as fast as he could. Tears were streaming down his face.

By 2016, policing across the United Kingdom was being affected by austerity politics. Enforced since the start of the decade by the Conservative–Liberal Democrats coalition government, the shredding of public services was becoming very evident.

'There were a couple of points in 2015 and 2016 where I was like, this can't go on. This is just so lean, so ridiculous, we're on the edge here,' said Chief Inspector Jack Rowlands, who has worked his way up the Met's ranks having trained in 2003, based mainly in south London. He is the founder of Divert, a programme working out of several south London stations, which hires youth workers to intervene in young people's lives when they are arrested.

'Back in 2010, 2011, 2012, the cuts hadn't really kicked in yet because the Met were still getting funding for the Olympics. During that time, I felt that I could walk on to my ward – Ferndale in Brixton – close my eyes and tell where I was purely because of the feeling under my feet. I know it sounds corny, but when you're doing good police work you *absorb* your ward, and in turn you get to know people. I'm a social person, I'd have people talking to me all day. It was the best job I've ever had. But that became harder to do when the cuts started to kick in. It was all diluted. By 2015, we might have the same number of people who would have looked after one ward before looking after three wards. When that happens, what do you really think we can achieve?'

The rise in street violence in the years following 2016 has often been blamed on funding cuts to police. The assumption is that less funding equates to fewer officers on the streets, and therefore more violent crime. However, the way funding cuts have actually impacted policing in London is not primarily to do with raw numbers of officers on the ground – it is more the fact that officers have been given less time and fewer resources to do proper community policing.

'Compared to the rest of the country, the Met has done a reasonable job of protecting its officer numbers in the capital,' explained Gavin Hales, an independent researcher and the former deputy director of the Police Foundation think tank. Statistics show a fall of just 3 per cent in Met officer numbers between 2008 and 2018, but because of the reduction in support roles, officers are being pulled in more directions than ever before. 'The bigger loss is how cuts have affected *police staffing*,' he said, referring to community support officers, intelligence analysts, receptionists and administrators. Staff workforces have nearly halved over the same time period. 'Work-per-officer is going up. They have to be reactive, instead of building links in the community, doing preventative work or investigating increasingly complex crimes,' Hales continued. Traditional neighbourhood policing has been dismantled, rendering the goals of community engagement and harm prevention as uncoordinated, separate entities.

The physical element of land control, of having a place for

officers to retreat to, has been drastically hit, too. Rowlands explained that the Met's human resources function is now out-sourced to a call centre in Newport, South Wales. There has been a loss of architectural infrastructure in which police might congregate, organize and discuss the demands of their role.

'The thing that breaks my heart is that we've sold our crown jewels. When I joined Lambeth police in 2008 as a sergeant, we had Frank O'Neill House on Clapham Road, we had Streatham police station, we had another covert building in Lambeth, we had Kennington and Brixton. We've still got our base in Clapham Common, just about. But Streatham's shut and Kennington's shut – although it is actually going to reopen. Increasingly, we're losing physical environments where before police officers were parading all day, every day. The whole design of being a trauma-informed community is that you have safe environments, but those have been sold off. All of these stations used to have twenty-four-hour canteens. They provided a space for people to sit together and say things like: "Mate, you've still got blood on your sleeve" – and then have a laugh or cry about it, and so on. That was a really important part of our culture.'

The polarization and digitization of British life has meant that the nature of policing London has changed in the twenty-first century. Modern criminal activity has birthed online, invisible and cleverly guarded avenues in which to operate. Meanwhile, layers of the Met have been hollowed out in the name of shrinking the state since 2010. Decisions of political leaders to reduce funding for law enforcement in our country, alongside drastic cuts to more fundamental state systems such as healthcare, education and welfare, have created a multiplier effect for social breakdown. When people face crises but have fewer lifelines for support, they are more likely to call the police. And if the police are struggling, they will be less likely to respond appropriately.

However, in 2015 Britain still had the second largest budget-per-capita spending on public order and safety in Europe. By highlighting the way austerity has made it harder for the police, I am therefore not arguing that we need to grant police endlessly greater financial powers. Far from it. In an ideal world – where other public services are funded properly, giving people a universally supportive start in life – we would not have much need for the police. But even in our imperfect world, if the most vulnerable or socially excluded young people were not left traumatized or wanting, and if the UK were less unequal, there would be a reduced motivation to commit crime.

A renewed call to defund the police would explode across the US following the racist police killing of George Floyd in Minneapolis in May of 2020, during the Covid-19 lockdown. America spends 2.04 per cent of its GDP on public order and safety, a rate that is far higher than European states and any other developed country. On a per-capita basis, the US spends more than twice the amount of money on prisoners than on its public school students. Evidence of inherent racism in American policing is rife: roughly one in every 1,000 African-American boys and men can expect to die at the hands of police, slightly higher than the chances of an average American dying in a motorcycle accident.

America is not the same as the UK. But following the success of the US campaign, people in the UK have reproduced the argument for defunding the police here. It is worth considering: focusing on the belief that, ideally, we as a developed society ought to be empowering community-based initiatives rather than pumping a demonstrably ineffective and discriminatory penal system with the little public money that remains.

'Campaigns to defund the police and prison system do not argue that every prison should close tomorrow and every police officer be sacked the day after – they argue that social problems

are better addressed through social responses,' wrote Adam
Elliott-Cooper, an anti-racism activist and UK defund-the-police
campaigner, in the *Guardian* in July 2020. When we spoke over
the phone the following month, he argued that the real problem
remains the lack of value placed upon systems of care, and the
overvalue placed upon systems of control and punishment.

'Before austerity began the police were continually being
funded more and more. They had more weapons, they had more
powers, there were more police on the streets. Did that lead to an
increase in public safety? Did having less stressed-out police officers, better resourced police officers, make them any less racist?
Any less violent? Have they been more effective at making communities safer? The answer is no,' Elliott-Cooper said. 'Violent
crime peaked before austerity, during which time we saw a litany
of scandals in the police, from Stephen Lawrence all the way up to
the killing of Sean Rigg in 2008, and everything in between. So
there is clearly no correlation between improvements in public
safety, reductions in racism or police violence, and investments in
policing. Regardless of whether we have more police or if we
make even relatively minor cuts to them, we still don't really see
any significant changes in the areas of life that the police are created to deal with . . . Angela Davis [American political activist]
says that prisons don't deal with problems, they don't lock away
bad people. They lock away unemployment, they lock away illit-
eracy, they lock away mental health problems and addiction. So
having "efficient" police services, with administrators and support staff and comfortable canteens, doesn't in any way address
the fundamental problem with policing, which is the idea that
violence is the best way to deal with things. The best way to prevent violence happening in the first place isn't violence. It's care.'

Chief Inspector Jack Rowlands pointed out that the psychological impact of the policing job is rarely captured in wider
discourse about the imperfections of police work. Signing up to

be an officer carries with it an accurate assumption that you are going to come up against extreme situations. But when this is placed in the context of the Met's staff base being stretched thinner, it explains yet more about the mismanagement of policing, and the therefore heightened likelihood of malpractice and lack of accountability.

'Policing throws up things that you *never* thought you would see in your life,' Rowlands told me. 'I had one week where someone got stabbed to death, there was a suicide, there was a four-year-old boy who got his head caught in the door frame of a car and died. I dealt with a road traffic accident. That was all within six working days. I woke up on my rest day and I felt absolutely nothing. That was the scariest feeling, the fact that it didn't bother me. Then there is all the stuff in between, operational policing: you see someone who you arrested before for carrying a knife, so you ask them to take their hands out of their pockets, they become aggravated, you have to use force to stop and search them, but you find nothing so you're seen to make a mistake. Ten a.m. you record a burglary. Eleven a.m. you deal with a sudden death, an elderly gentleman has passed away and you need to be there to sort everything out. Then you need to arrange a raid on an address because there is intelligence to suggest that there is a shitload of different drugs being dealt from there. You've got a young person in the station who is involved in gangs, so you need to arrange support for them. Then there is the worst possible scenario. There's been a fight outside a chicken shop. You turn up and someone's been stabbed. They're taking their final breaths. You dive on them, and you're cutting all their clothes off to work out whether it's one stab wound or ten, and you're calling backup, you're getting an ambulance there, you're administering first aid. Friends and family have already turned up and they're all yelling at you to save his life, right in your ear, on your shoulder, begging you to save them. Then they die in front of you and the only thing you can do is put a blanket over them, put a crime scene in place and begin the professional mode of saying we've now got a victim of a murder. Then you go home and you have your dinner. The next day, you get in your police car and you ask: what's London going to chuck at me today?'

He explained that this barrage of stress takes its toll on the way police officers behave. 'I've had to stop and ask myself before: why is it that when I open my drawer at home I get a little bit edgy when I see a knife? Why am I having such primal reactions to things? Maybe I've started going from zero to ten very quickly, whether it's being vigilant, whether it's having a debate with someone down the pub. There is no mediation taking place. I'm conditioning my body to go, go, go, all the time. Without the right support for dealing with that, it's very difficult to do your job properly.'

Sympathy for these hectic ordeals, however, can only go so far. Funding cuts alone do not explain away the mistakes that are made in practices like stop-and-search. A recognition that stop-and-search does not solve street violence has sunk in over the years. Its use has reduced significantly: in 2017/18 there were 277,378 stop-and-search incidents in England and Wales, a rate of 5 per 1,000 people, down from 23 incidents per 1,000 people in 2009/10 (although its use shot up again during the Covid-19 lockdown in 2020). But regardless of its prevalence or lack thereof, it is still racist, and arguably getting more so. In 2017/18, there were three stop-and-searches for every 1,000 white people, compared with 29 stop-and-searches for every 1,000 Black* people; Black people were nearly ten times as likely to be

---

* This includes those who identify as from Black Caribbean or Black African origins; it does not include mixed-race people, who are still policed disproportionately but at a lower rate.

stopped-and-searched as white people. The previous year, they were just over eight times as likely. In 2014/15 they were just over four times as likely. The type of violent racism that plagued the Met in the years of Tony's adolescence may now be regarded as an exorcized ghost. But problems identified in the Macpherson Report in 1999, following an investigation into the racist killing of Stephen Lawrence, remained alive and kicking in the 2010s. Evidence of this has been typified by the deaths of Black men at the hands of police, such as Mark Duggan – whose killing in Tottenham, north London, sparked riots across British major cities in August 2011 – Sean Rigg, Sheku Bayoh and many others. The Met's institutional racism ought to be stamped out as a priority by investing in initiatives where young people and community leaders can have a consistent dialogue with local officers, comprehensive inclusion training for forces and grass-roots efforts to attract and hire more diverse cohorts into the policing profession.

I described to Rowlands what I saw when the police arrived at Jacob Sawyer that afternoon in April 2016, searching the young man's car and confronting Tony in the process.

'I get it. The very nature of stop-and-search isn't an ideal situation in any stage in life. Even if you've got a firearm or a knife on you, or loads of drugs on you, it's still, by the very nature of what it entails, pausing your liberty for that moment, not a good experience for anyone,' he replied. 'But as a police officer it's often the case that you can't share the full extent of the intelligence that made you decide to search people. What if the intelligence suggested that there was a knife in that car? But then the people in that car don't have a knife on them, and you've got it wrong, but you can only go on what you've got. We're trying to make sense of whatever intelligence we have, and we can't risk having people flailing around with a weapon. It's really tricky to explain to young people we stop but also to members of the public who watch what we're doing. I still believe the Met are under-resourced, and we're getting there with that, but from a geographic point of view we're still always quite close together. So when you do need urgent help from your colleagues, it can come fast, and it comes from all different directions. It can be quite dramatic. If I'm near, I'm not going to wait to see if another unit goes, I'm just gonna go. It just so happens that now there's loads of cars at the scene.'

I asked him to tell me about some of the less obvious gains that are made by stop-and-search.

'What people forget – because it's never really talked about – is that stop-and-search is used a lot on people who burgle houses, defraud people, con their way into homes and cause criminal damage. You get car thieves walking around with a jemmy in their pocket wanting to screw cars, and it makes up a huge proportion of people we stop and search. When I've got a particular person walking down the street who is a career burglar, and we are getting hammered for burglaries in the local area, and I stop this person on my ward and they've got nothing on them, that would be recorded as a stop-and-search with no outcome. But the flipside to that is: what have I prevented him doing, just by being there? There is always a greater context to it. If I've literally just received a call from a member of the public, or I have other intelligence, I have to act on that information, then I have to protect the public. It's humans doing this role. Humans get it right, but humans also get it wrong. What I do know is that we get a lot of feedback from young people saying: I'm uncomfortable with you doing this, but I do understand why you're doing it, because my cousin got stabbed to death last year and the violence is making me feel unsafe.'

Jacob Sawyer was not just an escape from a troubled home or road life, or a place to go to after school. It was a neutral space and a font of elders' wisdom; a sanctuary where altercations with law enforcement might be contained. What's more, witnessing police surrounding the centre had granted me a simple logic about my own identity within the space. Tony soon explained it to me bluntly: 'The boys are not gonna expect anything different from someone like you unless you give them a reason to.' This no-nonsense truism helped Rory and me to realize that by putting in time at Jacob Sawyer we could aim to disrupt the existing narrative about newcomers to Brixton, and outsiders to the centre. Tony explained that a lot of the attention that boys in Loughborough Junction received from people who might look like us came from figures of authority such as teachers and police. Could anyone blame the boys at the centre for having initially calculated the assumption that Rory and I, too – until we proved otherwise – might be of the same ilk?

Our first project at Jacob Sawyer was by now getting off the ground. We'd received funding to start a weekly discussion group with boys at the centre. I invited a local artist called Ben Nugent to come in so that Carl and his friends could brief him to create our logo. They suggested aesthetic qualities they felt should be involved in its design.

'Street lamps?' suggested Carl.

'Big tower blocks!'

'The roads . . .'

The resulting logo was a black-and-yellow mask built by the shapes described by the boys: rectangles containing rows of squares, like Loughborough Estate's tall towers, hinged open to look like a window into the mind; circles for eyes to capture the roundabouts; arrows to denote navigation.

For the first planned session in early March, we went to the corner shop near the centre to buy some sweet snacks and cans of fizzy drink to use as small motivational carrots. We handed them out and sat in a circle in the centre's classroom next to the staff office. I'd brought along a big, hardback photography book called *Don't Call Me Urban! The Time of Grime*. It contained images taken by photographer Simon Wheatley documenting grime music across the 2000s. I figured that the book's images would be relatable enough to be interesting for the boys, but foreign and challenging enough in their depiction of a past London to spark conversations. I held up photographs and asked questions about them. How did the images make the boys feel? Where and when did they think they were taken? What was surprising or familiar about what they saw?

One image showed a group of boys standing in the street looking up at a surveillance camera, all with their middle fingers raised. A couple of the boys yelled out in glee.

'Those are like the CCTV cameras in town!' commented Carl, leaping out of his seat.

'You never know whether they're real or not. Anyone could be watching,' someone else noted.

Another image showed a group of boys sitting on office chairs. Three of them scribbled with pens in notebooks and one boy reclined back with headphones on. His eyes were closed, his mind cocooned in a private musical experience.

'That's like the studio here at Sawyer,' someone commented. 'Is it a youth club?'

I explained that it was someone's bedroom in a flat on the Isle of Dogs, in east London. His question sparked a conversation with the boys about how much they valued Jacob Sawyer as a place they could visit.

'It's one of the only places I can be myself. Here, I don't worry about other things that happen outside or when I'm at home,' said Carl.

Another image showed a close-up of a group of teenage boys in baseball caps and hoodies, their foreheads sweating while they fought over a microphone. Their mouths were open and hands stretched out to be the next performer to clash. The photo was taken in 2005 at the Lansbury Youth Club in Poplar, east London, next door to Langdon Park School, where Dizzee Rascal had created his legendary album, *Boy In Da Corner*, two years earlier.

'They look free,' expressed one boy.

Finally, we told the group to look at a pair of images and identify the common theme between them. The first was a blurred, frantic scene showing a young man being restrained by two policemen inside a convenience shop in Thornton Heath, to the south of Lambeth, in the London borough of Croydon. The other showed two boys being stopped and searched by two policemen. The group erupted into discussion, some of them visibly irritated, others laughing and recounting memories.

'It's like when feds stop you and ask you to take your hands out your pockets even though you've done nothing wrong. But you don't actually have to say anything or tell them your name.'

'Yeah, it's jarring when that happens. But they have to do their job. If no police searched anyone, more people would walk around carrying a shank.'

'Bare man hate on police, but it's not helpful. Not all of them are bad people. And let's be real, around Brixton there are so many GMs!'

'Nah, I know they need to search us . . . especially when bare people have been stabbed. But it's more about how they speak. One time I was coming home from school and they stopped me. I was so calm because I remember what happened last time, when I got angry and they just held me down on the floor and one of them pushed their knee into my back. But even when I didn't say nothing, my man shoved me up against the fence! He went way too hard! It was a violation.'

'It's like them "sus laws" that used to exist back in the day. Feds used to just arrest whoever they wanted. These times they had the Brixton riots. Stop-and-search don't even bother me now, cah it's happened so many times I can't even count. I just keep my mouth shut, fam.'

We awarded Carl the 'Hero of the Week' prize, a bag of sweets, for his intelligent contributions to the session. It received some protest from the others, who tried to wrestle the sweets from him. The boys ran through the main room to play football on the astroturf outside. Rory and I popped our heads into the office to debrief with Tony.

Carl's mum asked him to go to the shop to buy some milk. He put on a tracksuit and trainers, walked down the stairs of his block and across the car park. The olders were standing in a group. They looked agitated. The opps were taunting them on socials; they'd caught one of the mandem lacking the day before.

So the group started walking north. Carl went with them. He knew the others were carrying their knives. They entered quiet roads, where Carl saw one boy on his own. Carl recognized him from his year at school and realized he needed to help. 'It's calm, he's my cousin,' Carl told the olders. He was lying to protect the boy and he felt good about it.

After the group split up to look for opps, Carl heard sirens, so he turned down a side road and jumped over a fence. He landed hard on the pavement, then walked past the tube station, slowing so that he looked like a civilian. He was sweating and he knew he looked bait. Plus, because of his dark skin and the way he dressed like a GM in a tracksuit with a pouch, Carl felt like he was more likely to get stopped anyway. He felt like the police always stopped darker skinned boys like him more than lighter skinned ones because they associated dark skin with knives and drugs. He wondered whether the others had scored a point.

Suddenly a police van swung round the corner. Out jumped loads of feds. They grabbed Carl, put him in handcuffs and shoved him into the van. Carl became scared that he was in trouble. What if the olders cheffed up someone? What if somebody died? What if the feds thought it was Carl? Were they taking him to prison?

When they got to the police station they took Carl's details and fingerprints, then they waved a handheld metal detector over his body and searched him. They took him into a room for questioning, where he said he didn't know what happened. They asked if he wanted a solicitor, and Carl said yes.

The officers put Carl in a cell where there was a camera in the corner of the room. As he sat on the hard bed, his mind was racing. Is this what prison was like? *Maybe they thought Carl had done a murder.* What if he was going to spend years here? Would he ever see his mum again? He dropped to the floor and started doing press-ups, then sat on his bed panting until one of the police officers knocked on the door and brought him some dinner on a tray, gooey lasagne that had no flavour. Carl ate a few mouthfuls of the food then fell asleep.

When Carl woke up the next day he did some more press-ups. Being in cells reminded him of being in the isolation room at school. There was nothing interesting to do and nobody there to help him, even though he was only young.

When the solicitor came at 3 p.m. she asked about what happened. Carl said he didn't know and she advised him to say 'no comment' in questioning. Carl would never snitch, anyway. He kept his mouth shut. When he looked at the solicitor he felt like she cared about him, because she was the only person who seemed to want to help him. Afterwards he was allowed to leave, and when Carl got home, his mum was upset. Carl felt bad, because he knew he should have just got the milk and returned home, like she'd asked him to.

A letter arrived the next day through Carl's door which said: 'No Further Action.'

5. Diligent

Education

Carl sat in the isolation room for the first time since joining his new school. He'd been permed from his last one just as he was about to start his GCSEs. His friend got caught with weed and claimed that Carl helped him get hold of it. Carl denied it, because this time he really hadn't done that, even though he'd brought in weed other times. But the head teacher didn't believe him. Carl had started messing around more since his dad had left his family home. He'd stopped taking life seriously now that there was nobody at home giving him rules to follow. When the school called his mum in to speak to her, Carl could see how sad and angry she was, and he felt ashamed. He felt like he was a failure, and that there was no point trying any more, because his record was tarnished. He knew he would never make it to university now. That's what his teachers kept telling him. But nobody had looked out for him properly, or talked to him about his dad leaving, or asked him why he was getting into so much trouble. Now it was too late. Carl knew loads of boys who'd been excluded like him. It was normal in Brixton.

At his new school, Carl was being punished for selling snacks and drinks in the playground. By being in isolation he was missing History, which he was happy about. He disliked History because he didn't see it as relevant to his life. He hated writing and reading for long periods of time. Carl thought the teachers probably wanted him out of their classes because they knew he'd been excluded from another school. He knew they didn't like him, even though they didn't know him or what was going on in his life.

At his old school there were only detentions, which lasted for three hours every Friday afternoon. Now, in the isolation room, Carl could get away with doing nothing. When the teacher wasn't looking, he'd go on his phone to watch videos on You-Tube, or rest his head in his arms to pretend like he was working. He thought isolation was making him *less* smart. School was supposed to teach you things, so what was the point of school if they were just going to leave kids like him on his own? Carl felt like a lost cause. He suspected teachers were looking for reasons to send him to a PRU, like other boys he knew. Plus, there were more bad kids at this school than his last one, more gang members, so he ended up fitting in with them. He knew a few of the boys in his year already, so he was popular. People in his year thought he was funny. The olders rated him. He'd won some fights. He was starting to get attention from girls. His face was becoming bait.

In the summer Carl had started shotting small bags of weed. He hid stashes in a plastic Tesco bag and tucked it behind a dustbin. He learnt to hold baggies inside the same Lycra shorts he wore to football, or in some boxers which had small pockets in them, so that if he got patted down the feds wouldn't find them. Every time he moved food he made £40, £50 if he was lucky. Carl just wanted money. Money was all he could think about. If he had money he could buy meals, clothes and trainers himself, instead of coming home hungry to an empty fridge.

His mum was stressed out more than usual since she'd told Carl's dad to leave. Carl had sometimes listened to his dad, but now with him gone, he could do what he wanted. His dad made promises he couldn't keep which made Carl trust him less. Carl knew his mum didn't understand his life. She was becoming more suspicious. She kept saying he was changing and asking

Carl where her kitchen knife was. He told her he didn't know, but he took it in case he saw any opps and had to defend himself. He was always alert when he was in public. Carl didn't want to be stabbed like other people he knew. Lots of boys had got hurt or died in Brixton over the years. He wished he lived somewhere where nobody carried knives or got stabbed.

In the isolation room Carl was still high from lunch break. His new group of friends always hid behind the bushes to smoke. The teachers probably knew but they didn't stop it. The only day when Carl didn't smoke was when he had PE. He always liked exercising. His auntie, who loved athletics, had recently encouraged him to go to boxing sessions at Carney's community centre in Battersea. She was a big inspiration for Carl because she always told him about the importance of keeping his body healthy. Carl was naturally good at sports, and football and running made him feel positive about himself at school. On sports day he would win any race he entered.

Carl had recently started group discussion sessions at Jacob Sawyer every Friday night. He and his friends would sit in a circle and chat about their lives. Carl liked those meetings because he could talk about school and police and music. It felt good to get stuff off his chest and hear other people's perspectives.

The exclusion room made Carl feel bad about his life. When he deeped it, he realized it was evil. Any time he tried to speak to the teachers they just ignored him, or made out like he was being stupid or aggressive. Carl knew he just needed help. He didn't understand why more adults were trying to punish him than help him. His behaviour needed to improve, but wasn't school supposed to educate people? Why had the teachers given up on him already?

Carl laid his forehead on the desk. He closed his eyes and started to daydream. He wanted school to finish so he could smoke some more. He didn't want to think about the future because it made him feel depressed. Carl reckoned that deep down all boys like him felt like that.

Having turned fourteen, Jhemar was old enough for us to meet outside of the IntoUniversity centre. We convened by the plane tree that has stood for over a hundred years casting cooling shadows over Brixton's Windrush Square – the strip of land named after the passenger liner that brought the first wave of West Indian immigrants to the United Kingdom in 1948. Next to the square stands the Ritzy cinema, Brixton library and Black Cultural Archives (BCA). The BCA was founded in 1981 with the aim of securing better historical representation for Black people in Britain. It has archival rooms, an exhibition space and a cafe selling small plates and cakes.

The previous October, during Black History Month, Jhemar had expressed boredom at the repetitive content he was being presented with at school. Rehashed lectures rarely veered far from Martin Luther King, the transatlantic slave trade and reggae music, he said. 'There's one teacher who switches it up but otherwise it's the same thing every time. It feels like they're just doin' it cah they have to, then it's back to business as usual.' Both of Jhemar's parents were born in Jamaica, and growing up in Brixton meant that he had been surrounded by Caribbean influences his whole life: the dancehall-and-soca-filled block parties taking place in the summer; the colourful Rastafari lion or island flag murals painted on walls and shopfronts; the loaves of coco bread, patties and bottles of punch served in the market. Jhemar had learnt about the HMT *Empire Windrush* at primary school. He told me about what it was like in Jamaica when he visited his grandparents: the jerk BBQ pit smoke; the swarms of mosquitoes that kept him awake at night; the crowded streets of Kingston, where his dad was from, and the paradise beaches in Falmouth, the seaside town where his mum grew up. In other words, he could easily derive pride for his transnational identity. Yet he saw Black History Month as a gimmick.

I asked what he felt about the history he learnt during the rest of the year. He shrugged his shoulders in despondency. I mentioned how I used to switch off during history lessons at secondary school because they never felt relevant enough to my own experience. Given the student body I belonged to, at least 50 per cent of which was British Asian – Indians, Sri Lankans, Pakistanis, Koreans, Chinese and more – the preoccupation with whitewashed European history – the Romans, Tudors and Nazi Germany – never wholly satisfied my intellectual curiosity. This is not to downplay the importance of these traditional history subjects. It is to critique their presence at the expense of all else. In a city as diverse as London, and a country whose identity depends upon a history of global command-and-conquer, such a focus seemed short-sighted. As a teenager I never saw it like this, of course: I just misbehaved and took the subject less seriously. But I didn't learn properly about the term 'colonialism' until my early twenties, while reading at university. I was never formally educated about Britain's role in colonizing the Indian subcontinent, the Indian people's two-million-soldier-strong presence fighting in the Second World War, the arbitrary, bloody Partition of the states of Punjab and Bengal at independence from British rule in 1947 or the invited migration of South Asians like my grandparents to the United Kingdom in the mid-twentieth century. Jhemar and I had debated how suitable the contemporary history curriculum is for serving people like us, whose existence is a product of a global empire. We concluded that Black History Month shouldn't need to exist, because its contents should already be presented as British history in the broader subject curriculam.

The BCA was hosting an exhibition called 'Black Georgians: The Shock of the Familiar'. It was a room full of historical artefacts – illustrations, letters, newspaper cuttings – narrated with captions, organized so that visitors could walk anticlockwise and absorb collated stories about the presence of Black people in Britain during the Georgian era, between 1714 and 1830. We spent an hour inside reading about different people from across the class spectrum: from escaped slaves and labourers to wealthy land-owners, aristocratic lovers and popular sportsmen. At the exit, one question written on the wall underlined the purpose of the exhibition: 'Why have these stories been omitted from British history?' Before leaving, visitors were encouraged to write their final thoughts on a Post-it note. 'This is the beginning of the fight to find out more about Black life!' Jhemar scribed neatly. His enthusiasm underlined to me the importance of creating educational experiences that are responsive to the identity of the learner. I was meeting Jhemar halfway, on his own terms, as well as my own. This principle, of mentoring via collaboration, quickly became foundational in my makeshift pedagogy as a youth worker. I'd learn that boys like Jhemar, Demetri and Carl, each different, were desperate to challenge what they saw as the demeaning confines of the British education system, and there-fore wider society's structures.

Months later, in the summer holidays, I met Jhemar by Brix-ton tube and we travelled south to Tooting Broadway to eat lunch at Dawaat, a Pakistani karahi house. Jhemar's eyes wid-ened with excitement when the sizzle of our tandoori mixed grill was plonked on our table with naans. I'd printed off an unmarked map of South Asia to show Jhemar where my dad's family are from and where I'd travelled to. On our way back to Brixton afterwards, I asked him what he had planned for the rest of the break from school.

'Michael's been moving a bit mad recently, you know,' he replied, digressing from my question with no explanation, awk-wardly playing with his jacket zip. Jhemar spoke about his older

brother with admiration. His voice always carried unwaver-
ingly, like their fraternal bond was unbreakable. But he also
mentioned once or twice that Michael would sometimes get
into trouble at school. Now his tone was more solemn. 'It's a bit
sticky . . .' he continued, looking disappointed. Then he spoke
up, returning to his upbeat demeanour. 'But I'm sure it'll be
calm. Michael can look after himself! Anyway, we gotta go for
more of that food soon, you know. It bangs!'

I would estimate that at least 50 per cent of Willow's students
were Black British (West or East African and Caribbean in broadly
equal numbers). The rest were made up of recently emigrated
Latin Americans (Brazilians, Colombians, Ecuadorians), smaller
groups of East and South Asians (Chinese, Indians, Bangladeshis,
Afghans) and white children of British and Eastern European des-
cent. In other words, it was extremely multicultural, perhaps to
an extent that is incomparable to any other city on the planet.
    The school belonged to a multi-academy chain – a charitable
organization which creates and takes over schools across the UK
in areas of socio-economic disadvantage. Academy schools are a
definitive feature of education policy that began under the New
Labour government in 2000, as part of Tony Blair and his adviser
Andrew Adonis's strategy for making the inner city more attrac-
tive to the middle classes. They were then ramped up under the
Conservative-led coalition in 2010; Michael Gove, the former
education secretary, spoke at an assembly on Willow's launch in
front of press cameras. His plan was to push academies until they
became the norm: in 2010, of the roughly 24,000 schools in England, only 203 were academies. By January 2018 there were over
7,000. This was the British manifestation of an establishing global
trend of 'autonomous' schooling, in which neoliberal thinking
has generated a belief among policymakers that the more independence headteachers have, the better. Their equivalents are

charter schools in the United States, free schools in Sweden and independent public schools in Australia.

Multi-academy chains, or trusts, can run like charities and businesses at the same time. They are driven by a philanthropic normative mission underpinned by corporate structures. They govern by their own set of codes and hierarchies. They conduct teacher-training programmes and boast slick brands. Schools connected by multi-academy chains share practice and face stand- ardized internal inspections. While they retain government funding alongside private sponsorship, academy leaders have more control over what they teach and how they pay their staff. They are designed to compete and succeed or fail and restart, rep- resenting the marketization of state education.

Academy status is granted when new schools are formed afresh with the help of a funding sponsor, when schools are rated 'outstanding' in their Ofsted report and successfully apply to convert into an academy, thus earning the right to greater independence; and when failing comprehensives are deemed in need of a reboot away from local authority control. Willow's journey fell into the latter of these categories.

In 2008 Willow's multi-academy chain took control of Wil- liam Shakespeare, dubbed one of Britain's worst schools in newspapers. In its murkier past, one senior teacher turned a profit running a nearby brothel for night-crawling City workers. I have heard from those who attended the school in its worst years that another teacher was a high-level drug dealer, known to cocaine- slinging older students as their 'plug', the original source of their product. Weapons seizures and assault peppered term life. Staff were reportedly robbed by students on their journeys home.

While talking to Monica and the few other teachers remain- ing from the pre-academy days, I heard countless horror stories of what the school used to be like. Samurai swords, machetes and nunchucks were stored in lockers, brought in by students whose families had alleged triad links. Lit fireworks were thrown loosely into classrooms by students wandering the corridors; one was placed in the hood of a girl's jacket during assembly, which burnt her back. A group of boys once urinated down the middle of the central staircase. Life before Willow was not the desired learning environment of a wealthy capital city.

'It wasn't an institution for education. It was an institution for surviving,' said Caleb Femi, London's former poet laureate and author of *POOR*, who attended the school throughout the 2000s. He grew up on the North Peckham Estate, on the same block as Damilola Taylor, the ten-year-old stabbed to death with a broken glass bottle as he walked home from Peckham library in November 2000. 'As a kid I wanted to go to Shakespeare because it was an environment that I was well aware of; it represented more than a school. Damilola had just died. I knew that on ends there were two ways of living: you can live like him and stay out of everything, and end up as the victim, or you can get involved and become someone who never has to worry. I remember seeing him go to the library and deciding that I was going to go another way because I felt like assimilating was a better form of protection. I turned up on the first day of Year 7 and I could see Year 10s and 11s driving their cars into school. Nobody was saying anything to them. Growing up in such a poor environment, there were seven of us living in a one-bedroom house. We had nothing. So at Shakespeare I saw there was a way of living that was not only for safety, but *really* living.' In other words, by learning to fit in with whatever illicit money-earning activity was available, achieving quick access to material items like cars (before they were legally able to drive them) and clothes became an obvious temptation for new pupils willing to try their hand.

Violence became normalized during Femi's school experience. 'In Year 9, a friend of mine brought in a little gun. It's crazy to think about now, but that was normal. By then two of my friends had been stabbed, one of them for a new pair of trainers. At that point you're starting to have problems with other schools, who are going through the same thing, so you know if you get caught slipping, if you wanna be the one to opt out of carrying something, you're really putting yourself in danger. You're living in a war zone, drowning in anxiety, and you're experiencing that at home and at school. School is supposed to be a respite, but instead it was an introduction to a particular lifestyle. And you can't be like, guys, I'm not involved, because you might be an innocent kid and someone asks where you're from, or what school you go to, and that has a default affiliation just by having a uniform.'

By Year 10, he had sat more than half of his GCSEs. 'I got my first GCSE in Year 8. They used to identify the smart kids, or the ones they didn't think would last until Year 11, and put them into GCSEs as early as possible. So for me, there was no motivation to continue being in education other than to come to school and get involved in other things. I was academically achieving, and that was something that was taken for granted because the school themselves, the way they emphasized needing to achieve, wasn't to go to university or become prime minister. It was: "achieve this to stay in the school; do this in order for us to not call your parents; we don't see you ever going to university or doing that job, but do this for serving *our* purpose". It was data manipulation. It allowed them to play with their numbers.'

Femi was excluded from school in Year 11. By then he was barely going to lessons, but teachers wouldn't chase him to attend and his parents were never called. He was simultaneously embedded in street life. He would visit a scrapyard in Deptford with his friends to buy second-hand cars, which they would drive around Elephant & Castle, unlicensed, during school time. 'In Year 7 I had £5 to last me the week. By Year 11, I don't even know how much money I had. Enough to be stupid with,' he recalled, smirking. 'The staff were equally wayward. Teachers would leave after a couple of terms. One time I saw a member of the senior management team walk past a student who dropped a knife on to the floor and act like nothing happened. They were all aware of what was going on. Teaching was out the window.'

In the years following its academization, Willow improved dramatically. It received improving Ofsted reports and helped increasing numbers of students get 5 A*–C GCSE grades. Before I started there, it opened its first sixth-form college, aiming to help students pass all the way through the school to university.

Despite the purpose of my job for The Access Project, I was sceptical about the obsession with trying to funnel *all* young people into higher education – a practice that seemed to hold across the charity's partner schools, other organizations such as IntoUniversity and secondary education in general. This ideal reflected the trend over recent decades of business-minded, profiteering universities cementing themselves as the end goal that all pupils should strive for. Indeed, degrees have become a prerequisite for entering large chunks of the modern workplace. But the rising debt that now came with pursuing a degree compared to when I attended in 2009, after the controversial tripling of tuition fees from 2012, made things complicated. Prospective students, especially those who were poorer, now had more difficult decisions about whether a degree was value for money. I remained loyal to supporting students who were suitable for and determined to access university study. But I started to see from the other angles of my youth work and volunteering that university might not be for everyone. I felt that opportunities for less academic students – or those faced with too many barriers to tick the narrow boxes of exam results – to pursue high-quality apprenticeships, or creative or sporting endeavours, or even to go straight into the workforce, ought to be regarded as equally valuable for producing productive, self-sufficient and fulfilled adults.

Willow's intake was sourced largely from social housing estates in the most neglected pockets of nearby areas: Kennington, Walworth, Vauxhall, Borough, Bermondsey, Peckham, New Cross, Camberwell, Brixton and Stockwell. Many students hailed from the same communities as people, like Caleb Femi, who had attended during its less glitzy past. Sure, the school had since gained a post-modern sheen. The potential for total anarchy had been rooted out. But the harsh context which orbited the school was still clear. Willow pupils were among the most socio-economically disadvantaged in the city, and therefore the country.

Students at schools serving impoverished communities face an array of social barriers to learning. Symptoms of societal fragmentation – a dire underfunding of support for children with Special Educational Needs (SEN), overwhelmed single parenthood at home, the influence of grooming from drug-dealing elders, undiagnosed trauma from street or domestic violence, poor mental health – trickle into conversations, corridors and classrooms. Only a portion of these cases are ever addressed head on, let alone acknowledged. The impulse of pretending that everything is fine in such institutions can trump answering messier questions about how some of the more at-risk students are faring.

The attempts of schools to serve their most vulnerable and disruptive pupils are one of their greatest uphill battles. Of course, years of austerity, which between 2010 and 2018 reduced per-pupil funding across the United Kingdom by 8 per cent, have made fighting this battle in the state sector even more difficult. In many schools the allocation of staff and resources is permanently shifting and precarious. Externally, the draining of support wells like youth services, the NHS, early-years help for mothers and other state benefits have further compromised the education system's chance of success.

To my mind, this raises the broader question of whether schools in twenty-first-century Britain are places that should be conceived of as mere educational institutions. Given the life-changing role that any adult working where young people spend their time can have, perhaps schools should be framed as broad-church support systems? But austerity's impact also means that the neglect faced by communities and their young people now needs redressing by more than just a school budget and an 8 a.m. to 3.30 p.m. timetable. Should schools and their underpaid, overworked front-line staff be expected to pick up *all* the pieces from a child's shattered life? Probably not.

To problem-solve on these perpetual conundrums, school leaders experiment with new pedagogical styles, incentives and punishments. The reality of high staff turnover becomes a dark, shared running joke among the few teachers who have managed to hang on. Each year a cohort of new teachers joins staff bodies as part of the 'Teach First' programme, which places graduates in challenging schools with only a few weeks of training. Pastoral heads of year, aided by small inclusion teams, face the task of ensuring the safe, calm intermixing of hundreds of hormonal students. But some students might not have had dinner the night before, let alone breakfast in the morning. Others may be unwashed or without clothes that fit them. Many speak different languages at home to their parents, who have a potentially non-existent understanding of the contemporary education system. Students with roots in other countries and cultures are often left navigating important decisions about their futures alone. A deceptively high proportion of school students across London hail from disparate rival estates and territories that remain invisible to most staff. Yet all of them have to sit still in lessons, stare at a smartboard for hours and chase exam results dominated by mechanically tested Maths, English and Science.

Schools can serve some students – those often labelled 'gifted and talented' in academies – brilliantly. I have met pupils like Demetri who possess resilience, critical thought and emotional intelligence, and who manage to apply these qualities to achieve academically. TAP students spread across my schools were immovably motivated. They responded well to the opportunities, pressures and security granted by their school regimes. Such students might aspire to study at a Russell Group university as the first person in their family to do so. The tireless work ethic of teaching staff during term time ensures that the aim of sending teenagers out into society as qualified adults is made possible. None of this could have happened even half a generation ago at schools like William Shakespeare. I have been proud to work for institutions that are clearly facilitating life-changing transformations.

Yet this neat impact can only reach so far. In the zero-sum game of the education market, gains made in some areas generate losses elsewhere. Not every child benefits from academization. Caleb Femi argued that because schools like Shakespeare were so bad before, 'anything now will look like a five-star resort'. He trained as an English teacher and taught for two years at an academy school in Tottenham, north London. 'But the bureaucratic game is different now. It's not as potently fucked up. It's a different sort of fucked up. There is still a level of manipulation, but it is cultivated in a cleverer way,' he continued. 'I would question the way in which students are valued in academies. It's the students at the top who are given value. I think academies are one of the biggest symbols of that; of carrying that sense of who is or isn't valuable as a student, who we care about. Students are just data: who is making it and who isn't? And if they aren't going to make it, how can we gently usher them through without causing substantial reputational damage?'

By July 2016 our discussion group had become a feature of Friday evenings at Jacob Sawyer. Carl and the other boys would turn up to greet us with a handshake, organize themselves on seats in the classroom and wait for their favourite can of drink to be handed out. That year we engaged with over thirty other teenagers – almost all male. Some sessions might have only three or four young people in them, generating rich, open and calm conversations. Others reached double figures and would need chairing more carefully, sometimes with the help of another youth worker or older member of the centre who could offer a more seasoned, relatable perspective. Rory and I would plan and debrief every session with the help of Tony so that attendance and any noteworthy or concerning comments from participants were monitored.

One evening Rory and I brought in a large A–Z map of London and stuck it on the wall. We set the boys the task of placing a small, circular sticker somewhere of their choice. One Arsenal fan located the Emirates stadium. Another placed his sticker over the converging train tracks of Loughborough Junction. One boy placed his sticker over Brixton Hill – traditionally a rival area for Jacob Sawyer regulars. I'd assumed that anyone from the Hill could not visit the centre, but I soon realized this breaking of territorial norms was common for those with familial ties or close friendships represented locally.

Another newcomer reached towards the east of the map. He placed his sticker over Stratford, where the Queen Elizabeth Olympic Park is situated, explaining that he enjoyed going to Westfield shopping centre. I hovered my hand over east London, explaining that I was soon to start working at a secondary school there for TAP.

'Aren't there bare p*kis in east?' said one member of the group. This was the first time I'd heard someone use this racial slur since my time at university in Bristol, where some of my white, male peers would say it to describe the man who worked at the local shop or other South Asian people in my year, and I would become numb with suppressed fury (I was called it as a child growing up in

Surrey). Following the EU referendum in June 2016, one month before this session at Jacob Sawyer, my partner, Yasmin, had been called it by groups of white men while travelling on public transport on three separate occasions. Brexit had opened a Pandora's box of xenophobic language that was evidently circulating far and wide around British society during this time, its proverbial chest puffed out as a result of the divisive rhetoric used by many senior politicians over recent years. The charity Stop Hate UK saw a 60 per cent increase in hate crimes reported to them within three weeks of the vote and a 32 per cent increase across the year quarter.

Hearing it now hit me like a tonne of bricks. It was the first time I'd ever heard a Black person use the slur, let alone a young person I was working with. When I opened my mouth to respond, Carl beat me to it.

'You can't say that, fam!' he said, frowning with disapproval.

'Why? There are bare Pakistanis there!' the boy replied.

'It's offensive,' Carl continued. 'It's not about what the word sounds like, it's how it's been used *back in the day*,' he added. He turned to face me in solidarity.

I thanked Carl and told the group about my negative experience of the p-word growing up. The boy who used it apologized. I explained that the word stemmed from the racism that South Asians faced while arriving in the UK in the mid-twentieth century; how they would be attacked by National Front thugs who went out 'p*ki-bashing'. This prompted a wider conversation about racism and its history in London.

'Some of the white teachers at my old school are proper scared of Black youts, you know!' one boy chuckled, receiving a round of agreement from the other boys.

'I'm not being funny, but the Asian man in the shop near my school proper thinks I'm gonna rob the shop every time I go in there,' Carl muttered.

★

The following week Carl explained to me how he'd been permanently excluded from his previous school a few months beforehand, after being accused of helping his friend to bring in weed. He'd been at the end of Year 10 and approaching his GCSEs. I wondered how much had been done to help him before it was too late. It saddened me how anyone, let alone Carl, who was excelling in our sessions, could be given up on, banished from the matrix of whatever data system his school used to store information about its students.

Whether they had experienced temporary or permanent exclusions or not, the majority of boys who attended our sessions at Jacob Sawyer often spoke in negative terms about education. School was the bane of their lives. The repeated expression of this was on some level a performative groan of moody, anti-establishment adolescents. Yet I was continually struck by how, with the exception of a few late starts, our sessions seemed to be a positive experience for the boys. They responded proactively to topics Rory and I would throw at them. Something about the atmosphere at the centre, and the non-hierarchical, discussion-based format we had established, was plugging a humble but important gap. It cemented the idea in my mind that youth services are a vital institution in public life, especially for young people who resented school.

In one Friday session we played a short clip from *The Wire*. It showed crowds of African-American students pouring into their Baltimore high school on the first day of term. The protagonists pass police officers, get told off by teachers for walking on the wrong side of the corridors and wearing jewellery, and talk jovially to one another over the new, fresh-faced teacher as he fails to wrest control from the students. We asked the boys about their schools compared to what they'd seen in the video.

'There's a fed who used to walk around my school,' Carl noted.

'It's so jarring when they get on to us about uniform! At least in America they don't have to wear ties,' expressed his friend.

I asked the boys what they believed school was for.

'It's dead. I don't learn like that. I don't see why it's necessary for someone like me,' said one of them.

I pointed out that the group seemed to enjoy our sessions.

'Yeah but that's because I can see why these conversations relate to my life. It's not boring, you get me? There's no teacher telling me pointless things to do.'

'School makes you learn to be social. You make friends and you learn rules,' Carl followed. 'But them teachers can't hack it! It's just a pay package for them at the end of the day. Some youts learn more on the roads than we do in school. The olders understand what we're going through.'

The boys conceded that they were likely to make more money when they were older – money that was legal and consistent – if they stayed in school. But they expressed frustration that school and university took such a long time, whereas they were interested in quicker ways of making big money like footballers, rappers and social media influencers.

'The thing that jars me most is the way teachers focus so much on negative behaviour,' said Carl.

'Word!' exclaimed one of his friends.

'At my school, they have this points system where they mark you down on everything,' Carl continued. 'But when a teacher doesn't like you, they give you *even more* negative points. It's like a trap! So, even when I'm feeling positive and I'm trying to not mess up, all it takes is one teacher to ruin my day. Most of them don't let you explain. If you argue you get more negative points. Then they keep adding up until it's like a dark cloud hanging over you, and you can't even get rid of it. That's you for the rest of the term!'

'Facts!' muttered another boy. Carl was leading the group's

critical charge against the data-driven tendencies of academy schools, and their impact on boys like him.

'If they had more points for positive things it would be better because you could work your way back up. But the teachers barely ever give them out, especially if they see you as a bad kid. Schools are like prisons. Nobody listens. It makes me just want to give up.'

Carl was describing a mechanism used at many schools across the UK: a table ranking students in each year group based on performance data. Each year, university, A-level and GCSE league tables are printed in newspapers to publicize institutions at the very top, and those at the very bottom, thus creating incentives for innovation and high standards (despite statisticians widely condemning the practice as an inappropriate way of measuring the 'success' of the institutions themselves, given the variability of student cohorts year to year). Student performance scores in schools take this same logic to rank the lives, characters and perceived value represented by each young person. It represents how competition has been pumped into the state education system, moulding the way schools operate not just in relation to one another, but internally, too, in the way students are organized.

Stuck to the corridor walls of some schools, including Willow, are lengthy Excel spreadsheets listing students by name in order of their data scores. Attendance and punctuality are usually two key metrics: if a student has consistently strong attendance and turns up on time, their score stays high; if they have poor attendance, or turn up late, their score falls. Another two metrics, working in inverse correlation, are good and bad behaviour or effort points. All of these pieces of information are merged into a single numerical quantity which is displayed vertically, pitting students against one another. At the top are the best, the elite, the celebrated, the 'gifted and talented' and most improved. In the middle are those who are doing moderately, but who have room for improvement. Towards the bottom of the table are those who are late, unattending, poorly behaved, unmotivated in their work, or if they are literally in the last few names, some dire combination of all four.

In turn, students at the bottom face certain punishments or interventions, such as staying behind after school for a number of days or being excluded from the luxury of fun activities and trips. They have the humiliating visibility of their name displayed at the bottom of the score rankings on the corridor wall, which acts as a form of punishment in itself. In some schools, things are taken a step further: students' portraits are placed beside their names, alongside their most recent set of grades. In these circumstances, everyone knows exactly who is failing and who is succeeding. Such schools are therefore either ignorant or uncaring of the internalized shame that they're inflicting.

'It made me feel like shit,' said one student called Hema, who I mentored during my employment at TAP. She would go on to complete a degree in History and English Literature at a top-tier university, against the odds of her low performance score during her A levels. 'The worst thing is that by the time I got to sixth form I had serious mental health problems. I was barely sleeping. So of course I was late a lot. My school knew all about it, but they still put me at the bottom, and put my picture and my grades up there in the corridor for everyone to see. Then I wouldn't be allowed out at lunch. If I came in, I'd have to stay until five p.m. every day, instead of going home at three thirty like everyone else. Then that made me want to be at school even less. It's weird even talking about that year, to be honest, because I've tried to block it out of my mind ever since. It was traumatic.'

'I can only speak for myself, but I reckon it's kinda pointless,' said Demetri when I asked what he thought. We were meeting for our first one-to-one of the new academic year, after the summer holidays in 2016. He'd done well in his GCSEs, achieving a range of As, Bs and Cs – despite admitting that he didn't do as much revision as he should have done. He was now studying Psychology, Sociology and Geography A levels. 'I've always been near the top cah I know how to play the game. I muck about sometimes, but I'm always on time. I never miss school. I stay up high on the list. But other than that, I honestly don't care. It's not making me do things because they are good. It's making me do them to stay out of trouble.'

I played devil's advocate. Surely, I suggested, the ranking system existed to create an orderly pattern and principle of motivation in his life? Presumably, it did drive people – others who were perhaps more self-conscious, wary of failure and punishment, or inspired by competition – to behave better and work harder?

'Yeah, I guess,' he replied. 'Some people do everything to be top. They live for it. But it's still dumb. It's a way of controlling us. Take detentions. Some people are in them because they're proper mad! They're rude, they fight, they disrespect teachers. They are the "bad kids" everyone knows. But others are in there because they've not been at school. Maybe they've got stuff going on at home, so they've been late a few times, because of things out of their control. But all these people are at the bottom, even though they are bare different.'

There is clearly merit in using technology to collect and process data to track student progress. I was doing this with my TAP data in order to keep tabs at each of my schools. But Demetri's criticism was valid: collapsing a young person's overall school performance into one metric like this – let alone publicizing it – can be simplistic and dangerous. What's more, a young person who is doing badly on the scoring system might internalize their powerlessness in the face of this metric in a way that makes them want to give up, like Carl had expressed. For some students, it therefore causes the opposite of its intended effect. By deciding upon and then plastering a student's failing performance around school, it weaponizes shame.

Academization has allowed slick phoenixes to rise from the ashes of burnt inner-city comprehensives which are able to send their most able and compliant students to the top universities – those, like Demetri, who I was working with on TAP. All the while, it has turned schools into robotic market stalls which behave like they are competing businesses. Academies strive to achieve the best exam results, university placements and PR opportunities at all costs. One such cost is the way that a reliance upon subjectively defined data can punish individuals who struggle to conform by ranking them at the bottom of the pile and rendering them as disposable.

Students at the top of the score list thrive. For them, academy systems serve as a useful, efficient and validating way for teachers and school leaders to spark, monitor and evaluate progress. They have their praises sung in assemblies. They are invited on work experience schemes and trips to visit top universities. They are allowed access to certain privileges, such as being able to leave the school to get lunch. They win the game. Meanwhile, those at the other end of the spectrum lose it. The data, insensitive to social circumstances or psychological well-being, universal and non-specific in its algorithmic methods, writes failing children off. These children are those who are most likely to finish school with few or no qualifications, or be sent to PRUs or AP (Alternative Provision) schools (which saw an expansion in scope and the funding they receive across the 2010s). Indeed, in a September 2020 report titled 'How Black Working-Class Youth are Criminalised and Excluded in the English School System', the Institute of Race Relations noted how there is a 'two-tier' state education system which creates a dichotomy: between 'deserving' and 'aspirational' students performing well in academies, and 'defiant', 'lazy' and 'undeserving' students performing poorly, who are therefore most likely to end up being excluded and sent to specialist institutions.

The decisions being made in academy chains and management consultancy conference rooms affect, in startling ways, how the poorest, most vulnerable students are experiencing childhood and adolescence. Much like their schools in the marketplace, if pupils do well, they reap the rewards. Some pupils can excel, experience social mobility and access university, well-paid careers and a bigger world. But pupils who don't do well can be both left behind and actively demeaned. Their score is too low. They become valueless, too expensive – a rough irritant beneath the shiny surface of marketing posters and branded leaflets. It is at this stage that a child might be deemed better off if they are educated elsewhere. To me, that looks an awful lot like giving up on these children.

6. Verified

Social Media

'Look at this donny!' Jhemar exclaimed. His phone screen displayed a boy in a school blazer running away from the camera. 'Allow it! Please!' the boy yelled, passing a bus stop. The person filming the scene was giving chase, panting into his phone. He held it in his left hand so that its camera captured two things: his fleeing target and a kitchen knife clasped in his right hand. The ten-second clip, short enough to have been sent on Snapchat, ended abruptly. 'Look how reckless these man are moving! These times people are losing their minds on social media!' Jhemar continued.

We were meeting in November 2016, in the autumn term of his Year 10. Jhemar had grown and was nearing my height. His voice was breaking. He was showing the first signs of manhood. He had short hair merged into a tight skin fade. We'd sat down to write our aims for the session in 'The Book of Wisdom', which was tattered and creased from being at the bottom of Jhemar's school bag for over eighteen months.

Jhemar explained that one boy he knew had been permanently excluded from his school within a term of being there – having already been excluded from at least one before – for bringing in a knife from home. The boy was being taunted and threatened over social media because lots of boys in his new year group were from a rival part of south London. Thinking it was only a matter of time before someone tried to harm him, he'd armed himself in preparation for being attacked. I couldn't fathom how hard it must have been, at the tender age of fourteen, to be living with such anxiety. He was later sent to a Pupil Referral Unit.

It had made me think yet again about the profile of boys who were experiencing these fork-in-the-road moments. Their 'value' in their school system had been compromised; the level of risk they posed deemed too great. How aware were school staff bodies that their students were being threatened like this? Was there any intervention that might make boys feel safer? I wondered whether, all things considered, the decision to carry a knife, motivated by self-defence, could be prevented. I was also becoming sure that social media was a key lubricant in the cycles of exclusions taking place.

'Guys have *been* getting permed for knives. It's happened to people in my year and the year above. I keep telling this one boy in the year below me to stop moving like that cah he's gonna get caught out soon, but he won't listen! It's a mindset. It's difficult to reason with them man because they're seeing things differently, you get it? It's real life for them. They're stubborn. Check that video I showed you, yeah? There are *hundreds*, nah, *thousands* of clips like that being sent around all the time! I see mad, violent things on my phone every day. Most parents and teachers don't have a clue. Even for me it's so hard to keep up with, especially on Snap, because it disappears. Then there are videos of youts being violated by their opps getting uploaded to YouTube every day. Sometimes they get hundreds of views and then everybody writes comments below them. That's where all the rumours start. So if you are involved and you respond, you get drawn out, things can get *peeeeeak*!'

The impact of digital technology and social media on human life has been well analysed. Advertising is more targeted than ever thanks to a previously unthinkable amount of data harvested from consumers. News is increasingly disseminated by anyone, anywhere, without the editorial filter of major news media. This has 'democratized' information available to us, and it has also opened the door to so-called 'fake news'. Events towards the start of the 2010s marked a leap in social media's evolution, as it was successfully used by cultural and political movements to advance their aims. The so-called 'Arab Spring' in North African and Middle Eastern countries, for example, in which populations filmed and shared protests, and organized across vast geographies via the internet, proved that an internet connection could be leveraged to topple regimes of power. The riots coordinated across British cities in the summer of the same year demonstrated a similar rebellious effectiveness. The advent of social media has affected all of these trends, and more, on a macro scale. But it has also affected individuals, on a granular, micro scale – often in ways that have been overlooked or distorted in our common understanding.

In my youth work in London, and at a time when we were all waking up to the effects of this new, powerful tool, I could see how these technologies were changing the behaviours of adolescents. Teenagers use their smartphones to communicate with one another at unprecedented rates and speeds – sometimes in positive ways, and sometimes in negative, dangerous ways. Such usage is barely comparable to even my own generation's teenage use of platforms such as MySpace, Bebo and Facebook in the 2000s. Children now traverse gigantic interactive universes on online games like Fortnite, virtually meeting new people from around the real world as they go. They know how to create, share and hide content on rapid-fire and potentially untraceable applications like Snapchat and TikTok, while simultaneously sitting in a classroom or at the family dinner table. They make music, film videography and broadcast gossip and memes to forever diversifying, intricate and adaptable extents. Some teach themselves musical instruments or how to fix a bike, learn about quantum physics or philosophy, by sitting on YouTube. Others open themselves up to grooming, exploitation and bullying. Those I was working with, who belong to 'Generation Z', born from the late 1990s onwards, are digital natives: they understand concepts like coding, screen navigation and instant messaging with drastic superiority in relation to their slow and outdated carers and educators. This set of circumstances presents a deep challenge for parents trying to protect their children, teachers attempting to control their classrooms, youth workers maintaining community safety and intelligence teams trying to prevent criminality.

There are obvious educational and social gains that can be made from a young person spending time online. A sociable or inquisitive child growing up throughout the 2010s was able to discover a whole new world of information and knowledge at the click of a touchscreen button, quickly and while on the move. They could exchange ideas with like-minded individuals, be creative and expressive in novel ways, and socialize with their peers without needing to travel or risk placing themselves in physical harm – a genuine concern for teenagers living in areas where violent crime is prevalent.

But an entrenched dependency on screens and internet culture brought with it a whole matrix of risks. The Organisation for Economic Cooperation and Development found by surveying more than 250,000 teachers in 2019 that cyberbullying was more likely to affect young people in England than in any other industrialized country. The specific extent of the impact of screen time on a person's well-being is contested across the globe. Many healthcare researchers, however – such as in papers produced by the Canadian journal *JAMA Pediatrics* and the American journal *Preventive Medicine Reports* – have linked more screen time among young people to higher rates of depression and anxiety. In 2019, the Royal College of Paediatrics and Child Health (RCPCH) surveyed 109 people in the UK aged eleven to twenty-four: 88 per cent felt screen time had a negative impact on their sleep. Such studies confirm what many parents suspect. A modern lifestyle of video gaming, being able to stream television shows and films at ease, and staying glued to smartphones to socialize outside of school is increasing young people's capacity to remain physically inactive.

I asked Jhemar to come up with more examples of how social media was changing the world for young people like him.

'Well, there's hella music coming out right now!' he replied, turning to YouTube on his phone. 'You heard of 67*, from Brixton Hill?' he enquired, nodding out the first-floor window ahead of us. 'Or 150†?'

Over the summer I'd heard boys at Jacob Sawyer playing a type of rap music I didn't recognize. Intrigued, I'd gone home and started flicking through music videos on YouTube of the artists they were playing. I'd recognized young men who I'd seen around Brixton in several homemade videos accompanied by their own style of punchy, menacing rap songs. Some of these videos and others like them had hundreds of thousands, or occasionally millions, of views. The artists' lyrics often seemed directed at their local enemies. Other lines referred to the intricacies of drug-dealing, struggles of survival in poverty and material showboating. This new sound rendered local London genres like grime – which started in the early 2000s – and road rap – a slow type of gangster rap pioneered by Peckham MC Giggs in the late 2000s – old news: sonic timestamps of a previous generation.

The new breed of music was being labelled 'drill'. It was an emulation of Chicago drill, a type of rap that grew to global attention in 2011 with the rise of teenage rapper Chief Keef, who hailed from the city's hollowed-out South Side. Keef and

---

* Pronounced 'six-seven'
† Pronounced 'one-fiddy'

his contemporaries became superstars in a matter of months by filming DIY videos and uploading them to YouTube, giving hip-hop fans across the globe a crisp window into the ghetto of America's most infamous city. Their songs were both a treacherous, high-risk means of sustaining territorial violence, after decades of splintering gang politics, and a vehicle of socio-economic mobility for African-American men and women trying to escape the hood. Chicago drill – its deep basslines, tinny, marching-band drums and haunting melodies – was not only a soundtrack to the way that racism and economic forces dovetail to oppress Black lives in the contemporary American city. It was the mobilizing anthem of artists harnessing new technologies to tell their stories at all costs, and survive. Its cry – war cry and cry for help – cross-pollinated to London and other Western cities across the planet.

The British version being made and listened to by young people in London – 'UK drill' – borrowed from the elements of its US birthplace. But by 2016 it was quickly evolving, having spawned its own impatient tempo and cryptic lyrical lexicon to reflect its new grey environment. What's more, UK drill was initially hyperlocal and geographically bound in left-behind pockets of south London, specifically my own neck of the concrete woods. Via my work with young people between Brixton and Elephant & Castle, in which I'd consistently use music as my go-to connecting point, I'd stumbled upon the early tremors of the English capital's next subcultural earthquake. I soon realized that UK drill was a goldmine of conversation starters that I could use to learn about my home city and utilize to affect change as a youth worker.

'These videos are doing the most because we're all watching them and wondering what's gonna come next! Like, how are they gonna respond? Who is gonna get drawn out? You hear about all the rumours at school and on Snap – who got cheffed by who, who's gone pen,' Jhemar explained.

UK drill music amounted to a narration, a war report, of what was going on in the precise environments that made up Jhemar's world. The territories defended by young men in the newest generation of rappers had splintered across region: instead of a divide that might be defined by north London versus south London, as in generations of the distant past, or between towns like Brixton versus Peckham, as in the 2000s, now it was southern parts of Brixton versus northern parts of Brixton. The turfs and their ruthless underground politics had shrunk. A level of bespoke relatability to rap artists' output was therefore drawing boys like Demetri, Jhemar and Carl in, transmitted over a personalized, explicitly digital wavelength.

Drill music was giving young Londoners a voice. Judging by the number of views some videos were racking up, it was gaining a growing audience all over the world, even if mainstream British society hadn't noticed yet. Thanks to the widespread ownership of smartphones, this music could be shared by young people without the knowledge of parents or school staff – a key component to its insidious rise.

At the end of our meeting, I asked Jhemar how Michael was doing. He gulped and his face sank. He replied that he'd not seen his brother since the start of the summer holidays.

'I don't know the details,' he told me. 'But I'm probably not gonna see Michael for a lickle bit while things calm down.'

I gathered that he didn't want to talk about it any longer. We shook hands and I climbed on my bike to ride down the hill back to Loughborough Junction.

While spending time with gang members on the South Side of Chicago to conduct fieldwork for his 2020 book, *Ballad of the Bullet: Gangs, Drill Music, and the Power of Online Infamy*, Professor

Forrest Stuart, a sociologist at Stanford University, would regularly check Twitter and Instagram.

'I discovered all this flexing on social media,' he told me. 'I'd be standing right next to these guys and realize they were posting things that had nothing to do with what we were actually doing.' Some of the young men didn't own and had never used a gun. They simply borrowed them to stockpile photos and videos of themselves holding weapons, curating an intimidating social media profile that they would drip feed on to the internet over the coming days and weeks. 'I'd be driving them across town in my car, and when we'd pass a rival block they'd start taking selfies out the window, pretending they were on their way to do a drive-by.'

It is tempting to take all apparently violent social media content – Snapchat clips of men brandishing knives, YouTube drill music videos depicting groups of masked boys throwing up hand signals into the camera lens – at face value. But like Stuart found in Chicago – and as I have found in London – there is as much exaggerated bravado as there is inconvenient truth woven into the tapestry of online video content produced by teenagers. Legitimate concern and calls for removal ought to be paid towards the outpouring of substantively violent content: abuse of boys and girls in the street, bloody stabbings and robberies captured on film and shared intensively. But across the mid-2010s, the capacity for cleverly establishing a believable personality on social media opened up to young people, via music lyrics, photos, DIY videos and livestreams, that might or might not equate to the truth. Like brand influencers distorting their appearance to fit a desired aesthetic, or a holidaymaker only sharing fun or ostensibly expensive experiences with their followers, young creatives are able to manipulate how they represent themselves on social media.

'Generally, and this applies to kids across the race and class spectrum, social media is becoming a new forum for working out the same kinds of identity issues as before,' Stuart continued.

Many of his principal findings from Chicago are applicable to what has been happening on British shores and in other cities across the world. A universal shift has been taking place in human development and technology, which started in the new millennium and has gathered steam since. 'Kids used to work these things out in the lunch hall at school. Now these conversations have been taken online. If before you had spaces to try out or perform identities and wear different hats – the tough kid, class clown, jock, soccer player – in the past you could go to school, perform your identity, then go home and take that hat off. Now you have to perform these things online, and they become sticky and durable. They are harder to disprove and move on from. Lots of people are looking and commenting. If you wanted to be seen as an athlete last month, the ability for you to transition into a new identity is made more difficult because of the mounting evidence about you being someone else.'

Alongside this identity crisis, for disadvantaged young people in poor pockets of London – indeed, British young people everywhere – there has been a disintegration of an old socio-economic order. In part due to the expanding opportunities of the gig economy, unemployment in the UK fell from 8.1 per cent in 2011 to 3.8 per cent in 2019, after rising steeply across the 2000s. But precarious working arrangements such as zero-hours contracts and the expanded, increasingly expensive requirement to go to university have become norms for those making the transition into adulthood. Meanwhile, austerity has removed funding from schools and closed youth clubs, making it harder for those who cannot fit the mould of formal education to succeed. It has been all too easy for innovative young people faced with such unpredictable futures to turn to the internet to start carving out their own ways of earning money, gaining respect and being valued – away from the trappings of school performance data.

'In this new influencer economy, it is a mischaracterization to suggest that these dynamics are unique to young, poor or gang-affiliated kids,' said Stuart. 'So many people are online, and there is so much noise. So the question for everyone – adults too – is: how do you cut through the noise? It might just be a kid who is trying to be popular at their school, but it might also be an artist who is trying to stand out and stay relevant. Every channel owner, anyone who is trying to make it in this digital economy, is facing this. And how you break through the noise is directly related to the resources that you have available to you. For some young people in the inner city, who live in poverty with few resources, it therefore becomes a competition about who is able to do the craziest thing. Who has the biggest gun? Who is willing to video themselves walking through their rivals' territory?'

UK drill performed this function for poor (mostly) Black British teenagers in London. The British iteration of the music has swept through in the slipstreams of garage, grime and road rap, whose pirate radio stations, self-made CD mixtapes and televised music videos gave underground music visibility across the 2000s. UK drillers such as 67, Harlem Spartans, OFB and many more over the latter half of the 2010s carried the DIY lessons of their forefathers into the new generation.

In the UK equivalent of the genre, however, instead of bragging exclusively about guns, it has been a person's willingness to rap about and prove they are wielding the biggest knife that has arisen as a currency of social value. UK drillers use tens of different words denoting a knife and the act of stabbing someone. Some are borrowed from previous generations while others are brand new: shank, nank, dipper, ramsay; to ching, to chef, to poke, to splash, to wet, to dip. These deadly linguistic symbols of London's young underworld are shocking to those outside of it, but like an Inuit has tens of words she can use to refer to snow, they reflect the knife's importance in day-to-day life. As years have passed since its inception, UK drill has matured and commercialized into a marketable, semi-mainstream subculture. Its artists have become more at ease rapping about topics such as post-traumatic stress disorder (PTSD), the futility of street violence and the advantages of making legal money through the pursuit of a successful music career.

'When I've spoken to men who have served long prison sentences, they often say to document your criminality back in the day was to go against the code,' said Craig Pinkney, a criminologist and Director at Solve: The Centre for Youth Violence and Conflict, based in Birmingham, which is known as England's gun-crime capital. 'Now this has changed. Being quiet actually means you're irrelevant. Young people who are marginalized and invisible, all they have is themselves and their postcode. If it's the only way you can be heard, why not go on social media and rep your area?'

As both an academic and youth work practitioner on the front lines, Pinkney argued that, from an educational perspective, adults need to take much greater steps to understand social media.

'We need to learn about what is happening before we go and lecture young people about how they should be using social media. Start with the social media companies. On the BBC's *Panorama*, they interviewed the person who invented limitless scrolling. He said the aim isn't to make users addicted but conceded that one of the main objectives is to keep consumers using platforms. So, really, are they making people addicted to their platforms? Are young people getting more addicted? These technologies are creating environments dominated by narcissistic behaviour.'

I asked Pinkney what educators and youth workers ought to be focusing on.

'I don't think social media has to be a bad thing, and I also don't think we should censor anything because it will just push young people on to the dark web and into spaces that are even more hidden. I think this is more about identity. The dangers of social media aren't the core issues. Young people's identities, their popularity and self-image are. Why is it that some young people feel that they need to get half naked to get likes? Why do some young men feel they need to act in hypermasculine ways to get likes? In that instance, the education we provide needs to be about understanding what masculinity is; or how to develop self-esteem and confidence from other sources. Distorted forms of these ideas are leading young people to social media to document their lives in a particular kind of way that can then be damaging. We need to be thinking of other ways for young people to get positive affirmation.' This might be achieved by creating more non-academic and flexibly creative modes of gaining useful qualifications in schools and at university, providing safe spaces for the most at-risk teenagers to open up about the complexities of the digital world and road life, along with paying youth workers properly, in schools and youth centres, so that they are able to forge long-term and impactful relationships with young people who lack them.

The instant, easy access and public nature of the online world has opened up endless opportunities for young people to reinvent themselves away from real life. This fact has created a large scope for potential danger and conflict when digital provocations spill on to the roads or the school playground. But it also presents a rich, fertile ground for having an efficient, positive impact in education and community safety – for forging life-saving dialogues with excluded young people. The British education system should be redesigned to embrace digital technology to meet vulnerable teenagers organically in their own virtual spaces online and on their own terms in critical, authentic conversations about their experiences as navigators of twenty-first-century city life.

In September 2016 I set up an intervention for boys at risk of permanent exclusion at Willow. Demetri expressed his desire to assist at each session. I figured it would be a natural fit for his interest in applying his A levels in Sociology and Psychology. It would also grant him responsibility around the school that he could record on his personal statement for applying to university.

Almost all of the chosen participants for the intervention were at the bottom rung in their data scores. I reasoned that a safe, positively reaffirming weekly space for those who were not getting on with school could help them to engage better. I focused on male students, starting with Year 9, on recommendation from Demetri, who said that it was this year in which boys went through 'their bad-man phase'. As I did for TAP, I prioritized names who were eligible for free school meals and therefore formally regarded as living below the poverty line. All research about permanent and fixed-period exclusions suggests that boys are excluded at roughly three times the rate of girls. Students receiving free school meals, despite only representing roughly 15 per cent of the population, account for 40 per cent of all permanent exclusions. Combining these trends suggested that boys hailing from the poorest households who were exhibiting persistently poor classroom behaviour – the main reason cited for school exclusions – were most in need of preventative support. I was assigned a core group of six boys. I tracked them down to introduce myself.

'Who else is coming? Let me see the list!' one boy asked, glancing at the sheet of paper in my hand. 'You've just picked all the boys who get in trouble!' he scoffed, skipping off down the corridor.

'Will there be any snacks?' another boy asked. I told him there would be, making a mental note to buy some chocolates as a bribe for the first session. 'Say no more! See you there, sir!' he added respectfully, saluting his forehead cheekily with his right hand.

Three of the six students showed up for the first session.

Despite their initial scepticism, they seemed appreciative of the attention. They bounded into the classroom and took part in a conversation with an enthusiasm that surpassed the boys at Jacob Sawyer. Being slightly younger, however, their level of respect needed a lot of work. All were bursting with a natural energy that I presumed they'd been suppressing during the school day. Two of them had come straight from being 'parked' – sat in the monitored, silent 'isolation room' – during their final period of the day. These sessions were therefore a new series of tests of my behaviour management ability.

Demetri sat mostly in silence to observe the boys' behaviour while they talked. A couple of times they were uncontrollably loud, and conversation spiralled out of control, prompting me to end it and refuse to dish out any more chocolates. But those introductory sessions proved to be some of the funniest, even if they were exhausting. At times I struggled with their collective energy and fearless disruptions, taking their temptation to become distracted too much to heart. It was a baptism of fire. My respect for teachers – who had to deal with this all day, for five times the number of children, while imparting a curriculum – increased markedly.

One boy who had not showed up was called Freddie. He was short and well-built, and wore plaits which dangled down his neck. I'd tried to speak to him in the corridors at break a few times. He would snigger and walk away. His non-compliance became a challenge. He attended for the first time in the fifth week of the half-term. This was likely because of a combination of my persistence and the hearsay that had circulated from the others. It seemed, to my delight, they'd reported back to Freddie that far from being like detention or an after-school subject intervention, participants would be handed pouches of Capri Sun to drink and then be given the chance to talk about their school lives without judgement. I was pleased that I had finally succeeded in creating a space which all six now found at least intriguing. I had small badges made, decorated with the black-and-yellow mask designed by boys at Jacob Sawyer, which the Willow boys wore on their blazers with pride. They were useful tools to increase the visibility of the programme for teachers and to weave my weekly discussion space into the social tapestry of the school.

The first workshop I planned for Freddie's attendance was based on the utilitarian philosopher Jeremy Bentham's 'panopticon' – an eighteenth-century prison design used to examine power, surveillance and control. I printed off a diagram showing a tall, thin tower at the centre of a large circular building. A searchlight would be shone from the top of the tower on to the hundreds of cells facing inwards towards it. Prisoners would each be placed in their own cell. They would look out on to the others and the single stream of light, which was moving continually, unpredictably, highlighting one cell at a time. None of the prisoners knew who or what was manipulating the light. They couldn't know which cell would be lit up next. The main function of the panopticon would be to adjust the behaviour of prisoners to make them more law-abiding. The mere threat of the light would, in theory, suppress their temptation to break rules.

I explained that the panopticon had influenced the thinking behind many things in society.

'Can anyone think of what these things might be?' I asked.

'It's like when a teacher threatens to get you in trouble!' one boy replied. 'If you're messing around, and they say they're gonna mark you down on the computer, sometimes you might stop and pattern.'

'It depends which teacher it is,' interrupted Freddie, contributing for the first time. He'd not put his hand up. I told him if he wanted to say something he needed to raise his hand. He glared at me for a few seconds, before raising his hand. 'If it's

Mrs Stuart then yeah, I'll pattern. But other teachers aren't serious! Miss Russell is a joke!'

Whispers of excitement from the others unravelled for a few
seconds. Demetri was suppressing a wide grin.

'The searchlight reminds me of CCTV cameras!' another
boy added. 'The ones in the playground. I always look at them
and wonder if someone is watching.'

'Yeah or like on Snap, when you put your location on. People
can see where you are, so if they really wanted to they can come
and find you.'

'What about an undie's whip?' one boy posed, generating
another buzz of excitement from around the room.

'Yeah! But the feds think they're not bait, even though it's *so*
obvious it's them.'

Demetri raised his hand slowly for the first time. I chose him
to speak.

'How can I put it? In this, there are no blind spots. Apart from
when the light isn't shining on you. But it always *can* shine on
you, so there's nowhere to hide, you get me?' he said. 'I know
where all the cameras on my block are. If I really wanted to do
something, away from the cameras, I could do it, because I know
the blind spots. So I think if there are blind spots in CCTV, and
the people being watched know about them, it doesn't work. It
undermines the power of the cameras. Also, I reckon it's mad
that you have no idea who my man in the tower is. It could be a
toddler holding the light, and you could be some tapped, violent
criminal. But eventually you're gonna get shook of the light. It
controls you. You don't want it to shine on you. So whoever
holds the light has got mad power because you don't know what's
behind it.'

Demetri paused. He had the attention of all the boys. He
kissed his teeth to collect his thoughts.

'You know what else it reminds me of? How certain man are

copying GMs on social media. Cah bare man front on socials, but others are really living that life. Some youts put up pictures of themselves in ballies, or they rap about being on crud. But it's fake for so many guys. So what they put out on social media for people to see is like their own light. It gives them power, because even if they don't actually live like a gang member, if they do it for long enough, people start to believe them. At some point they'll start to believe it themselves.'

Carl was sitting at the back of the bus to Brixton travelling from school with two friends. He was wearing his big puffer jacket that he'd got from Primark. It was freezing cold outside, so there was condensation on the inside of the bus windows. He was travelling home having spent his final lessons in isolation.

Carl knew the other kids on the bus were scared of him. Nowadays he was feeling more confident. He'd gone to a video shoot the week before and the guys there made him feel like he was part of a big family. The video had dropped on to YouTube earlier that day and already had a few thousand views. Everyone was talking about it in detention and sending it around on Snap.

'We need to catch an opp *right now*!' Carl yelled. His back was against the window. His legs were reclining on the cushions of the two seats next to him. Carl didn't have many opps yet, but because his face was getting known on Snap, he knew people would come after him if they saw him. Recently, he'd started moving with a flicky. Now, because he was in the video, he felt like he was ready to start setting pace.

Carl's olders on his block knew him as a good yout. They kept telling him to stay out of trouble. But he found it more fun travelling to hang out with his new batch he'd met at school. They were giving him mad love. Now that he was in their music video, he knew he better treat their opps like they were his opps.

'If I catch anyone lacking it's gonna be *peak* for them!' Carl said confidently. Sure enough, after they got off the bus Carl recognized a boy who was his age across the road. He was an opposition. He was walking with some friends, but they were just civilians. Carl couldn't let this slide.

'I swear that's a paigon!?' Carl said.

The opp was pushing a bike. He seemed scared of Carl. He looked down at the floor. Not wasting any time, Carl punched him in the face, and he stumbled backwards without falling over. He wasn't even fighting back. Carl felt sorry for him for a split second.

'This is mine now,' Carl said, taking the bike. He grabbed the handlebars of his trophy and started wheeling it away.

Carl rode the bike around Loughborough, showing off his new ride. Then some of the others came to check him. Carl took a photo of the bike on his phone and shared it on Snap, mocking its previous owner. Within hours the Snap had been shared by loads of people. Carl was getting messages from people sending him love. Now he felt untouchable. Now he had opps, for real.

Demetri designed his first workshop around the theme of reputation. He chose this focus because he felt that it permeated all of the boys' concerns about how they were viewed around school by teachers and other students, worsened by their publicized data scores. I agreed, reasoning that it would be a good way of talking about how social media was playing a role in their lives, too.

Most of the boys seemed to value the intervention of our weekly group. I felt that it was slowly having a positive effect. I knew their commitment to the space was strengthening. We'd held over ten sessions. I'd also started a second group for another year.

On arrival, Freddie was in a visibly bad mood. He slouched backwards with his arms crossed and chin resting on his chest. He was having a bad week. During lesson time he'd arrived at my desk shaking with rage, tears streaming down his face after getting into an argument with one of his teachers. We talked the incident through and he calmed down, but he was subsequently parked – sent to the isolation room – for the rest of the day. I knew he was dealing with a great deal from basic information I'd heard about his turbulent home life. It gave me an insight into how easily a boy with legitimate reasons for disruption could be dismissed from education for the day. He expressed frustration about never being given space to posit his side of the story when he got into trouble. I made it clear that, if he wanted, he could bring his issues into our discussion forum. His rapidly developed loyalty to the weekly group implied the sessions had started to mean something to him. Together, we'd marked out the boundaries of a rare sanctuary in which he could vocalize his thoughts without fear of being reprimanded or having his performance score dragged down further.

The first exercise Demetri planned was to ask the group what they felt their reputations were, and how these impacted their life.

'My reputation has been bad since Year 7,' mumbled Freddie. 'I try to fix up but everyone knows me as a bad yout, so it's hard. The teachers expect me to be bad, so they assume if people are talking in class it's me, even if I've got nothing to do with it. Then if I argue, I get in more trouble. They don't give me second chances like they give other people. They speak down to me,' he continued, slouching back in his chair and frowning harshly.

'Word. It's like that with me. I'm late all the time,' said another boy. 'Now I can't ever get out of the bottom of that list. I get in trouble because I answer back, too, but I feel like if the teachers wiped the slate clean I'd be better. Like, sir, you can see that me and Freddie are always respectful to you, nah? But some of the other teachers are too stressed. It's like they like to see us fail!' he complained.

I replied that it was, of course, easy for me to be relaxed and unstrict with such a small group and no subject curriculum to teach. Our sessions were not comparable to lessons.

'It was sometimes the opposite for me. I'd always be near the top of the table, so the teachers would get on to me *more* if I did mess about,' Demetri said. 'If you're in top set they say things like "you're acting like you're in bottom set" if you don't act perfectly the whole time. So reputations can impact your life in school. You should remember that teachers are chatty patties! When you get to sixth form you realize they all talk in the staff-room and that. So it's no good being calm with one or two teachers and then messing around with the others. Your reputation will carry around places. It will stay with you and then you have to work harder to impress people. You gotta be consistent.'

'I always play football at Kennington Park on Saturdays,' said another boy. 'There is this guy there who apparently brings a shank. I've never actually seen him bring one. But because it's his reputation, it makes me scared of him. It makes me want to stop playing football.'

Demetri asked the boys about the reputations of local musicians. He started with the artist Dave, an up-and-coming young rapper from Streatham, to the south of Brixton Hill, who was making a stir because of his emotional and political lyrics. He played the piano to a grade 7 standard. Only Freddie had heard of him.

'Dave's hard, still. His reputation is that he's mad smart, even though he came from a bad background. He raps about shotting and shanks. His brother's in pen. But he is still positive with it,' Freddie said.

Next, he used 67, the leading UK drill crew, as an example.

'67 are active!' one boy exclaimed, receiving nods from Demetri and Freddie.

'Do you think that makes their music better?' Demetri asked in response.

'Yeah, because you can believe them. Their reputation is that they are certi! I wouldn't ever go near Brixton Hill! I don't want to die!'

It struck me that despite the fact Brixton Hill was, to my mind, a pretty calm and leafy part of London, to which I would travel a short bus ride to meet Jhemar every fortnight, these boys – all of whom lived in estates around Elephant & Castle, Peckham, New Cross and Kennington – viewed the area as a faraway, dangerous place to go.

'I rate 67 more than Section,' Freddie added, referring to Section Boyz, a rap group from Thornton Heath, in Croydon, to the south of Brixton, who'd been blowing up in the London music scene.

'Why?' chuckled Demetri.

'Because their music bangs! But also, on Snap, in YouTube comments . . . everyone is saying they're top of the scoreboard,' Freddie argued.

'Loski is in prison, he's *verified*,' another boy added, referring to one of the main members of Harlem Spartans, the Kennington-based drill group who were starting to make a buzz in the local UK drill scene. Because of the school's proximity to where he was from, Loski was especially popular among Willow students. I took note of the fact that the word 'verified' had become a colloquial way of describing someone who'd proven themselves on the roads, appropriating the language of social media influencers. This was similar to how drill rappers – with echoes of the data-driven policies of many academy schools – referred to 'scoring points', or stabbing enemies, and the 'scoreboard', an imagined ranking system for the most feared local gang members, in their lyrics.

The boys agreed that Stormzy, the grime artist who would go on to become a global superstar in subsequent years, was making songs that were becoming popular in the mainstream. But they all shook their heads when I asked if they rated his music. I was surprised. Surely they thought he was a talented MC? He was just attracting more attention now as a result of his ability to speak to a wider audience and achieve commercial success, I reasoned.

'Exactly, sir. He's not making music for youts like us,' Freddie replied.

They sought music which spoke to and for their individual experience. The boys placed the most value on an artist aligning their character and actions in real life with their lyrics detailing their lifestyle.

'It's all about verifying yourself,' Demetri said. 'It's like adults trying to get a blue tick on Twitter or Instagram. If you can prove you are on stuff, you can get more views and followers. People look at you because they are interested in what you do and say. It's more entertaining. Some rappers are in prison. So that means people don't even question whether they are on stuff, everyone just assumes it. That means people are more likely to listen to them. When people live what they rap, it draws people in.'

After the half-term break, Freddie was permanently excluded. During the holiday a few boys in his year group had got into an altercation at a gathering in Burgess Park, a grassy stretch of land which students would pass on their bus journeys home to Peckham and New Cross in the south-east. The argument had led to a flurry of threats back and forth on social media in the days leading up to the start of school. The rival group of boys were from another local school and they'd been threatening to come to Willow's gates to hurt Freddie. So on the first Monday back, Freddie had brought in a knife from home. He was caught playing with it in a lesson by a teacher. Within two days he'd been excluded. Nobody came to tell me. It turned out that he'd brought in a fifteen-inch bread knife, which only added to my impression of his helplessness. I would never see him again.

Another permanent exclusion from school was tearing through the progress of my youth work. I was trying to offer a solidifying route for boys to exist more meaningfully in their attachments to formal education. I was not kidding myself that my mentoring was a magic wand; there are plenty of pieces to the puzzle of why a young person may struggle to learn and behave, and how they might be supported, from parental relationships and peer pressure to poor mental health and special educational needs (SEN). I also understood the main thrust of the decision to permanently exclude boys like Freddie or Carl for bringing in a knife or illegal drugs. It is a strict principle that school leaders have to stick to in order to keep their community's environment safe. By holding their line, it deters other students from thinking they might get away with taking such risks, and sends a message that carrying a dangerous weapon is both an inherent moral wrong and an act that comes with consequences. If awards and opportunities granted to the students at the top of the performance data charts are the carrots, detentions and exclusions are the hardest sticks for students at the bottom.

But I also knew an injustice had been done to Freddie, in the same way as had been done to Jacob Sawyer boys who had been excluded from their respective academies. These children, and the thousands of others hailing from dysfunctional homes who suffer the same fate every year, are often not given a fair chance to thrive before they make a zero-tolerance mistake that affects the trajectory of their lives.

I was starting to see – and have since come to firmly believe – that not enough has been done in the British education system to truly understand and cure the unique struggle of the most deviant young people *before* it is too late. If someone who has barely entered their teenage years feels the need to bring in a knife to defend themselves, even when they know full well they will be excluded if caught, what does this say about their relationship with their school? What does it say about their sense of safety while moving through wider society? Schools should not have the power that they currently do to freely brand children as 'bad' without question and exclude them so easily.

In a 2017 guidance document written by the Department of Education titled 'Exclusion from maintained schools, academies and pupil referral units in England', it is made clear that a 'permanent exclusion should only be used as a last resort, in response to a serious breach or persistent breaches of the school's behaviour policy; and where allowing the pupil to remain in school would seriously harm the education or welfare of the pupil or others in the school.' Bringing a knife into school is clearly a serious breach of behaviour policy and has the potential to harm the welfare of students. So on these grounds, Freddie's exclusion makes perfect sense.

The document recommends that 'the decision to exclude a pupil must be lawful, reasonable and fair'. Excluding a pupil who brings in a sharp instrument – that is, crucially, illegal to carry around, inside or outside of school gates – is, of course, lawful, reasonable and fair. So on these grounds his exclusion makes sense, too.

But the document also states that schools 'should give particular consideration to the fair treatment of pupils from groups who are vulnerable to exclusion'. Not enough was being done – whether by youth and social services, or schools and their inclusion teams – to open up a dialogue with the most vulnerable teenagers on their path to exclusion. Instead of receiving care and support from staff members who ought to be trained to detect early signs and provide an appropriate service, students who perform badly are too easily ignored, branded as failures in robotic data metrics, publicly shamed across school communities and disposed of when they eventually – inevitably – take a step of no return.

'Disruptive behaviour can be an indication of unmet needs,' the document continues. 'Where a school has concerns about a pupil's behaviour, it should try to identify whether there are any causal factors and intervene early in order to reduce the need for a subsequent exclusion.' Instead of continually punishing those who struggle to engage in mainstream education, thus entrenching the cyclical prophecy of their bad reputations and low self-esteem, their disruptive behaviour should be taken more seriously as an indication of unmet needs.

This could be achieved by setting up clearer links between schools, families and youth hubs in local areas. An opportunity for the students deemed most at risk to succeed in and be rewarded for something, even if it falls outside the remit of traditional exam results, and therefore to be valued, ought to be woven into every state school. I strongly believe that a significant solution to preventing school exclusions and improving badly behaved or disengaged teenagers' engagement with education is to have more youth workers based in schools – or more youth workers trained and paid a respectful wage, full stop. I could see that the work I was doing with Freddie and his peers had value; I could only imagine what might happen if the role had been sustainable, and had this sole group session been complemented by interventions from other specialist professionals.

Of course, this is impossible to do when funds have been drained from public services such as schools, and the unsympathetic, invisible hand of the market is left to determine what and who is worthy. Intercepting rising youth violence – stopping lost, misguided, lonely children carrying and using fatal weapons that belong in their mother's kitchen drawer, after bouts of paranoia and pride – should be possible in one of the richest nations in the world. But priorities lie elsewhere.

Freddie was a victim of a point-scoring system: at school, on social media and in Westminster.

7. Them Pretty New Blocks
Gentrification

Demetri said goodbye to his friends at the bus stop. They'd been hanging out after school for a couple of hours. He crossed the New Kent Road and passed where Heygate Estate used to be. There was nothing standing of it now. He peered through the open door in the blue wall surrounding the building site. Cranes and builders wearing hard hats populated the empty space. He read a noticeboard on the blue wall: 'Elephant Park'. It showed computer-generated diagrams of what the area would look like when the building was finished. Chain restaurants, shops and bars lined the virtual pedestrianized street. Photoshopped avatars drank coffee with Bluetooth headsets wrapped around their ears; a mixed-race couple nursed a baby over lunch at an outdoor table; a woman read her book; two toddlers played in a sandpit; a group of teenagers lounged on the grass. The buildings behind them looked like they were out of a futuristic film. This was not the Elephant & Castle Demetri knew. He couldn't believe in its vision of the future. It seemed to be condensing all of London into one type of look. The buildings and people were clones of one another. He'd learnt a new word in his Geography A-level lessons, 'gentrification', and how it applied to Elephant.

He crossed Walworth Road. A man was walking about ten metres in front, in the same direction as Demetri. He wore a black trench coat and smart shoes. After a few minutes the man turned the corner towards Demetri's block. The man – white, in his thirties, with stubble and a mop of hair – neared the front door. Demetri had never seen him before. He started fumbling in his pocket for his keys. He glanced around, looking briefly at Demetri. Then he placed his key fob on to the door to enter it. He let it swing slowly shut behind him.

Demetri could see through the door's slitted window. The man had stopped to wait for the lift. He was looking back at Demetri through the glass. He felt that the man should have been polite enough to keep the door open for him. This man was new, Demetri wasn't. He'd lived here his whole life. Yet the man was looking at him with a mix of fear, disgust and confusion. He was shook. It was the same look that Demetri received getting home late at night from work recently, when a woman pulled her child close and gripped her bag tight as she saw him approaching with his hood up. She was shook, too. But Demetri was only small. He'd never robbed anyone. Why would he harm an innocent woman? Did she think he would kidnap her child? Did she really think he was a danger to her? Did the man inside his block think the same?

Demetri made a motion with his eyes towards the door's lock. The man saw him through the glass but turned his head towards the lift. He was acting as if nobody was there. Demetri kissed his teeth, pulled out his key fob, unlocked the door and entered the hallway. He looked at the man as he passed him and ascended the stairs, trying to catch his eye.

'Gentrification' was coined by the sociologist Ruth Glass. In her 1964 book, *London: Aspects of Change*, Glass studied the transitions taking place in some of the capital's historically poor, inner-city neighbourhoods. In its post-war recovery, London was growing at an unprecedented rate, in both population and financial power. 'As London becomes "greater", the dislike, indeed the fear, of the giant grows,' she observed. She employed the word 'gentrification' – whose etymology stems from the term 'gentry', or people born into a higher social class – to describe the process by which working-class urban areas were losing their affordability. Glass was interested in the impact this was having on the shifting demographic in towns which were becoming available only to 'the financially fittest, who can still afford to live and work there'. Her conclusion was simple: 'Once this process of "gentrification" starts in a district, it goes on until all or most of the original working-class occupiers are displaced, and the whole social character of the district is changed.'

Glass's field work was partially conducted in Notting Hill, in west London. As in Brixton, many of the Windrush generation from the Caribbean had settled there, alongside White British and Irish families. Glass wrote about the racist housing and employment policies that affected arriving West Indians. The community suffered from anti-Black violence during riots in 1958, against a developing political backdrop that Glass argued had become polluted by intolerant, exaggerated claims about immigration from distant parts of the British Commonwealth. Following the end of the Second World War, families had been arriving in London for nearly thirteen years from parts of the Caribbean and South Asia in particular, on invitation from the British government. It would be a decade later that the Conservative MP Enoch Powell gave his infamous 'Rivers of Blood' speech against mass immigration, reflecting the growing tension in increasingly multicultural areas of cities. And while parts of Notting Hill remained locked in poverty, dilapidated terraced houses were being refurbished and sold off. It soon became full of middle-class people seeking a trendy urban base. It then started to transform into the plush, whitewashed hinterland of today.

Glass's documentation is evidence that the texture of London life has long been restitched. The Notting Hill she wrote about is apparent in Sam Selvon's 1956 novel, *The Lonely Londoners*. The recently arrived Trinidadian protagonist Moses becomes trapped in a cold cycle of day-to-day subsistence. 'London divide up in little worlds,' he reflects, 'and you stay in the world you belong to and you don't know what happening in the other ones.' The idea that, in London, disparate lives are forced to reconcile with one another, is not new. But across the 2010s, this reality made itself known in particularly shocking ways.

On 14 June 2017, Grenfell Tower – a twenty-four-storey high-rise social housing block near Ladbroke Grove tube station, a stone's throw from where Glass conducted her ethnography work and Selvon penned his classic six decades before – went up in flames. Seventy-two people lost their lives and hundreds of others lost their ways of life. Thousands were forced to self-mobilize to pick up the pieces in the absence of any comprehensive support. The building's blackened carcass was left peering over the vicinity for months. Mourning families and children were expected to carry on despite the reminder of neglect peering back down at them. The fire had travelled fast because of cheap, flammable cladding installed in the building's walls. The material had been purchased to save money rather than to maintain the safety of its residents.

The London borough of Kensington and Chelsea, where Grenfell stood, is one of the wealthiest authorities in the United Kingdom. It contains some of the most valuable properties on the planet. The tower's specific ward, however – Notting Dale, to the north – has remained among the poorest in the capital. Charles Booth's London Poverty Maps, published at the end of the nineteenth century, noted that the ward's poor fed pigs on rubbish dumped in the West End and then boiled down their fat to use for engineering and brewing. Back then they lived in tiny shacks, metres from some of the world's most luxurious mansions. The contrast is no longer so stark, but my point is that inequality in London is timeless.

On 14 January 2020 I attended the thirty-first silent walk in memory of those who passed away in the fire. Walks take place on the same day every month as a ritual of commemoration and peaceful protest. Traffic stops as crowds carrying green placards loop Notting Dale. The names of the fallen are read out over a loudspeaker. Surnames are repeated, reflecting the family members who perished.

'What created Grenfell was deregulation. What created Grenfell was Thatcherism,' said Daniel Renwick, a local writer, filmmaker and Grenfell activist. Renwick has spent years documenting the fallout, lending a hand to the community's recovery and working to bring those responsible for the fire to justice. He explained that under a governing ideology of unrestrained capitalism that favours shopping out services like social housing, policing and healthcare to private companies, there has become an absence of responsibility. He described a 'drive to the bottom' to save costs. 'It's the market state – the fact that profits and budgets mean more than people do.'

The Grenfell fire sent shockwaves across the city. As local residents had warned in blog posts, letters and protests years before it happened, a tragedy as epic as this had been a long time coming. Grenfell would stay dominant in media headlines, although nobody has been held accountable for it. Countless young people I worked with in the months after it happened spoke of a palpable sense of loss. 'It felt so close to home, 'cause it's just like the block I used to live in,' one political activist from Brixton would tell me.

By the summer term of 2017, I'd become sensitive not only to the inequality in Elephant & Castle, but to how this inequality was changing. Contrasting value systems and life patterns existed on the same tiny stretch of land that was becoming one of the most sought-after in the city. Glass's conception of 'gentrification' has been exported around the Western world – from San Francisco and New York to Berlin and Copenhagen. Since the turn of the millennium, however, there can surely be few places in the UK that have transformed as Elephant & Castle has done. The speed of the makeover is remarkable – something I'd previously associated with cities in China and India, whose economies and populous middle-classes are growing unlike anywhere else on the planet.

Week-on-week during my commutes to and from Willow, I felt like I was witnessing a remodelling of London's future: the constant din of pneumatic drills, the paving of shiny paths, the gleam of outdoor escalators, the plots of immaculately cut grass, the shipping-container pop-up shops and cafes. What appeared to be 'pseudo-public space' started to fill the centre of Elephant & Castle: land in the form of squares, parks and pavements, presented as easily accessible and publicly owned, and therefore free to walk on, that is in fact owned by private companies with their own ledger of rules and regulations. From walkways around the Olympic Stadium in Stratford to the canalside seating of King's Cross, it represents the insidious tightening of the private sector's grip over life in the capital.

In July 2018, the shopping centre containing local businesses – nicknamed an 'anti-Westfield' for its old-school charm, with its market which sat in the 'moat' circling the main building below ground level – was announced as pending demolition. A decision taken by the Southwark Council planning committee gave way to the development firm Delancey, who planned to build new retail space. Long-standing Latin American hubs Distri-Andina and La Bodeguita would be set to close. It was a struggle to imagine any of the small, family-run stalls or cafes near the roundabout surviving Elephant's flux, as has been proven in countless other gentrifying parts of London, from Brixton to Dalston, where 'developments' simply mean that rents become unaffordable for locals.

'It's concerning because the change is too fast and if we can't adapt fast enough then we get moved,' Demetri said. Inspired by the daily interactions I was having with young people often themed around their frustrations about the regenerative changes taking place in south London, I wanted to create a piece of collaborative journalism platforming their perspectives. I presented the idea to various groups of students at Willow. Five expressed an interest in taking part. We met one afternoon in a classroom after school for a round-table discussion. The room buzzed with impassioned debate and free admission. Afterwards, I typed up our conversation and let each student refine their respective comments.

'My mum used to take me to Elephant & Castle as a child, and on our way there we would see how many people she knew – aunties, uncles – she would be able to just freely say hello to people. There was a sense of community,' explained one sixth-form student I was mentoring for TAP – a member of the school's poetry collective, who went on to study English at university. 'Now you can see it in her behaviour when we go out on the Walworth Road, she is more closed off, even if we see [other] Bengali people, people just look at each other and move on,' she continued, highlighting what she saw as the breakdown of her community. 'People are forced to do their own thing now. It would be amazing if new residents and existing ones helped each other and there was lots more mixing – if there was more unity – but it's not happening, it's not the reality. People work on their own self-interest. I definitely think that there is meaning behind the types of people that are coming in, and the people who are being pushed out.'

'When I look outside my classroom sometimes I see a new building growing in the distance. It builds my anger, but also my aspirations for if I want to still be living somewhere like here in ten, twenty years' time. It's an injustice, so I write poetry about it, I speak out against it,' explained sixteen-year-old Joshua Adeyemi, a Year 11 student, another poet, from Brandon Estate in Kennington. Weeks before taking part in our group conversation, Adeyemi had been granted a full scholarship to attend Eton College sixth form. He would later attain a place at Cambridge University to study Human, Social and Political Sciences. 'There is not a lot of social or community cohesion. My mum has recognized the change. She asks me, "Have you seen that new neighbour?" and I am always on the lookout for new people. Gentrification is not always in the form of new buildings, sometimes it's in the form of a new class of people. So I'm like, how come you chose here? It's not the fact that I don't want new people here or anything but it's how they don't try to interact with other people who have lived here for so long. They move in and seclude themselves in this little bubble. I think if both sides did more to understand each other it would work out better.'

One of Demetri's friends expressed that he was pleased about new aspects of the change. 'Before people wouldn't let their kids go outside alone or stay in the park without them being there. With new people moving into the area I see parents letting their kids go out now. And with my parents as well, they actually trust more people,' he said, referring to how he feels like his native Walworth has become safer for families and young people as it has been redeveloped. 'But whereas before you had big groups of people who used to hang around together, who knew each other and where each other lived, and if you needed something you could go to your neighbour's house and ask for it . . . I don't feel like I can do that as much now.'

'Sometimes the change is good, but I feel as if . . . it's not for the benefit of the people who already live in the area, it's for the new people,' said fifteen-year-old Tatiana Walker, from Brixton. 'It bothers me that [the people moving in] only want to get the good stuff – carnivals, like Brixton Splash. They probably wouldn't want to listen to the intensity of the bad stuff that actually happens.'

'Recently, in the construction site where Heygate Estate used to be, I keep noticing a new thing every week, like new windows and fresh trees. It makes me feel scared about how much longer our community will last,' Demetri said. He told us the story of how he'd recently returned home to his block, only to be ignored by his new neighbour waiting for the lift.

Built in 1974, the wide concrete blocks and raised walkways of Heygate Estate – cherished by visiting urban explorers and many of its 3,000 former residents, feared by those who saw its maze as synonymous with overcrowded social failure – amounted to one of the most recognizable public housing structures in the UK, if not Western Europe. It was known to many as a location for countless gritty films and television shows over the years, including *World War Z*, *Harry Brown* and *Attack the Block*.

Completed in 2010, Strata SE1, the tall skyscraper that Demetri looked out on to from his bedroom window, stands a few hundred metres away from Heygate's former grounds. Heygate and Strata might be understood as clashing symbols of the past and future. Heygate was demolished in 2014; Strata represents the post-modernist, new-era version of Elephant & Castle.

While working at Willow I heard a few students make references to the way their family, friends or former classmates had been rehoused and reschooled elsewhere in the city as a result of Heygate's demise. And knocking it down was a means to a bigger end: harnessing prime real estate for rich new tenants seeking a central, Zone-1 base. Lendlease, the Australian developers of Elephant Park who had been chosen as Southwark Council's partner, claimed to be offering the right-to-return for people previously living in Heygate. Former property owners or renters would, they promised, be 'decanted' from the estate after its demolition, then come back when the project was complete. But this commitment was a myth. The company could take advantage of

Southwark Council's weak position after central government cuts had further eroded its limited standing in negotiations about the rights of its residents. In its last months, makeshift signs of protest reading 'Lendlease STOLE MY HOME' were pinned with tape to Heygate's metal fences.

A local action group called the 35% Campaign found that only one in five secure tenants – 216 out of 1,034 – found new housing in the SE17 postcode after the decant. The rest were scattered across south-east London. Of the leaseholders who the campaign gathered information about, none stayed in the same postcode; around 50 per cent of those displaced were relocated to other south-east postcodes, including many distant ones. The other 50 per cent moved even further out, in all directions. Some bought new homes tens of miles away in satellite towns outside of London like Slough, St Albans and Cheshunt. They received criminally low compensation for their former homes which made it impossible to return to live anywhere near central London, a city whose average monthly rent of £1,673 is nearly twice as high as the national average of £959.

The Heygate was home to 1,194 social-rented flats at the time of its demolition. In the end, Elephant Park would provide only 74 social-rented homes out of its 2,500 units. On paper, Lendlease were legally obliged to guarantee a minimum of 35 per cent 'affordable' housing to replace the estate. This later dropped to 25 per cent due to loopholes in legal accounting practice. The 'affordability' of even this quarter of homes is questionable, too, because it is calculated on market rates, which fluctuate and tend to hinge on the inflation of London's price-distorting housing crisis. It was under conditions of central government austerity, during the London mayorship of Boris Johnson, from 2011 onwards, that 'affordable rents' for social homes would be introduced as 80 per cent of market rates, thus birthing an equation that would write in stone the subtle pricing-out of poorer tenants for years to come. Westminster Council would write to Johnson to clarify that, to meet this rate, households would therefore have to earn an annual income of £58,000 to pay for a one-bedroom flat, and £109,000 per year for a three-bedroom house. A household income of £40,000 would be required to live in the cheapest London borough of Barking and Dagenham. The mean household income of the whole of London in 2018 was £36,421. Johnson's successor, Sadiq Khan, has since failed to lower the 80 per cent rate as he promised to do during his mayoral campaign. The 'affordable' label is in many cases now meaningless; a clause which serves property developers and those with the purchasing power to rent privately, rather than members of pre-existing low-income households.

Heygate tenants who exercised their right-to-buy in decades prior were forced to sell for a pittance as part of something called a Compulsory Purchase Order, or CPO. The 35% Campaign found that the average compensation paid for a one-bedroom flat during the Heygate decant was £108,164. One leaseholder received just £32,000 for their one-bedroom flat in 2008. By contrast, the cost of a new studio flat started at £569,000. Two-bedroom flats started at £801,000. Southwark Council had originally sold the Heygate site for £50 million and spent £44 million on emptying the estate. After redevelopment, it would later be valued at £1.2 billion. Over the same transitional period across the 2010s, according to Hamptons International estate agents, house prices in Elephant & Castle rose 76 per cent. The erasure of Elephant & Castle's past and its diversity was underway.

'Elephant was always one of those areas, like Bow in east London, that was viewed by its council as lacking a mix — as pure council estates. For people like Peter John, the former head of the Labour council in Southwark, vast, sweeping change was completely necessary to save the area,' said Dan Hancox, author of *Inner City Pressure: The Story of Grime*, which focuses on how regeneration in east London boroughs around the turn of the millennium birthed grime music. Hancox has researched and written extensively about the intersections of British politics, life in London, music culture and gentrification. He explained that since the New Labour government of the late 1990s an accepted truth has seeped into council decision-making: 'They will argue that you get a better outcome for people in council estates if they live in a mixed area. And there might be some truth in that. But my critique of it would be, at a fundamental level, that the first thing you should be doing is ameliorating existing social problems: increasing public spending on schools and services, making sure there are good mental health provisions, and so on. Not replacing people with other people, and allowing the selling-off of council housing, youth clubs and playing fields to private companies.'

Tony Blair's first speech after being elected Prime Minister in 1997 was at the Aylesbury Estate in Walworth – another sprawling, infamous social housing complex like Heygate. 'Police were scared to enter it,' Tony, who was in charge of its youth service in the 1990s, once told me in one of our chats at Jacob Sawyer. Several Willow students lived in Aylesbury, although its buildings have been steadily emptied and demolished.

'Aylesbury was a symbol of everything Blair felt that eighteen years of a Conservative government had left: social decay, crumbling tower blocks, these remnants of Thatcherism,' Hancox explained. 'The transformation of the Heygate, the Aylesbury, the roundabout itself and the shopping centre – not to mention the building of Strata and various other towers – those plans are about enacting the New Labour vision of a "mixed community". What that means in practice, of course, is the dispersal of the working class, disproportionately BAME residents and businesses – gig venues, clubs, restaurants, cafes, all sorts – to the outer boroughs. It's worth mentioning that a lot of the post-war

estates were built with a utopian idea that these would help lift
up the communities in them, out of poverty. And the Heygate
and Aylesbury did not create a utopia, as many people who lived
there will tell you. But their communities were loved and valued. I think that's part of the reason so many people defend
estates like the Heygate, not because it was a perfect place to live,
but maybe it *could be* if it was kept up properly, and the lives of
the people in it were treated with more respect.'

Hancox is sceptical of those who argue against change in the
city. But he maintains that regeneration in places like Elephant
& Castle has been for the few, not the many.

'People deserve to live in better homes. Being critical of gentrification doesn't mean thinking that cities shouldn't evolve and
transform and regenerate. I'm not against regeneration. The
question is: who are these places regenerating for? For me, it
wasn't bad, per se, that they tore down the Heygate; it was bad
that they tore it down without absolutely ensuring that people
had the right to remain or come back to the area, and that the
social mix would stay the same as it was. They didn't do that,
though, because they didn't want to.'

The story of the Heygate is the story of a housing crisis in
which prices have soared due to rising demand and faltering
supply. Nowhere near enough social or affordable homes have
been built across the United Kingdom by recent governments.
In the end, this reality benefits asset-rich landlords and the
wealthy. It has allowed working-class life across the city to be
trampled on by the sturdy-footed middle classes moving in and
remote, elusive foreign investors seeing profit. Local councils
should be standing up to companies that swoop in to make profit
out of poor people's loss, not simply cosying up to them to
attract chain commerce and monied inhabitants.

For local young people, the arrival of new-build flats, chain
shops and pricey eateries in places like Elephant & Castle and

Brixton was having an insidious effect on their sense of belonging. The social problems that have existed largely on the backstreets and behind closed doors for decades among the poorest households have been strategically displaced and covered up in the name of trendy regeneration. Many teenagers experienced gentrification by acknowledging the improving aesthetic of their area around them. They might comment on the attraction of new, glistening grassy areas or pedestrianized walkways. But they would simultaneously hint at a loss of freedom, self-esteem and ownership over their homes. Boys, in particular, already looked over their shoulders when they navigated particular parts of town. Yet because of forces out of their control – austerity, big business, Westminster policies – their claustrophobic world was shrinking even more.

Equality is not just socio-economic: it is also about the spectrum of people's personal liberties, imaginations and dreams for the future becoming more inclusive. The glossy veneer of marketing jingoism, pricey cafes, shared workspaces and fetishized 'mixed communities' has helped to make everyone blind to the injustices that entrench social division, and therefore further enable anger, displacement and violence on London's streets.

Carl had recently finished Year 11 and it was the summer holidays. He hadn't revised for his GCSEs. He was going to football college, anyway, so it didn't matter that he'd done badly in them. He'd been smoking and shotting more. He felt strong and confident but more people he knew were getting stabbed. Every couple of days a new madness happened.

He was leaving the chicken shop with one of his friends at midnight on a Saturday. They walked out of the door and turned left to go towards the Loughborough blocks. Carl never had much reason to turn right and walk towards Brixton mains. He didn't really care who he bumped into any more because he

would firm it no matter what. But the closer he got to Somerleyton*, the more careful he had to be. He felt calm up to the
soup kitchen, but past that it could get sticky. The same was
true towards Stockwell, Kennington and Lower Tulse Hill. He
had opps everywhere. He'd got into more fights and become
more active on socials, meaning his face was bait. By staying in
and around Loughborough he was fine, or so he thought.

Within seconds of leaving the chicken shop Carl and his friend
walked past someone he recognized. He was an opposition, a few
years older than Carl. Carl had seen him on Snap and in music
videos. Carl wondered if he might try something for the clout.

'Where you from?' he asked Carl.

'Loughborough. So what?' Carl replied. His heart started
pounding.

The opp reached into his tracksuit bottoms and pulled out a
mini Rambo knife with serrated edges. He lunged at Carl, who
jumped backwards to dodge the blade. Carl turned and ran with his
friend. Carl was too fast. He would never get caught in a foot race.

After he got away, Carl said goodbye to his friend and headed
home. He felt a bit shaken up but also angry. How could this
one yout come to Loughborough and ask where Carl was from?
Carl had never been g-checked like that before, especially in his
own ends. Carl g-checked *other* people. Carl always moved a
certain way, like a boss, because he never wanted to be a victim.
But he felt like a victim now. It frustrated him. He nearly got
caught. He was annoyed at himself for leaving his flicky at
home. He didn't usually need it around Loughborough.

Carl passed the old Fields† blocks, then the pretty new ones.
For years the area had been a building site, with cranes and diggers
and metal fences. Now it was called 'Oval Quarter'. Carl thought

---

* A housing estate off Coldharbour Lane, near central Brixton
† Myatt's Fields South housing estate

the flats looked proper. They'd built a big new park which was lit up at night. The basketball court had bright-blue tarmac. There were outdoor seats next to stone tables. He liked the park and the new flats. The old flats were depressing. They made the area feel like the slums. Now it looked better, less dangerous.

Carl looked up and saw adults walking towards him. They were the kind of posh people he was seeing more around Brixton. They looked like his teachers. They were dressed in shirts and jeans and dresses. They were all white, apart from one man, who was Asian. They were joking around with each other. They looked drunk and Carl thought that maybe they'd been at a party at one of the new flats.

Carl became aware that his hood was up. He softened his face and feigned a smile. He didn't want to seem intimidating; he would never harm civilians. The group stopped making so much noise as they neared him. Maybe, Carl thought, because of his dark skin and his tracksuit, they thought he was a mad man or a drug dealer. Maybe they thought he was going to rob them. He stopped smiling. But he didn't want them to think that he was a bad yout. He had manners and he was always polite to his elders. He kept his head down. The people parted to make room for him to walk on the pavement. He looked up and one of the women caught his eye. She tensed up and looked down at the pavement. Carl carried on walking. Seconds later he heard their laughter resume.

'As a teenager in the nineties, we had more freedom to move around, total freedom. That's probably why so many people turned crackhead and ended up in prison. We had access to wherever we wanted. But there were no platforms. No opportunities. We had nothing to do *with* our freedom,' explained Elijah Kerr, better known as Jaja Soze, author of *The Power of Love: My Personal Notes*, who grew up in Angell Town housing estate, where he now runs Brixton Recording Studios. Over the years some of the biggest names in the contemporary UK rap and drill scenes have passed through its doors to receive mentorship. He is an established community leader. When we met at his studio, I'd asked him to explain the difference between growing up as a teenager in Brixton now compared to when he was young. 'Now, it's the reverse. Kids have got the platforms, but they lack the freedom. They've got more grants and funding. There are young people writing books and starting magazines or businesses – whereas back in the day, in the hood, you only heard about drugs, robberies and fights. But now there is less freedom than ever, because the gang problems are so bad.'

At the turn of the millennium a gang called PDC – Peel Dem Crew, later rebranded to Poverty Driven Children – ran Brixton's streets. Jaja Soze was its founder. PDC succeeded earlier generations of so-called 'Yardie' gangs made up of British-Caribbean men and women. They rose in the 1970s alongside other ethnically defined subcultures: the Mods and Rockers, National Front skinheads and South Asian gangs in Southall and Newham. Brixton's most feared criminal outfits such as the Raiders Posse, 28s and the Younger 28s were influential in the 1970s, 1980s and early 1990s as crack cocaine became a lucrative drug market. But whereas these earlier collectives operated across large swathes of south London, PDC were based mostly out of Angell Town. The shift between the generations saw jurisdictions shrink. Sets formed narrower identities – a contraction continuing to the present day.

'Before, there was no boss,' said Corey Johnson, a former member of the Younger 28s. 'One man from each estate in Lambeth borough made up the whole gang.' Like Soze, Johnson now runs a successful music studio in Lewisham, called Digital Holdings, as a means of steering young artists away from the roads. His studio got the nickname 'Switzerland' because of its neutrality for visiting rappers. Later, Johnson explained, when people started to make serious money, people wanted tighter control. 'Out of nowhere you had PDC in Brixton, Peckham Boys in Peckham, SMS in Streatham, G Street on Wandsworth Road, SUK in Clapham Junction, Ghetto Boys in New Cross . . . all these different gangs. It all changed.'

This splintering did not happen in a vacuum. Failing state schools and widespread unemployment meant that young adults in poor parts of inner cities were dependent on the drug game and other illicit ways of making money to compete in the capital's rat race. Under Soze's leadership, PDC became feared and influential across Brixton and beyond. They 'steamed' banks and shops – a practice in which tens of robbers would overwhelm a building and steal things at once. They robbed other drug dealers.

Yet Soze explained that because of the reach of his social network, he could still move around the borough of Lambeth largely without worry. 'If it was a sunny day, we used to call it "the walk". At the start I used to walk to Myatt's Field, round to Vassall Road, up to Stockwell. On the way I'd be meeting people, smoking, chilling. We might do a little robbery. We'd go to Acre Lane, Brixton Hill, Tulse Hill, Norwood, Somerleyton.' As Carl and other boys' experiences had shown me, all of these parts of south London that were in theory once more civil, or at least on some level united by familial ties and community socializing, are for the most disenfranchised young people now ruthlessly guarded territories, each with their own unique reputation on the roads, drill outfit and relentless social media presence. These entangled webs of risk weren't always there. 'We'd just walk and hang,' continued Soze. 'We had the freedom to do that. Especially if you was popular, like me, you could just walk everywhere. You'd go to one estate and someone's mum would give you food. It was a totally different ball game.'

Both Johnson and Soze stressed that earlier iterations of gangs prioritized money.

'We just wanted to make money and get the fuck out of here. We wanted to look fly and buy some dope cars and clothes, because the people who were respected were the people with money. People were scary and violent but being bad for the sake of it wasn't the main goal. You were only bad *to make money*. That's changed now. Now you have bad boys who don't care about their clothes. It's become more about just wearing a hoodie and Nikes, and having a gun,' Soze argued. He maintained that gang members now are driven by other ways of attaining status and surviving, not just money. Beefs of the past have multiplied and intensified as they've been inherited by young people following the codes of their elders. Now, young potential gang members must, for example, decide whether to avenge events in which they or their friends were violated over social media. So-called gang warfare is less predictable. Although fundamentally always entrenched by the poverty of its proponents, this reflects an even broader church of societal problems whose roots have dug in deeper over time.

'It's less about money now and it's more about *emotions*. It's more mindless now,' Corey Johnson told me.

I asked Soze how he thinks Brixton has changed due to gentrification.

'Before, middle-class people – whether they are Black, white or Asian – would not come on to the estate. Their kids wouldn't engage with us. You had those kids on one road, where all the big houses are, and us on this road. We didn't even know each other existed. Now things are more visible. The other day, I was driving around the estate at night-time and I saw a lady riding her bike, with a basket and everything. She looked like Mary Poppins! You wouldn't have seen that before: on the one side of the street, the mandem with their hoods up, bunning a spliff. Then a few metres later, Mary Poppins! That took me some time to get used to.'

What frustrated Soze most about gentrification was the displacement of people who helped make Brixton the culturally rich town it is today.

'In the 1990s they knocked down some of the blocks and a lot of the families weren't given the opportunity or the education to buy property, so they got relocated. Then the middle classes started to come in. Even though not much has changed – it's exactly the same area, the crime is still high – suddenly, it's all worth millions! It's cold, when you start deeping it, because the people who built Brixton got sent out. They had dope businesses, but they just needed help. When local small businesses get into problems with high rents, the bailiffs come around straight away. The new class of residents in Brixton want these offices now, so they'll kick people out. Then you see posh people come in with their business, but it doesn't serve people on the estate and they don't try to reach out. They don't come and knock on your door and say hello, and ask how we're doing when they move in. They can come into Brixton and enjoy what the community built. They can afford all the stuff. They can buy up premises and go to all the bars and enjoy themselves every night. But we can't afford to do that. So now, when you go out, you see a certain type of person enjoying all the music, the graffiti, the clothing – the things that *we made cool*! When we *do* go to the bars, *they* look at *us* funny! Like we're not supposed to be in there! Even though we made this place cool in the first place! And it's not like we built all that quickly. We had to go through blood, sweat and tears.'

He stressed, however, that good things can come from gentrification in Brixton if people moving into areas make an effort to forge local relationships and commit their privileges to causes that can benefit those already living there.

'It's not putting blame on anyone, it's just knowing that people who come into these areas – Brixton, Shoreditch, Peckham – should be building bridges with the foundation people who are already here. That's when gentrification can be progressive. When a middle-class person comes to me and asks how they can help, I say: you build bridges. You've got access to another world. Now you're coming into our world that we've built. The problem isn't that people are coming in, it's that they need to be giving us access to things they have access to. But in Brixton that's not happening a lot, and it should be. The access works both ways. All of us who have been here for years have access to stuff, creatively – business, music, fashion, art, poetry, literature – but we're just lacking finances. We don't have assets. Our elders didn't leave us assets. When our parents died, most of us just got bills.'

At the end of our conversation, Soze posed a powerful question, as well as its answer.

'Do you know that exercise, when they get people to line up like they're doing a race? And then they ask you questions. Like, who's got a dad? Take a step forward. Who got taught to do goal setting? Come forward. When I saw that exercise, I was like, oh my God! That's how I felt my whole life! I swear, there was a little tear in my eye. Because as a kid, I'd be at the starting line, still waiting for them to ask other things. Who got taught to buss a gun? Who knows about drugs? So when the starting pistol finally goes, the guys at the front, who got taught all them things, are practically at the finish. Whereas we're starting all the way at the start. Some people have finished the race, but we're still running.'

Rory and I had started doing trips with our group at Jacob Sawyer. We completed a workshop about local history with the education outreach team at the Black Cultural Archives. We took the boys to eat in places they wouldn't usually, such as

Franco Manca, a sourdough pizza restaurant in the bustling Market Row, which brought about groans from a couple of the group on account of the menu's lack of barbecue base flavour. But such trips served to further solidify the breaking down of boundaries between our world and theirs.

None of the boys had ever dined in Brixton Village, despite it only being a short walk from Loughborough Junction, so we ate at a Thai restaurant there. The Village is an undercover emporium which forms one part of the town's busy markets, where small businesses have served local people since it was built in 1937. Since the area started diversifying with immigrants in the 1950s, mostly those from the Caribbean, and later West Africa and Latin America, it has long been a popular place to spend time and shop. For sale are spreads of fresh ingredients like fruit, yams, ackee and plantains; plates of Trini roti, Ethiopian injera and Colombian steaks; and vintage clothes, vinyls and books. But its steadily drained affordability and the fight against property developers, much like the situation in Elephant & Castle, has not been easy for those trying to uphold their staying power.

I'd heard Tony and other locals comment that some older businesses they'd known as children had disappeared; others, forced to evolve to compete, managed to survive as the area's vibrancy attracted wider audiences. Some were positive about the change, glad that Brixton seemed to be attracting new, monied customers and interesting places to eat and drink. But others had heard how family friends who owned shops in the railway arches by the high street could no longer afford the rent and had been forced to close. Rumours and stories of this type of frustration circulated in the local newspaper and online blogs. A 'Yuppies Out' protest against the 'Champagne and Fromage' bar took place inside the Village in 2013, garnering support from those who felt such pricey new ventures symbolized the pompous exclusivity of new arrivals.

On one Friday evening at the end of the summer holidays, Rory and I hosted a discussion at Jacob Sawyer entitled 'Society'. Rory wrote the word on a whiteboard we'd brought from our flat. We wanted the boys to verbalize any observations they might have about inequality. As an icebreaker, we asked the group to say the first word that popped into their heads when they read the word 'society'.

'Generation', 'people', 'hierarchy', 'organization', 'communities', 'authority' and 'surroundings' came their replies. Rory wrote them in a list beneath the title.

Next, we asked them to describe the structure of society.

'There's upper, middle and lower class,' said one boy. The others agreed. Rory wrote each class level in a rectangular box, stacked on top of one another vertically in the middle of the whiteboard.

I asked the boys to place themselves in this system.

'Let's be real, we're all lower class.'

'I reckon I'm middle class, you know,' challenged someone. 'Both my parents have good jobs. My mum's a carer, my dad works in transport. Plus I live in Herne Hill, which is a wealthy area.'

The others erupted into complaints and started shaking their heads.

'Fam, you're lower class just like the rest of us, don't get gassed!' lectured Carl. A couple of the others laughed. The boy looked at the floor and became shy.

'Lower class is sometimes called "working class", init? So just because your parents have jobs doesn't mean you're middle class. Also, just 'cause you live in rich ends doesn't make *you* rich. If you live near some of the new blocks, but you still live in an estate, you're still poor, fam,' another added.

I asked what sort of jobs they associated with the different classes. For the upper class, they suggested: the queen ('I swear she owns the country?' queried one participant), anyone in the government, accountants and judges. For the middle class, they said teachers and police.

Rory asked the group if they felt the structure they'd come up with was useful.

'It's useful because it's honest. It's the way the world works,' one boy stated.

'It can proper affect your mindset,' muttered another.

I put forward the idea that there must be different ways of defining how someone fits into the different classes, and therefore different ways of valuing people or deeming them important or powerful. I asked them to suggest some ways people can differ between their positions in society. The boys responded with a range of metrics: age, race, job, income, where you're born, where you live, your living standards, your education and how many 'houses and cars' you have. Rory wrote all of these down on the left-hand side of the whiteboard.

To finish, we asked the group if they thought it was possible to move between the classes. A couple of them agreed that it was if you earned more money, and that one way of doing that was studying at university and getting a good job. Carl shook his head and said he wanted to earn money quicker.

'What's the point of all that debt, fam? That's moist! It's better to start working right away,' he scoffed, getting animated. 'You see me, yeah? I want that money *quick*!'

On the one hand there were those in the room who had clearly come to accept the prescribed route of gaining grades at school and moving on to a university degree before entering the workplace. Like students I was working with as part of my job at TAP – and the ethos of academy schools and the charity itself – university was perceived by some young people as society's most reliable route towards, and metric of, success.

But on the other hand, Carl was expressing a reluctance to fit the education system's mould. Success for Carl did not mean – arguably *could* not mean – following the mainstream, slow-burning and allegedly secure route of academic qualifications and a nine-to-five job.

'I reckon you'd still be lower class, even if you made a mill tomorrow from trapping. You're still the same person, init? You'd still be living that working-class lifestyle. So it's what you've grown up around. It takes time to move upwards, cah it's about how you act and who you spend time with, too,' one of Carl's friends contributed.

By the end of the session the whiteboard was covered in the boys' reflections and thoughts. We said our goodbyes to the boys and debriefed the session with Tony and other staff. Rory headed home; I'd been invited to a drinks party in Oval, roughly a twenty-minute walk away. It was being hosted by the friend of a friend who I knew from university. They'd both attended a prestigious private boarding school in their teens.

I headed north past Myatt's Fields South's aged and weathered low-rise blocks. The path I took past the estate was littered and bare clumps of dry, unkempt summer grass poked out of the ground. I walked past two souped-up hatchbacks parked on the pavement. A group of men were passing around a bottle of Courvoisier and pouring its contents into plastic cups. I recognized a couple of them from drill videos I'd watched on YouTube. They were playing their music from the car speakers.

I entered the new grounds of Oval Quarter. A man in boat shoes walking his dog wished me a good evening. I took the path across the open greenery of the park and could see people lounging on their balconies. All of them looked like young professional types, people with whom I would have attended school or university – those I was en route to spend my evening with. After walking further north I arrived in a mews. I buzzed the house number and passed through an electronic gate made from polished wood which slid open. It closed behind me seconds later.

It was roughly 9 p.m. when I was let into a three-storey townhouse. My friend showed me into a mood-lit living room where jazzy hip-hop instrumentals were playing from Bang & Olufsen speakers. I was introduced to the host, a man who was wearing a white shirt tucked into some chinos, loafers on his bare feet. He handed me a large glass full of red wine. My friend offered me a cigarette. We entered the back garden, surrounded by towering walls at least ten metres high.

I remembered that only a few hundred metres away from where I was now standing was Kennington Park Estate, where Harlem Spartans, the popular UK drill collective, hailed from. To the east of their estate was Kennington Park's multicoloured flower garden, and a few hundred metres to the east of that were the tall towers of Brandon Estate, where the drill group Moscow17 lived. Harlem and Moscow were allies. Many Willow students hailing from a similar part of town would sing their songs in the school corridors during term time. The pair of collectives were both fierce rivals of 150 and 410, of north Brixton. This meant that the precise walk I'd just done, up past Angell Town, through Loughborough, Myatt's Fields Park and Oval Quarter, had essentially involved crossing between two sides of a hidden war. I knew, deep down, this war was starting to become very real for people like Carl and his friends.

Demetri, who lived roughly one kilometre to the north, had been ignored by his new neighbour as he tried to enter the front door of his block. I looked around me, at people drinking and smoking and dancing at the party. Faced with the same scenario, would they have let Demetri in?

8. Sons of the Ends

'Knife Crime'

Monday 30 October 2017

'Guess what!?' Jhemar asked joyfully. He'd stomped into the IntoUniversity staff office where I was talking to two staff members. He nodded at them, shaking their hands briskly, before insisting we go into the other room to talk. He was sweating and out of breath. He'd been running, weighed down by a thick winter jacket. He was twenty minutes late.

'I'll guess what when you check your watch,' I replied drily.

'Oh my bad, I had a lickle ting to sort after school,' he panted. 'Anyway, fam, listen! I'm speaking to Michael again! This Sunday!' He held out his hand for me to slap. Then he danced an impromptu skank, bending his knees and waving both sets of gun fingers in the air, moving to the rhythm of his own excitement.

'Yes! How's he doing?'

'Michael's back in college. He's in a better place, still. Man's gonna chat to him this Sunday on the phone and see wagwan. Or maybe we'll see him at his yard. I'm gassed!'

The absence of Michael in Jhemar's life had taken its toll. Jhemar had stopped referring to his older brother's influence as a way to explain his most cherished ideals – cars, mechanics, PlayStation, being loyal, standing up for himself. He hadn't seen Michael since the summer before, over fourteen months. Hearing that Michael was returning to Jhemar's life was music to my ears.

My relationship with Jhemar was changing. Volume 2 of

'The Book of Wisdom' – we'd completed Volume 1, which to this day remains lost to the clutters of Jhemar's bedroom – was collecting dust on a shelf in the IntoUniversity classroom, near a photograph of our first meeting Blu-Tacked to the wall. Jhemar had hopped unscathed past the first hurdle of what Demetri had identified as the generic 'bad man' phase of boys in Year 8, 9 or 10. But he had arrived at the next hurdle: realizing early adulthood. Self-proclaimed independence was Jhemar's new-found fuel; a sturdier frame and argumentative voice his vehicle of autonomy. Society's imposing mould of hypermasculinity – the requirement to display confidence and the suppression of emotional openness – was entering the mix, too. Nonetheless, I was proud of Jhemar for managing to avoid caving to such social pressures compared to other boys his age.

Predictably, Jhemar had become more vocal about his fascin-ation with girls. They were apparently fascinated with him, too. Or, at least, that's what he kept telling me. Each time we met, Jhemar would relay bashful updates, seeking advice through reluctant grimaces about female friends he described as 'calm', or 'playing hella games', or plainly 'moving mad'. He insisted on trying to explain to me the micropolitics of his social media interactions. I set boundaries so he didn't delve too deep or ramble on for too long. I tried to reinforce moral laws that he might have overlooked without intervention. 'I know, I know, I know . . .' he tutted, rolling his eyes when I explained the importance of being fully communicative and respectful with romantic partners; of treating others how he'd want to be treated himself; of embracing vulnerability, if it felt natural to do so.

Jhemar was also becoming aware of his daunting GCSE workload. I questioned him on his revision schedule and plans for the future. He told me he intended to leave his school to go to a sixth-form college, but he was uncertain about university, insisting an apprenticeship would be better suited for his hands-on approach to learning.

I queried the lateness of his bedtime on school nights after his mum had told me that he was spending too much time on his phone and not getting enough sleep. He humoured me politely through sighs and glances out of the window or at his endlessly flashing phone screen. I'd become a subtle disciplinarian.

Jhemar talked about his adventures around London. He would take off on his bike to the BMX track in Brockwell Park in Herne Hill. He would visit local music studios to make beats and record raps. 'It's like nothing can harm me, because I'm part of God's army!' went the chorus of his most cherished song, 'God's Army'. 'Call it reflection time, now it's time to reflect on life. Growing up in London, south of the river, where it's a world of crime,' went the third verse. He showed me videos of him performing it on stage at church and school, receiving rounds of applause and calls for an encore. 'Fam, the next day I was like a celebrity! When I walked down the corridor, man needed security!' he cried hysterically.

The song's religious slant was evidence that Jhemar had started articulating his own fierce principles of daily life. He was convinced that avoiding groups of young people was the most responsible thing he could do to look after himself.

'I don't trust other youts. I'm just doing me, you get it? It's safer that way,' he reasoned. I'd heard Demetri express the same. The two of them had not met. But despite being opposites in demeanour – Jhemar the fearless entertainer, Demetri the quiet observer – I knew their respective outlooks were powerfully aligned. Discussions about survival while navigating city life were arising more across my youth work. 'Knife crime' had been appearing at an increasing rate in media headlines throughout 2017.

Jhemar spoke about impending violence as an intensifying

force. He described being stopped and searched by groups of police looking for weapons. A couple of times he was 'g-checked' by intimidating older boys wondering which part of south London he was from. He'd heard gunshots echo across his housing estate. He told me how other young people with whom he'd attended primary school had been kidnapped, or held at gunpoint, or stabbed, or excluded from school for selling drugs. When Jhemar had taken his brother Jerome shopping for a Mother's Day present in Streatham, they'd witnessed someone being chased with a samurai sword down the high street. 'Little bro is only thirteen. We almost witnessed a murder out here! London is a shambles,' he bemoaned. This extreme spectrum of incidents was, of course, distributed across a fun, love-filled school, social and family life that Jhemar was otherwise leading. Violence did not define his daily existence. But it was nonetheless happening all around him, forming an insidious forcefield for him to skilfully dodge.

Meanwhile, the social media feeds of young people like him became saturated with extreme photos and video clips. I'd heard yet more tales from youth workers elsewhere in London and teachers working at other schools of pupils being excluded from their schools for bringing in knives. Snapchat and Instagram's recently launched 'Live' function, in particular, allowed large audiences to watch as altercations between rival rappers played out in real time. I was seeing how some students *could not* switch off from their online mode, be that social media or video gaming. It made more sense of why some boys were struggling to free themselves from the trappings of their poor reputations at school.

What struck me about Jhemar's logic, however – that moving alone minimizes having to deal with the mistakes of others – was how it seemed to be a direct rejection of the temptation to be part of a group. It inverted the assumed territorial collectivism – the notion that banding together is the best way to protect oneself – that other boys like Carl were tempted by.

'You know what else? I'm never carrying a knife. Ever. If it comes to suttin' I'll firm it if I have to. I'll box it out with my hands or give 'em a kick. Or I'll play it safe, try and squash it. Or I'll just run. Running's actually smart, you know! I don't care what people say, I'm not getting cheffed for nobody!' Jhemar explained.

Faced with encroaching restrictions upon his personal liberty, brought about by the climate of fear in public life, Jhemar had conceived of his own complex practice for staying alive and fulfilled. But despite his shrewdness and bravado, as with any teenager, there were chinks in Jhemar's armour. He'd recently conceded that he'd been given a Friday detention for punching a fellow student. A boy was winding him up in a lesson and Jhemar lost it. He turned round and thumped him to the floor. 'My eyes turned red,' he explained. I let him talk it through without interruption or judgement. I had done this several times with boys at Willow who had lost their temper and been sent out of lessons. I'd learnt from Tony that the secret was to let young people feel heard in moments of raised temper; to give them a chance to tell their version of the story, and curate a space to openly feel shame without immediately punishing them. Really, this should be an opportunity that all young people with clear behavioural issues are afforded. After relaying what had happened, Jhemar said he was determined not to let this sort of thing repeat itself.

'I used to get angry occasionally but that time was different,' he would tell me years later. 'Teachers loved me at school! They must've known something was up. I didn't think about it like this at the time, but I guess I didn't wanna seem weak. You get it? I couldn't have my man undermine me like that. These times, there was no Michael there to protect me.'

Three Days Later: Thursday 2 November 2017

Jhemar got home from school at 5 p.m. His mum and dad were out. He threw his bag down in his room and started playing *Gran Turismo Sport* in the living room. He kept thinking about how he and Michael were going to catch up on Sunday. He was counting down the days.

His mum arrived home from work at 8.30 p.m.

'Did Daddy tell you what happened to Michael?' she asked.

'Nah, what do you mean?' Jhemar replied, pausing the game.

She told him that someone stabbed Michael in Betts Park, in Penge, round the corner from his home.

Michael was dead.

Jhemar dropped his controller on to the carpet. It made a thud beneath him. He walked to his bedroom to put on a tracksuit. He put on some trainers and didn't bother tying his laces. He told his mum he was going to Betts Park and went to open the front door. She told him to wait for his godmother to arrive to go with them straight there, so Jhemar sat down on the sofa and waited in silence. Deep down he knew who had done this. It must have been one of Michael's old friends. He could go to their house right now. He'd been there before. They must have set Michael up. Michael would never go to a park on his own at night, unless he was planning to meet someone he knew. There was no way Michael would take a chance with something like that.

A car came to pick them up to drive them to Betts Park. Jhemar sat in silence in the back. When they arrived it was dark and the wind was blowing through the branches of the big, leafless trees. The police were stopping people from going inside the gate. There was tape across the entrance. Jhemar met his dad, who was already there. He was crying. Jhemar had never seen his dad cry before. Jhemar started to feel angry and began to cry, too. There were people crowded around. A group of boys cycled by with their hoods up and Jhemar yelled at them to go away. They cycled off.

In the middle of the park was a big white tent with lights shining. Jhemar didn't believe it was Michael inside. Maybe they'd misidentified Michael.

They carried the body bag out of the tent and then out of the park to put it inside the ambulance.

Three Days Later: Sunday 5 November 2017

I was visiting my family home in Staines-upon-Thames when I received the news of Michael Jonas's death. I walked to the Thames footpath, at the end of the quiet cul-de-sac where I grew up. The river was moving fast after a recent downpour. The sky was grey. I sat on a bench and phoned Jhemar. He answered in silence. I said I was sorry and asked how he was feeling.

'It's funny! It's actually kind of funny, you know? That's the thing!' came his first words. His jolted scoffs and chuckles were too jagged, too loud to sound natural. 'These man think they can take life? Fam, *what* is going through their heads? Are they God? *Did they give life?* No! So how can they take it!?' We organized to meet later in the week.

After we said our goodbyes I sat staring at the flowing river for a few minutes before walking home. I felt solemn and numb. I couldn't stop thinking about the fact Jhemar had been intending to see Michael on that very weekend, for the first time in over a year. A death is a death. But the timing just made everything even worse.

Jhemar was spending the weekend in Penge. Family members and friends visited to pay their respects. When we'd spoken, he was sitting in Michael's bedroom, where the brothers had played

PlayStation, wrestled and scoffed their faces with pizza in happier times.

'I spent bare time in Michael's room that weekend. I slept in there. I could feel his presence. I could hear him telling me everything was going to be okay. But it was hard to see that,' he later told me.

Jhemar resisted every urge to leave the house to find the people who did it. He was receiving messages from friends who'd heard the news and were offering to help him take justice into his own hands.

'I don't know what I would have done if I'd seen them. I actually don't know. But I kept thinking about Jesus, my parents, my family, you. I kept thinking about the consequences of my actions if I did something. I decided staying put at my yard, with family, was the best thing to do. If I'd gone out on a vengeance ting I'd just be causing another family the same pain I was feeling. Moving like that wasn't gonna bring Michael back. You get it?'

After dinner with my parents and sisters that Sunday evening, I sat in my childhood bedroom, gazing out of a window glazed with rainwater. My elbows rested on the beech desk on which I'd revised for my GCSEs, one decade earlier. I thought about how carefree I'd been at the age of sixteen, compared to how Jhemar must have been feeling. I tried to imagine what it would be like to lose a brother to murder, and for life to continue like nothing had happened; for friends, teachers, examiners and employers to receive you with renewed expectations, while waiting for you to move on eventually. It was all new to me. The concepts of youth violence and loss had abruptly evolved into a more personal, urgent and emotional reality. Jhemar's life had changed in one evening. My responsibility towards him recalibrated in response.

I messaged my friend Suki, who I'd studied with at LSE. Suki knew Jhemar because he'd also signed up to be a mentor for Into-University. We'd attended our first mentoring graduation together, with our respective mentees, and then weeks later donned gowns and hats to qualify as postgraduates. Since I'd moved into Brixton, I'd often confided in Suki about elements of my youth work. Having grown up in nearby Kennington, he'd spent his teenage years around south London. He'd visited Jacob Sawyer with Rory and me to meet Tony and attend a Friday-night discussion group.

On receiving the news about Michael, Suki rang me. He asked me to pass his condolences to Jhemar. Then he paused.

'This is something we've never discussed. I don't like to talk about it that much, to be honest. But I lost my younger brother, Dayo, in 2011. He was stabbed to death, too.'

Suki explained that Dayo, who was fifteen, three years younger than him, had gone to confront a boy who'd stolen his phone by Myatt's Fields Park in Brixton. A fight broke out. The boy went inside his home to grab a knife, came back outside and killed Dayo. The perpetrator was later convicted of murder and sentenced to prison – as a minor, and therefore for a limited number of years. Suki was preparing to sit his A-level exams at the time. He still managed to achieve the grades to study law at Leicester University before successfully enrolling at LSE, where we'd first connected over our shared love for music and interest in the practical application of political theory.

It was hard to come to terms with the fact that Suki had been harbouring this experience for the entire time I'd known him, without sharing it with me. It was humbling evidence of how unknowably close we all are to painful events; how deeply connected seemingly disparate experiences can be, and therefore why it is important – essential, even – to assume little, if anything, as well as to show compassion towards typically cold headlines inked on our newspapers. Suki had woken me up to the need to pause and reflect. I would need similar awakenings in events to come.

'My immediate thought was of sadness on his behalf,

knowing what he was going to experience – despair, hopeless-
ness, shock,' Suki said more recently, when we caught up to
remember our conversation that evening. 'It's difficult to comprehend why someone would do such a thing. But I've come to
realize it's because they have no immediate reference point for
what a good life can be. They have no value for themselves and,
in turn, no value for others. Society has told them they're of little value.'

Suki said that losing a sibling to murder leaves a feeling of loss
and confusion which remains 'hovering around you. Not just in
that moment, but as long as you continue to exist. Even if you
get over it, you don't get over it. Sometimes you get triggered
and it might not be in your control. It could be a small memory
that comes up or you achieve something and that special someone's not there to celebrate it with you.'

I mentioned Jhemar's visions of going with Michael to the
car dealership to buy his brother's first car.

'Yeah, well that was clearly going to be an important milestone
for him. They probably promised each other they'd experience
that together, right? But it might come up later, too, in other times.
What about when he has a kid? Or when he gets married? Every
single significant milestone I've hit has been weird in some way.
Remember, I've still lived the majority of my life having a sibling
three years younger than me. So every milestone is a reminder that
things have moved on, that my brother is no longer there.'

Two Weeks Later: Sunday 19 November 2017

The rain was pouring when we shut the car doors. I'd been waiting for UK drill duo Skengdo and AM in the car park of their
housing estate in Brixton while darkness had fallen. I was sitting
in the back seat of AM's hatchback. Light from a street lamp

flickered in through the windows, revealing the pair's young, hardened faces. Skengdo removed his sunglasses, AM his balaclava.

'The area that we live in, the things that happen here, it pushed us in that direction,' Skengdo said, when I asked why they originally pursued music. 'We have to leave the estate to go to the studio. I prefer it that way.'

'In drill you have to represent something,' added AM from the front seat.

The pair's proactivity as part of Brixton drill crew 410 had shot them to the forefront of the London music scene. Their 'Mad About Bars' freestyle video on popular YouTube music channel Mixtape Madness, which aired in April 2017, had been viewed six million times – more than double the number of any other act featured in the series (it would go on to be viewed tens of millions of times). In the morning after it was uploaded on to YouTube, the corridors of Willow were filled with excitable whispers about AM's use of French and arithmetic in his lyrics. The pair would become two of the most successful – and censored – UK drill artists ever.

'Some people now do it because it looks cool. That's how it's changed. Before, the only people who were doing it were really in the field,' Skengdo said, emphasizing that an increasing number of drill artists had started making the music because it had become a trend. 'It changed for me when people started getting shows. Now if you think about it, people are getting excited over aggressive music, jumping up and down, getting all gassed. Everyone loves it. But how many people actually live that life? I've lived here my whole life. There ain't nothing here for me except for my bredrins who I want to take with me when I leave. South London is left in the shadows. This is why all these people on the block end up in crime, because there ain't nothing here for anyone. You have to want to get out of here or you just get consumed by everything going around in the hood – know what I mean? The government don't think about what can really lower the crime rate and what can change kids' minds a bit. No, they just leave it how it is. It's a cycle. As far as I'm concerned, it's always going to be like that. Some people go to jail, some people die.'

'The system is created to destroy us . . .' interjected AM.

'. . . they give us everything we need *to destroy ourselves*!' Skengdo continued.

I asked whether they felt a responsibility to their young fans – those who might be influenced negatively by listening to their music. Could the music be blamed for anything?

'In a place where people have low incomes, where they are struggling, respect becomes the most important thing. People want respect, they crave it. It makes a lot of people do crazy things. I do the most I can for the people around me but I don't feel like I can stay. I want to prove I can break out of the system,' said AM. 'I don't believe in telling my story a hundred times. If I did do that I'm always gonna stay the same person I'm trying to get away from. Revolutionists like Martin Luther King, what they were trying to push was acceptable, because it was about things that should have been going on that weren't. It's not my mission to make violence and my past acceptable in society. Drill is a good platform to get you recognized as an artist, but then you have to expand from there.'

'It is positive and negative,' said Skengdo. 'The positive out-come is for myself and AM. At the end of the day, it will be us getting the reward if we go far. The fans will be helping us on our journey – which I appreciate, fully. The negative side is what we're talking about, but the reality is: that's our life. If everything was sweet and flowers were growing and it was sunny every day, and then this music we're making came out of nowhere, I could understand why people might have a problem. They don't like it because we're speaking the truth.'

The debate about UK drill in public discourse was a timeless chicken-and-egg conundrum going back decades, to the inception of hip-hop. Do violent lyrics reflect an honest social reality and therefore serve the purpose of empowering artists? Or do they reinforce and exacerbate the issues they describe?

Skengdo and AM were addressing both sides of this paradox. On the one hand, drill was giving young men like them access to the catharsis of speaking on their harsh realities and the financial means to elevate out of their environment. Within weeks of our chat their first mixtape, '2 Bunny', beat both Stormzy and Jay-Z to the number-one spot in the iTunes Hip-hop/Rap UK chart. On the other hand, there was no doubt that their influence over the minds of young people listening to their music – its bleak descriptions of violence and drug-dealing, and threats directed at their enemies – was a responsibility to be handled with care. I knew many vulnerable, impressionable teenage boys who would spend all day listening and rapping along to their lyrics. But the pair continued, making me think twice about jumping to any simplistic conclusions.

'I feel like if there were statistics on this: we inspire more young people to start rapping than do violence. People hear one thing and think that's all we're about. I might be thinking: Hold on, I can actually get somewhere with this, let me keep pushing and try and make something positive out of it. But all a next man's hearing is: thugs, thugs, thugs . . .' said AM.

'The media portray us as negative people who don't have dreams or ambition when really and truly everybody wants something in life,' Skengdo added.

Around that time, Jhemar, Carl and his friends at Jacob Sawyer, and Demetri and other students at Willow, male and female, spoke regularly about Skengdo and AM like local heroes; leaders of their own subculture and role models for how to overcome a broken system. As London's underground music scene continued to blow up in subsequent years, I came to see Skengdo and AM – and, by extension, the majority of UK drill and rap artists – as providing a blueprint for what was possible for teenagers trying to navigate through life. They were doing more for themselves than the underfunded schools, demolished youth services, aggressive policing and the demonizing media.

It has been easy for onlookers to become preoccupied with UK drill music's shock value. But its rapid and global popularity over the latter half of the 2010s spoke to a deeper truth at its core. British society has left its most disenfranchised young people behind. Building on the traditions and innovation of transatlantic Black music going back generations, drillers have simply come up with their own way of staying relevant and surviving.

AM put on his balaclava. I took it as a sign that our conversation had come to an end. Holding his sunglasses in one hand, Skengdo glanced up at me to send a frank final message.

'I'm not being funny but you obviously listen to this music to get your facts and details. So listen to what we're saying. We're not just talking about being on ends.'

Four Days Later: Thursday 23 November 2017

The school clock hit 4.30 p.m. at Willow. I dismissed the boys from our latest session, debriefed with Demetri and went to my new office, which I shared with Monica, to type up my notes.

At the end of the previous academic year I'd nominated Demetri for a Jack Petchey Award, granted to British students in recognition of their service to their school communities. Alongside eight other Willow students he wore a light-blue waistcoat and attended a grand ceremony where he collected his certificate on stage to an applauding audience (which included Monica and me). He was granted £200 to spend on students at Willow so we selected a small group of the most improved boys to go for lunch at Nandos. We also commissioned a photographer, Tristan Bejawn, to come into school and shoot portraits of all the boys. I set a simple brief: make them look like kings. We set up a make-shift photo booth next to a first-floor classroom window, and the photographer used the light of the summer sun shining in against a silver reflector to highlight the boys' grins and pouts. I gained permission for them to miss lessons – allowing them to feel the reward of positive recognition. They spent the afternoon making each other laugh and pulling extravagant poses, forgetting all about detention and teachers, or the tide of London life lapping on the school's shores.

I had a deliberate strategy. As an active rejection of the fact that most of the boys remained towards the bottom of the perfor-mance data chart, I wanted to display their faces triumphantly on the corridor walls. For once, apart from in photos sourced from sports day, they could feel like the school valued and respected them enough to celebrate their identities in its communal spaces. I wanted them to believe they were leaders-in-the-making, just like students at the top of the chart did, whether by default or because their school told them they mattered enough for them to believe it.

Demetri was the greatest case study of my in-school mentor-ing. Over the two years since he'd applied to be on The Access Project, he'd constantly elevated himself, both via opportunities that were given to him and the way he took independent owner-ship of them. He was self-motivated to grow and reaped the benefits. In helping with mentoring younger students as a co-leader of our sessions, he'd given up over forty voluntary hours of his time. He'd held one-to-one check-ins with some of the boys when they got into serious trouble, and designed and led several of his own discussions. He'd analyse the behaviours of his mentees and come up with advice for them, and feedback for me.

I encouraged him to use formal language from his Sociology and Psychology A levels so that he became used to applying his learnt vernacular to practical scenarios. He'd engaged with at least one piece of extra reading per week that I would send him, usually on social issues stemming from our discussions: moral philosophy, gentrification, social media, drill music, youth violence.

By November 2017, Demetri therefore had an extensive list of proven practical *and* academic abilities to display having gone above and beyond his subject curricula. He was a worthy student for a top university. He studied for his exams in a quiet corner of the library every day. Yet he still remained a popular and sociable member of his year group. He'd mastered his work-life balance. Other TAP students – a number of whom were applying to Oxford or Cambridge, or various Russell Group institutions, for subjects ranging from English Literature to Politics to Biochemistry – were the same. Many ended up on competitive courses. This was in large part due to the efforts of Willow's committed staff body and the strict regime of the sixth form that raised expectations for a whole generation of students. Almost without exception, the TAP cohort in particular, as well as plenty of other students, excelled. This was Willow's greatest achievement.

I bid goodbye to Monica, who remained working at her desk long after school finishing time, as she often did, and left Willow to catch the bus home. The rush-hour traffic shuffled by, beeping and braking. I heard the thunder of trains passing above and the buzz of distant drills in Elephant Park's construction site. I put my headphones on so that UK drill music's rumbly bass thumped into my ears above the din.

I passed under the railway bridge by the overground station and the grocery and phone accessory stalls. On my left, a group of young men were walking up the long concrete ramp towards the shopping centre's entrance. They had their hoods up. They abruptly turned round. It was this subtle movement that caught my attention. I looked up from my phone towards them. One of the men started to walk down the ramp and I felt the hairs on the back of my arms stand on end.

The man who'd started walking down the ramp quickened his pace, leaping a couple of metres. In the same moment, another man, at the bottom of the ramp, turned his head on hearing the thuds behind him. He was just in time. The man leaping down the ramp towards him pulled out a big, jagged Kershaw knife from his hoodie and swiped it. He missed his target by what must have been inches. The targeted man, shoving his partner down the ramp and out of the way, pulled out a smaller knife. He swung back up the ramp at his attacker.

'STOP!' I yelled, without thinking.

'NO! PLEASE!' screamed a woman at the bottom of the ramp. Her shrill voice echoed into the moat beneath the shopping centre.

The man higher up the ramp looked up on hearing our voices. During the pause, the other turned and ran away. The other two men at the top of the ramp intercepted their friend, the original instigator, and started trying to restrain him. 'Allow it, fam! Allow it!' one of them said, shoving the aggressor backwards, up the ramp, blocking his attempts to give chase. But he was bigger and tense with adrenaline, so he pushed past, sprinting down the ramp and out of sight. His friends ran after him, passing the young woman, who I realized was the partner of the person being chased. She had her hands over her mouth and started to cry.

A few people around me stopped. One member of the public began consoling the young woman. I would estimate that during the ten seconds in which this entire scene played out there must have been over thirty people who'd somehow passed without hearing or recognizing any of the commotion.

I continued my walk, shaken up. Then I did a double-take. A

student from the discussion group I'd just chaired at Willow was standing glued to the spot, metres from me. Dressed in his blazer, his tie scruffily undone on his chest, he was looking over the railings at the woman crying at the bottom of the ramp.

'Sir, did you see that?' he asked me, smiling in awkward excitement, his eyes wide.

'Yeah, you did too? Are you okay?'

'I'm bless. My man almost got dipped! Did you see his shank!?'

I made a mental note to check in with him the following morning and to share what I'd seen with another member of staff. I told him to go straight home.

'I will, sir. Have a good evening.'

I put my headphones back on. I walked south across the round-about to the bus stop. I passed hundreds more people walking and cycling and awaiting public transport. How many of them had just seen what I'd seen? Which London did they live in?

On Saturday 23 November 2013, four years before I witnessed that knife fight in Elephant & Castle, ten children and teenagers were shot dead across the United States of America (seven are shot dead on average every day). British journalist, academic and author Gary Younge, who had been living in the US for roughly a decade, chose the date at random to form the subject of his book *Another Day in the Death of America*. Each of its ten chapters is an investigation into each death. They range from the result of gang warfare to extreme cases of domestic abuse. When Younge returned to live in London and to hold promotional events for the book, he found that 'knife crime' kept coming up in conversations and being raised by audience questions.

'People were asking me: would you do something like this in Britain?' Younge explained. 'And I would respond that there isn't the scale of death in Britain, which is true – there isn't. Knife deaths aren't even close to the level of gun deaths in America. But it kept coming up.' He'd long been suspicious of the term 'knife crime' but could sense a legitimate appetite from people wanting to learn more about it. 'Before then I feel like Damilola Taylor had been the sort of beginning of a massive awareness about it. I remember that because it was the first time I was ever invited on to *Question Time*. And I thought: no, I'm not going on to *Question Time*. What, a Black kid dies, and now you want me to talk about it? What about Black kids living? I wasn't hostile to it, but I was wary of it as a term. And now it was coming up again and again, from people in good faith; people who were engaged.'

At the start of 2017, as editor-at-large of the *Guardian*, Younge established the project 'Beyond the Blade'. His small team tried to unpack otherwise glossed-over issues underpinning youth violence, as well as solutions that might be employed to prevent it. He travelled to Glasgow – widely regarded as the world's greatest success story in reducing violent crime since 2005, after it was dubbed Europe's 'murder capital' by the World Health Organization, causing the city to launch a Violence Reduction Unit and embrace a gold-standard public-health approach towards combating knife crime. In London, Younge spent time with youth workers in hospitals and with bereaved mothers. He commissioned contributors like myself – I wrote an article arguing against funding cuts to youth services – to provide other perspectives. His aim was to deepen and shift the repetitive, sensationalist narrative and 'tabloid obsession' perpetuated by British news headlines.

'First of all, the media in a general sense has a very short attention span. It has been dominated by the notion of "if it bleeds it leads". If you look at most coverage of knife crime in the media, they cover the death, they cover the sentencing. That's it,' he explained. 'Secondly, there is a chronic lack of imagination,' partially because newspapers relying on drying-up revenue streams have to balance their limited resources against the prospect of gaining results.

When it launched in 2017, 'Beyond the Blade' gave professionals working in communities, like I was, something to grab hold of. Before then, I felt that there was a vast disparity between reality and the headlines inked on the front pages. Younge's editorial vision wasn't driven by the desire to generate clicks, but instead to become a bank of insights; a model of respectful, emotive storytelling and fact-checking. Over time, if subtly, it helped to shift the wider discourse away from sensationalism. Younge's respect for detail and care for the families affected shone through. He felt that the term 'knife crime' was a construct.

'I included any child, nought to nineteen, who was killed by a knife, because they were a victim of knife crime. And people kept saying to me: but that's not really knife crime, is it? And I would say, so can you define what knife crime is? Because I thought it was a crime committed by knives? So that's when you see the definition fall apart and the construct emerge. The first three deaths in 2017, none of them were in London. They were white girls in the North. But somehow, to some, that's not really knife crime.'

'Beyond the Blade' revealed the extent to which news reporting has been able to load stories about youth violence with racialized assumptions. Younge found that almost every time the term 'knife crime' appeared in the national press in 2017, outside of the *Guardian*, it was referring to Black young people in London. There was one exception, for the death of Sait Mboob, a Black eighteen-year-old stabbed in Manchester. This means that the term was not used to describe all crimes committed with knives, as it should have been, but only those where young Black men in London were involved.

From previously unavailable data spanning forty years, 'Beyond the Blade' found that roughly half of all deaths from stabbings have taken place in London, where Black boys and young men are disproportionately represented. It also found that the overwhelming majority of children and young people killed across Britain were not Black.

'For years, everyone had been talking about who was dying. It makes you think: what the hell were people talking about before, then? What authority are you speaking on? You can do anecdotal stuff, and you can branch out from that, but Tony Blair saying, "Let's not pretend that it's not Black kids doing this" – well, how did you know?'

Moving away from exclusively talking about murders – the sharp tip of a much bigger iceberg – crime analysis conducted by the Greater London Authority (GLA) in 2019 found that roughly 40 per cent of victims and offenders of serious youth violence in the capital are white, whereas 26 per cent of victims and 35 per cent of offenders are Black.

This reflects the impact that employing an overwhelmingly white journalistic lens to writing about poor, Black young men can have. A historic imbalance has skewed how we think, talk and *care* about violence, as well as those who harm or are harmed by it. The headline attention paid towards a specific set of extreme incidents involving a particular demographic of Black young males in London has perpetuated ideas in the wider, national imagination about this demographic being predisposed to criminality and violence – as opposed to being victims of a system which oppresses them from the moment they are born.

Throughout my youth-work career I have held many individual and group conversations with Jhemar, Demetri, Carl and other Black British boys of various global origins, about how they think race plays a role in affecting their treatment. Common observations have arisen that some white people will habitually avoid sitting on a nearby seat while travelling on public transport, or shopkeepers follow them round in anticipation of thievery. Carl and others regularly expressed feeling that they were more likely to get thrown out of lessons, or excluded from their school, or stopped and searched by police on the street, on account of having especially dark skin. Carl later explained to me that he felt although Black people in general, of all skin tones, would be targeted more than other racial groups in instances of suspicion and punishment, a spectrum nonetheless existed. The darker a teenage boy's skin was, Carl reasoned, the more threatening and guilty he was likely to appear to those in positions of (usually white) authority. He'd told me how he'd observed this at school, where he felt that many of his friends were being punished excessively, over time, for minor offences compared to their lighter skinned or white counterparts. It's a sentiment that I have heard countless at-risk boys like him express, a sinister sign of how many Black British children view their country and its institutions – based on their lived experience – and it's backed up by psychologists too, who have shown that there is a differentiation in stereotypes of Black people based on their skin tone.

Like many people of colour – whose radars are sensitive to the sorts of microaggressions that flow through daily life, invisible to the white gaze – I know that this detection of modern racism is not at all unfounded. I have seen teachers working in secondary schools act unfairly towards non-white and especially Black students, about whom particular narratives defined by non-compliance and aggression are allowed to insidiously develop. This is not to argue that unfair treatment is not dealt out to white children, but that, if such unfair treatment is dealt out, it is obviously not because of their skin colour or perceived racial identity. For example, harmless slang derived from Multicultural London English (MLE), disproportionately employed by young people of colour, is often punished without question by teachers trying to demand unnecessarily formal, top-down and narrow forms of language.

'Do you think speaking in a bad-man accent like that is funny?' a teacher yelled in the face of a Year 9 boy one morning, at one school I worked at. The student had excitedly spoken to his friend in disbelief during their private conversation: 'Say mum's!?' Or in other words, 'Swear on your mother's life!?' The teacher made the boy stand up and humiliated him in front of his peers. 'Well, do you?' the teacher pressed when the boy looked baffled. It was a bizarre over-exercise of power, but nonetheless one that I'd come to see as completely normalized in academy settings. Then the teacher walked out, leaving the boy, a bright-eyed class clown, sitting speechless, unable to comprehend his wrongdoing, his spirit crushed. Afro hair, too, is habitually dismissed as unprofessional. 'Barack Obama doesn't have cornrows, does he?' I heard one senior teacher say to boys I was working with at Willow on more than one occasion – including to Demetri, who has always worn plaits.

Collectively, we as a society have been unwilling to confront how media headlines demean the daily experiences of Black boys and girls. The mere idea of 'knife crime' has become a convenient proxy for people who enjoy racial privileges to avoid thinking hard about why violence in poor, multicultural communities happens in London; it is a simplistic and prejudiced term. The fact that young Black males are disproportionately represented in school exclusions and prison, let alone fatal stabbings in London, should be considered a societal injustice for which we are all responsible. Younge argued that, within the specific context of London, this disproportionality needs to be acknowledged, but not taken as representative of why violence happens across the country.

'There are lots of working-class white kids in London who are not getting stabbed at the same rate as Black kids. Which means there is something that is particular about being Black and young and poor in London that ups the chances of you getting stabbed,' he said. 'That doesn't make them representative of the Black population as a whole, but it does make it indicative of something about the experience of young Black people in London,' he continued. All but one of the young people who were stabbed to death in London across 2017 were Black and male.

However, only three of the nineteen killed outside London were Black. This means that the London picture is very different to the national picture when it comes to drawing links between race and youth violence.

A report by the Institute of Race Relations published in September 2020 called 'How Black Working-Class Youth Are Criminalised and Excluded in the English School System' would support Younge's nuanced, regional take on this racial disproportionality. It pointed out that in London white boys and young men are more likely than other ethnic groups to become victims and perpetrators of violence in London. But based on their low proportion of the population and over-representation in statistics relating to serious youth violence, young Black boys and young men are 1.5 times more likely to become victims and just under twice as likely to become offenders. However, less than 1 per cent of the total young Black population is involved in SYV.

> In part, statistics like this do confirm that young black boys and men are over-represented in SYV figures in London [the report read]. However, they do *not* explain the national picture, which is different, or provide insights as to why SYV or knife crime is more likely to be accompanied by tabloid front page images of 'menacing' black youth. It almost feels as though a political-commentator class is making a deliberate attempt to racialise the issue of 'knife crime' and link it to a stereotypical view of all young black boys mired in gang culture and prone to violence.

Taking race as an important component in discussions about London's violence is therefore reasonable, but the detail is crucial. What remains, and has always been, universal about young people who become involved in violence – especially perpetrators – is that they are typically poor, socially and educationally excluded, and traumatized from growing up in homes or communities where violence has been normalized.

Younge was awarded an Amnesty Media Award for his investigation into attempts by the mother of a boy to steer her son away from a path of violence. She'd written a letter to her MP begging for help to support him on what she saw as his inevitable trajectory towards criminality. Her son would go on to stab fifteen-year-old Quamari Serunkuma-Barnes to death on 23 January 2017, in Harlesden, north-west London. He was sentenced to fourteen years in prison. Embedded within Younge's storytelling, the mother's struggle said more about the failure of society and its institutions than it did about the troubled individualism of her son. Historically, the tendency in reporting cases like this, Younge said — a tendency he sought to combat — is to flatten what should be seen as complex human cases to the wrongdoing of the guilty.

'The way you stop the next one happening is at least by understanding that the last one was committed by a child, not a metaphor. So there are all these scripts and moral storylines that don't really match what's going on. And this was true in gun violence in America as well. Kids are poor, they are marginalized, and their lives are messy, and nobody wants to deal with messy. They want a clear moral landscape with goodies and baddies, and that is not how it works. They want a cause — parenting, schools, social media — as opposed to a confluence of things, most of which are getting worse.'

The 'Beyond the Blade' team tracked the number of knife-related child and teenage deaths throughout 2017 on a single, updated and animated page. Michael Jonas's death had been the forty-second of a minor by a knife that year. His portrait was added to the list. I'd been checking the website every couple of weeks. Seeing Michael's name appear changed everything.

★

Jhemar called the P5 the 'shuttle bus of the ends' because it went through Clapham, Stockwell, Brixton, Loughborough Junction, Myatt's Fields, Walworth and all the way up to Elephant & Castle. After finishing school, sometimes he rode it a few stops past his home because he knew the chicken shop there was cheap. He had a friend from school who lived nearby, so he'd hang out with her before walking back home down Coldharbour Lane. He'd only started going back to school the previous week, having taken two weeks off after Michael's death.

This time, he thought he would pop into Jacob Sawyer to play some table tennis. He'd visited the centre a couple of times before. En route there Jhemar noticed a group of four boys walking towards him. One of them was on a bike. Jhemar felt his heart rate quicken. He tensed his fist. He didn't recognize any of the boys, but they looked to be roughly his age.

'Yo!' one of the boys yelled.

Jhemar kept walking, looking straight ahead.

'Yo, what ends you from?' the boy's voice came again. The group stopped a couple of metres in front of Jhemar. He halted and pulled his hands out of his jacket pocket. He felt scared, but he was trying to hold his nerve.

'I'm from these sides,' Jhemar replied. Whenever he got g-checked he pretended that he was from the area. He was so close to home that he usually got away with it. It was a risk, but he'd got out of some sticky situations before.

'I don't recognize you, still,' one boy replied.

'I'm from here, fam!' Jhemar said, holding his line. It was also a tactic to buy himself some time. He was figuring out what they wanted from him. Were they going to harm him?

The boys were no bigger than Jhemar but because there were so many of them he felt overpowered. He considered whether he could take them in a fight. He decided it would be foolish to try. One boy reached his hand into Jhemar's jacket pocket. Jhemar grabbed his wrist and flung it away.

'Please don't go through my pockets,' he instructed firmly. He was trying to be authoritative but still polite and unthreatening. It was a fine balance. He could have swung for them or kicked them. He could have run. But it wasn't the right moment.

'Shut up, fam. Who you think you're talking to? You got any bread?'

'I've got one pound.' Jhemar smiled calmly, reaching into his pocket and holding it out for the boy to take.

'Back the shank!' ordered the boy, talking to his friend.

Jhemar's heart rate pounded faster again. His palms became sweaty.

But nobody pulled out a knife. It was a stalemate. The boy on the bike grunted. Either he had a knife, and didn't see the point in bringing it out, or it was a scare tactic.

The boy shoved his hand inside Jhemar's jacket and pulled out his mobile phone. Jhemar let him do it without fuss. He was trying to think smart: if they *did* have a knife, it wasn't worth it. The boy swiped up on the phone screen.

'What's the password?'

Jhemar shrugged his shoulders, maintaining eye contact.

'What's the password!?' the boy said again, squaring up to Jhemar.

Jhemar stayed quiet, holding the boy's gaze for a few more seconds. He was concentrating hard on the task of staying alive. He thought about how Michael must have felt when he was being chased across Betts Park. He thought about his dad. Jhemar couldn't let his dad lose two sons in one month.

'I don't need this phone anyway. It's shit,' the boy said, giving up. He turned round and threw it on to the roof of one of the blocks.

'Come,' the boy scoffed, and the others followed.

9. Park Bench Politics

British Politics

In July 1956, a thirteen-year-old boy called John Major was living with his family in a two-room apartment on the corner of Eastlake Road and Coldharbour Lane in Loughborough Junction. He'd moved to Brixton the year before from the suburbs, after his father's garden ornament business fell into decline. He would take trips to buy groceries and kippers at Brixton market – where, in later years, he would set up a soapbox from which to vocalize his political opinions. In the warmer months, he played cricket on a wicket against the brick wall at the back of his house. John had come to the end of his second year at Rutlish Grammar School in Merton, in the suburbs of south London.

At the start of the summer holidays, shortly before politicians would rise for recess, John was invited on a tour of the Houses of Parliament by Jacob Sawyer, the Labour Member of Parliament for Brixton. Sitting in the public gallery in the Commons, he watched as MPs debated the annual Finance Bill that had followed the spring budget announced by the Chancellor of the Exchequer, Harold Macmillan (Winston Churchill had stepped down as Prime Minister the year before). The bill sustained the belt-tightened austerity measures in public spending that followed the Second World War. It contained drier, finer details, too, on mortgage arrangements for colonial landowners in India and Pakistan, and taxes on tobacco, cider and perry. Britain was trying to reconcile underspending at home with keeping hold of a global empire slipping from its grip. Domestic politics was adapting to a new world order, the national story being rewritten. John became fascinated by what he saw. For the first time, he felt close to people who were truly powerful; those who belonged to what British journalist Henry Fairlie had first described as 'The Establishment' – those belonging to the social and political elite – in the *Spectator* in September 1955.

'I think what influenced me most were what Harold Macmillan would have called "events, dear boy, events". It was what I saw and what I experienced that made me realise that I would like to take part in public life to see if I could change some things,' John told the historian Peter Hennessey in *Reflections: Conversations with Politicians*. 'I always had a fascination for history, and the first time I ever went in the House of Commons . . . I felt that there is a special atmosphere in that building, and it reaches out and grabs you. And I thought to myself, this is where I'd like to work.'

In 1957, construction of the Loughborough housing estate was completed. In subsequent years a youth club would be built nearby. A short walk from the house where John Major lived, it would be named after Jacob Sawyer MP.

At the age of twenty-one, John Major stood as a candidate for Lambeth Council and won a seat. As Chairman of the Housing Committee he oversaw the construction of many large housing estates across the borough, including the vast Southwyck House of Somerleyton housing estate on Coldharbour Lane. He would later be elected MP for Huntingdonshire, near Cambridge, as part of Margaret Thatcher's Conservative government, before becoming Prime Minister in 1990.

Exactly sixty years to the day after the Finance Act of 1956 was passed, in July 2016, Rory and I had arranged to meet our group outside Jacob Sawyer. It was 8.30 a.m. and we were getting taxis to the Houses of Parliament. We climbed into an Uber XL and the boys scrabbled for the aux cable to play music. Dave and AJ Tracey's thumping new grime anthem 'Thiago Silva' came on, followed by Tottenham driller Abra Cadabra's 'Mad About Bars'. The music pumped out of the open windows as we sped over Vauxhall Bridge. Within fifteen minutes we'd arrived at Parliament Square, watched over by statues of Mahatma Gandhi and Winston Churchill.

We'd been invited by Helen Hayes, MP for Dulwich and West Norwood, the political constituency in which the community centre falls. After months of weekly discussions as a group on Friday evenings in the cramped classroom at Jacob Sawyer, we felt it would be interesting to allow the boys to see and feel close to the seat of decision-making power.

'It's mad how close Parliament is to ends!' Carl commented as we climbed out of the taxi. I thanked the driver, hoping the responsibility of booking transport for an excitable youth group playing loud music would not cost me a five-star rating on my Uber account. Thankfully, it didn't.

We queued to get inside. Politicians had risen for summer recess nearly a fortnight beforehand, meaning there were more visitors than normal. When our group arrived at the front, the guard stopped us. 'Hello, boys, what brings you here today?' he asked. I explained that we'd been invited for a tour by our MP. He turned to grab a sign showing various images of forbidden objects – weapons, drugs, explosives. The boys nodded their heads as we shuffled through.

'I swear he didn't do that to the people in front of us,' Carl grunted. 'My man moved quick to show us that sign. Don't pretend you didn't see it!' he said to me.

'I'm nervous!' another boy whispered as we walked towards the metal detectors.

The tour lasted approximately one hour. Our guide, a Goan Indian man who looked to be in his sixties, and spoke at length about the building's history, took a liking to the boys. They kept asking questions that were mostly money-orientated, such as how much pieces of art or gold decorative ornaments cost. They giggled at some of the more antiquated eccentricities. He seemed to appreciate the attention, blissfully unaware of their cynicism. He pointed to a strip of carpet and explained that its sole purpose was to ensure the Queen's feet didn't touch the floor, receiving gasps from the boys.

When we got to the Commons chamber, we lined up on a row of shiny green seats and looked out over the room's polished wood beneath the glimmering of chandeliers. Our guide explained that the two red lines marked out the boundaries of MPs from either side of the chamber. The distance between them was the length of two swords, to prevent a duel taking place mid-debate: an ironic norm to have carried forth into the present from the behaviours of governing politicians, given British society's repeated modern-day demonization of poor children carrying blades in fear for their lives. We moved into the House of Lords and discussed its function compared to the Commons. The guide noted that each Lord could opt to earn £300 per day just to turn up and sit down. 'What!? That sounds calm! I wanna do that,' one of our group exclaimed. He maintained for the rest of the morning that he'd think about going into politics if he could earn that much from making important decisions. 'So, even if I come on my Js, and just sleep on my chair, I get paid!?'

After the tour, we caught taxis to Sloane Square, in Chelsea, central south-west London – where the colloquialism of a 'sloane', or an upper-class, fashion-conscious woman, is derived from. During one session earlier in the year we'd asked the group about any parts of the city they didn't feel comfortable going to. One had named Chelsea as somewhere that he felt 'white people would look down' on him. He conceded, however, that he'd never been there. So we'd booked a table for us to have brunch at The Botanist, a plush restaurant with French windows opening on to the square to let in the summer breeze. We wanted to expose the boys to a new location, in a part of London they might not otherwise visit, let alone eat brunch at, and ultimately challenge their expressed assumption that they didn't belong. From supporting the many students I'd mentored during my job for TAP, I had learnt the value of empowering young people to spend time in spaces they perceived as elite. By confronting and removing barriers – the internalized fear of judgement, not to mention the excessive financial cost – the step sought to build their collective confidence, demystify an intimidating, unknown, yet nearby pocket of the city, and reward them for their commitment to our Friday-night discussions.

On arrival we took our seats at a table in the corner of the dining room. Carl returned from the toilet with news for the others that there were piles of fresh white towels. The boys balked at the menu. 'Nah, this is a piss-take,' one of them scoffed on seeing that the Full English Breakfast was £14. The waiter who came to take our orders nodded curtly as we made our requests.

'This better be the best breakfast I've ever eaten!' chuckled Carl.

'Word,' his friend agreed.

The breakfasts were slow to come. After a twenty-minute wait, I raised my hand and asked the waiter where they were. He snapped at me that they were on their way. When he brought them, one plate came with no toast. I asked the waiter for some. He became flustered. A few minutes later he returned with slices of toast and butter cut into cubes placed on a black slate plate. The boys found the whole thing hilarious. They were, however, unimpressed with the quality of the food: the homemade baked beans lacked flavour; the 'premium' sausages were too small.

'I'm not being rude, but I can get better than this at Johnnies,' Carl said, referring to a popular cafe on Coldharbour Lane.

For a moment I was disappointed that the boys didn't get to experience flawless fine dining. But on debriefing the day on our arrival home, Rory and I quickly figured that our imperfect meal had a silver lining. It showed that excessive pricing and fancy decoration did not always count for much. If anything, therefore, the average food and clunky service worked in our favour, shattering our group's perception that Chelsea's elitist branding meant anything worthwhile.

The following month, Helen Hayes MP joined us for discussion at Jacob Sawyer. Armed with cans of drink, which were still my trusty bribe for getting sessions to start on time – Hayes accepted one, too – the boys were able to speak face-to-face with their elected representative about their experience of visiting Westminster. The conversation quickly turned to how they were targeted by local police during stop-and-searches, and how they wanted better facilities at Jacob Sawyer.

The most memorable moment was when Hayes referred to the Prime Minister as a 'he'. 'I swear Theresa May is Prime Minister now!?' one boy interrupted, raising his hand and frowning, glancing around the circle. May had months before taken over the Conservative government after David Cameron's resignation following the unexpected Brexit vote. Hayes smiled and conceded her mistake, commending the boy, who received congratulatory slaps on the back from the others.

Hayes also spoke with Tony and other staff members. It was a long evening that dipped in and out of serious, emotional criticisms of the political system and institutional racism of authorities, and more light-hearted small talk about local life. She was at the centre for roughly two hours. I saw our trip to Parliament and her visit to our session as significant wins for our community group. Hayes could not promise to change the world that the boys, nor the centre's staff, experienced. She said this explicitly. Some members were left shrugging their shoulders, doubtful that anything positive would come from her visit. But, at the very least, the fact she came and listened showed the boys in our group that it was possible for them to have their voices heard. It also planted a useful seed in my mind about the sort of rich interactions that might come from curating a simple dialogue between young people and those in high political office.

Monday 22 January 2018

The first time Jhemar and Demetri met was in the queue to enter the Houses of Parliament. We'd been invited by Sarah Jones, the Labour Member of Parliament for Croydon Central, to contribute to the All-Party Parliamentary Group (APPG) on Knife Crime. A total of thirty-nine fatal stabbings of children and teenagers had taken place in 2017. Several young people were killed in street violence in the first hours of 2018. Jones set up the APPG to hold events with experts and young people about knife crime, investigate its causes, explore solutions and lobby the government. I'd been asked to sit on a panel to discuss if social media and music were playing a role in the ballooning violence. I asked if I could bring two young people. Given Jhemar's lived experience and Demetri's interest in the subject, I suggested they should appear on the panel with me. Jones welcomed the idea.

Jhemar was wearing a parka over his navy-blue school uniform, with his hood up over his hair, which he'd let grow into a small Afro. Demetri had come straight from college. He wore a black bomber jacket. In the first few seconds of us meeting, the two boys seemed wary, each for their own reasons: Jhemar had become closed off since the death of his brother in November; Demetri was always introverted and serious.

But I'd told Jhemar about Demetri's role as a mentor to younger students at Willow. I'd told Demetri about Jhemar's bold character and his recent loss of Michael. Demetri was two years older than Jhemar, but Jhemar, a head taller than the young man who would become the wiser, quieter half of their double act, was naturally more confident, a master of using smiles and subtle comedy to break the ice.

'You good, yeah?' Jhemar said to Demetri, nodding his head and holding his hand out to shake Demetri's. Demetri nodded, reaching his hand out slowly. 'Fam, it is icy!' Jhemar continued.

'Word,' replied Demetri as the three of us approached the gated entrance to Parliament.

The uniformed guard let a group of suited professionals walk through in front of us, nodding at them and smiling. When the three of us approached, his smile remained. I got déjà vu. 'Good evening, lads, have a look at this, won't you?' he said, pointing at the sign showing the forbidden objects as we passed through.

'*How dumb would you have to be to bring a shank into Parliament!?*' Jhemar whispered incredulously under his breath. Demetri burst out in sniggers.

The insides of Parliament are not meant for young people. Austere corridors and stern, tail-coated doorkeepers maintain more than tradition or Parliament's status as a historic visitor destination. For centuries, Parliament was a space accessible only to those of a particular colour, gender and class. The design of the space itself reinforces this purpose. The building seems at least 500 years old, but, in fact, most of it burnt down in the nineteenth century. When it came to the rebuild, the authorities shunned a more modern, accessible design for a neo-Gothic style most associated with the Middle Ages, with portraits of King Henry VIII and his six wives looking down on visitors. The past fifty years have seen some progress. But members of the working class, people of colour and young people are still under-represented among MPs, Lords and other advocacy groups.

Demetri and Jhemar looked around them as we proceeded through St Stephen's Hall. Staring down at us, unsmiling, were marble statues of famous parliamentarians like William Pitt and Robert Walpole. Not that Jhemar and Demetri were intimidated, but this was not a place that went out of its way to show them that they belonged. The impact of this lack of access on policy-making speaks for itself. The vast majority of those most affected by youth violence – indeed, any of society's most pressing social problems – have never stepped foot in the place where the laws to tackle that violence are debated and written.

We met Jones, her team, a handful of MPs and the other people who would be taking part in the roundtable in Committee Room 5. The list of experts joining us included policy managers from a range of organizations: Facebook, Google, Ofcom and Childnet International. It included representatives from the Mayor's Office for Policing and Crime (MOPAC), the Children's Commissioner's Office and a YouTube broadcaster called Andre Johnson, also known as Mr Montgomery. We sat in a horseshoe formation as the chairs in the other half of the grand room filled up with audience members. Jhemar was to my immediate right, Demetri to my left. Sarah Jones introduced the meeting.

The first of three topics was labelled: 'The impact of social media on knife crime.' Jones asked Jhemar to provide his own account of social media and drill music.

'The thing with drill music is that, to some extent, it does have an effect. But at the end of the day, it's all down to the person listening to it. Everyone has a mind of their own. If you are going to take that music and go and live that lifestyle because of what you hear, it doesn't really make sense. This music is a cry for help. These rappers are just talking about what they are living. It becomes a problem when other people see it and think,

"This lifestyle looks a bit fun, I want to join this lifestyle," because they don't see the consequences of being involved. So I think it should be about teaching the youth about certain lifestyles, and teaching them to have a mindset so they aren't drawn to it. It's their mindset that is allowing them to do what they are doing, so we should help them with things like critical thinking, rather than blaming the violent content.'

'What about the stuff you've seen that isn't always the music? Could you just give us a flavour of the kind of stuff you see every day, please?' Jones asked.

'Well, at first, social media is just somewhere for people to socialize. But on Snapchat, for example, you have people posting stuff they think is normal when it shouldn't be. Guns, people popping fireworks at people, people posting stuff like: "I just got a new knife." But no one *thinks about what they are doing*! One time, I was in Clapham and I witnessed someone with a machete in their hand, and they were running someone down, but they were holding their camera phone in the other hand, to record it. And I'm there just thinking, "That don't make sense! You are ratting yourself out to the police!" Just from living in Brixton, I've had situations where I'm coming from school and I'm seeing a bunch of guys running each other down, guys smashing glass at each other, guys with long knives. I've been at home playing PlayStation in my living room and heard a gunshot go off, and I didn't even think anything of it! That made me think to myself, "When did it become so normal that I'm not even bothered by this stuff?" And when you have rival gang members going to another person's area to show off, like "I'm in your area, what you gonna do about it?" and then they put it on social media — it's like they don't realize that you can have love for your surroundings without being prepared to *die for it*. Because that is what it is. You've got kids dying for their area. They don't literally run their area; they're not the council; they don't own anything or pay for it. But they still have it in their head that they *do* own it.'

'And what about you, Demetri?' Jones asked. Demetri pressed his mouth together in thought. His fingers were clasped together on the desk in front of him.

'Social media makes everything more competitive. So, because there are so many people doing music means that to be successful, to compete with everyone else and get noticed, you have to . . . kind of . . . set yourself apart. You have to keep on finding new ways of proving that you're badder than everyone else. I feel like the real issue is the perception of the music videos by young people. I listen to all this stuff, in the same way a lot of people play video games, too. But I don't feel the need to go and act in a certain way after I do it. It doesn't influence me. So it's about making sure young people perceive drill differently; that they don't see it as something to copy, they just listen to it for entertainment.'

'Snapchat is twenty-four hours! It don't cease!' Jhemar continued. 'It's so easy to spend all your time on social media, especially when you've got nothing else to do outside. So, another thing is making sure there is more stuff to do, so young people aren't just on their phones the whole time. Like it or not, all this stuff on the internet, it's still going to be there. That means we've got to help people deal better with it.'

The second topic was labelled: 'Preventing violent and dangerous content.' A discussion unfolded about how social media companies ought to try stemming the rise of this type of problematic online content. In April 2017, Mark Zuckerberg, the CEO of Facebook, had given a speech committing to an improvement in the way the website monitored its uploaded content. In December 2017, Google had announced that they would be hiring thousands of moderators to target violent video content uploaded on to YouTube. These companies had already been under fire from a select committee in 2017, which Sarah

Jones had been involved in, about the prevalence of online hate crime material.

In an attempt to neutralize the idea of competition that Demetri had outlined, one panellist suggested removing the views counter on YouTube music videos. This was rightfully rebutted on several grounds, one being that a step like this would simply penalize videos based on their popularity, rather than their content. It would thus likely miss the many thousands of videos being watched by a minority of viewers. It also assumed that drill music videos, and the competition driving them, were worse than non-musical violent content circulating online. To my mind, more fundamental to the problem at hand than the popularity of drill music videos was the endless, hidden occurrence of violence taking place among young people in the first place and the way this violence was easily transferring online through many forms of digital content that had nothing to do with music. In other words, while the music was by no means harmless, it was just the tip of a much bigger iceberg – one that social media companies were gaining from financially and failing to monitor, and therefore had a lot to answer for.

'You've got kids my age, younger than me, older than me, taking a knife from their kitchens in their homes and then walking out on to the streets like they are putting on their shoes!' said Jhemar. 'They think of it as living a certain lifestyle, and sometimes that's because of the music. But it's also because they might think, "Something may happen to me today, and I'm going to make sure I'm carrying something with me to defend myself if it comes to that." Some parents are thinking, "What if my child doesn't come back home to me today?"' Jhemar stopped in mid-flow to consider his thoughts, contemplating how deep into his own well of experiences to draw from. The whole room was hanging on his every word. 'In my family just last year I lost my eldest brother to knife crime . . . So it's like,

I'm seeing it happen in my family now. This ain't correct. Knives are there to either cut what you are eating or cook with.'

I had reassured Jhemar that he shouldn't feel pressured to mention what happened to Michael. Only days beforehand the case against the teenagers charged with Michael's murder had been dropped due to insufficient evidence. The Jonas family had not only had to come to terms with the tragic loss of Michael in the build-up to Christmas, but Jhemar was also having to cope with the regret that he'd not been able to see or speak to his brother before his life was taken. 'If I could have got to him first, maybe I could have stopped it,' he would say to me. And now, everyone mourning Michael was contending with the fresh, brutal knowledge that his killers were roaming free, unpunished. Michael's funeral – which had been delayed because of the murder investigation – was scheduled for the end of the week.

Now, by speaking his truth in Parliament, Jhemar was converting his pain and anger into a potent desire for social progress. His emotive delivery stunned the room into silence. After a few moments of letting his admission sink in, Jones thanked Jhemar for his candour. He nodded and sighed in relief. Demetri glanced a look of respect. I held out my fist for him to spud. The discussion continued, reaching the final topic: 'Youth-focused solutions.' Demetri raised his hand. Jones chose him to speak.

'We should talk about violence and treat it like a disease. Right now, it's more like we treat the symptoms. I don't think we should wait for the symptoms to show up. We should be nipping it in the bud – preventing it. Prevention is better than a cure. So, like, if the reaction of the government is "Oh, we're going to put more police on the streets" – you can put as many police on the streets as you want, but you are never going to catch everyone. You need to change the mentality of people so they say: "It's not okay for me to carry a knife." Then you won't need so many police on the streets. We need to change our entire approach to the way we are handling it. People who live like that, we should teach them what they are doing isn't only affecting them, it's affecting a broader scope of people . . . in their mind it's only affecting them, 'cause they are cut off from the rest of society. But we need to keep everyone included.'

I'd barely spoken, but Jhemar and Demetri had tag-teamed the debate, speaking more than anyone else. Rightly so. Jhemar made his final point:

'It's about coming down to the same level as young people and understanding how it really feels to be like us. If you've got strong-minded people like me and Demetri, who can actually speak to other young people, and they will listen, their mind might get opened up to a different perspective. I've had points where I've spoken to people at my school that may have been involved in carrying stuff that they shouldn't have been involved in. For example, one boy was walking about with knives, he was doing all sorts of things that he shouldn't have been doing, let's put it that way! And I sat him down and I had a nice little conversation with him. All I did was ask him questions. "Why are you doing this? How does it benefit you?" It's as simple as making them think about their life. Because no matter how crazy someone wants to say you are, there is always that element of common sense somewhere, in the back of your head. So if I can ask that question and be like, "Do you know what you are actually doing? Do you know how you are affecting the rest of the world?" – all it takes is a conversation.'

Adults around the room rushed up to the boys. They received compliments and business cards. After everyone said their good-byes, Jones offered to take us on a tour. Jhemar and Demetri posed for photos with her on the riverside Commons Terrace, where for nearly two hundred years MPs have gathered by the waters of the Thames to take lunch, hold drinks receptions and debrief debates. We ascended to see the roof, which has a unique view of Big Ben. Jhemar and Demetri both had their phones out to record everything on Snapchat in the moonlight. As we descended the stairs afterwards, I wanted to capture the three of us in our triumphant state. I held out my iPhone and took a short selfie video.

'Obviously, man's just in the Houses of Parliament and that, walking up the stairs,' Jhemar announced, providing commentary from behind me as we descended.

'We're going *down* the stairs,' Demetri corrected him from the back of the shot.

'That's what I said! I said we're going down the stairs, init?' Jhemar replied in upbeat rebuttal. 'Anyway, this ting's smelling all Victorian and that! We got Demetri in the background, you know already what he's doing, looking all confused!' He chuckled, segueing into harmless banter. Demetri laughed and shook his head at Jhemar's cheek.

'It was a weird vibe in there,' Demetri told me some time later. 'It's not like I go to places like that very often. Like, art galleries or museums, them places there. But I didn't feel awkward. I don't get nervous. I was just thinking how to articulate myself and keep it concise. I found it reassuring. Cah it made me realize that there are big people who can make change who are interested in the problem. Before that, I was like, they don't care. I still think most politicians don't, because it doesn't affect them. It's an isolated problem. But until then I thought they were all just thinking: "It's little Black youts running around stabbing themselves, it's not that deep, we need to worry about bigger things like the housing crisis or Brexit." It was empowering because suppose I'm just talking about all that stuff with the mandem, it's all well and good us discussing it on ends. But there, it was like, these man here have recorded what I've said! So I saw there was potential for change. I felt a bit responsible, you get it? When you experience that sort of thing, you start to deep yourself, as well. You start thinking about some of the things you do. You realize you've come a long way.'

An overwhelming number of London's teenagers feel unrepresented by political institutions. Like many adults, they do not see themselves written into the British social contract in any meaningful way. It is no surprise that the most disenfranchised exhibit a disregard for punitive rules and conformity: they are rarely the ones gaining from law and order, and often the ones suffering under it.

But my trip to Parliament that evening with Demetri and Jhemar showed me that this dearth of representation is not insurmountable. Even if we consider parliamentary democracy as flawed, it was obvious that the APPG on Knife Crime was in itself serving a public good. The first roundtable in November 2017 brought together fifteen young people who had been convicted, or suffered as victims, of knife offences. In subsequent gatherings, over several years, it would facilitate dialogues with hundreds of young people and front-line experts to address issues ranging from school exclusions to the role of the NHS.

It is undeniable that the government has failed poor communities in Britain when it comes to youth violence. But smaller cogs in the system such as the APPG, led by politicians like Jones who have committed to representing their constituents, play a role in shaping conversations and attitudes for the better. Jhemar and Demetri's contributions to this debate did not start and finish in January 2018. Their voices would be called upon to contribute again. Their roundtable presence in Committee Room 5 was recorded in Parliament's history books. I'd learnt that exposing young people to environments they perceive as elitist not only helps break down social barriers, it also performs a social good for wider society as it means debates and policy can be better informed by lived experience.

'I didn't think any of them would give a toss!' Jhemar reflected. 'But I was sitting there speaking to a room full of people I didn't know, and I could *see* them listening to me. I was *looking them in their eyes*! I knew they were taking it in.'

While canvassing during the General Election campaign in spring 2017, Sarah Jones got into a conversation with a group of young men on the street. 'They were saying, "You're just a politician, you're not going to change anything." And I was saying, "You should vote Labour, because we'll do x, y and z." They replied, "Well, what are you going to do? Are you going to reopen the youth centre down the road?" They were very sceptical about whether I was any use to them at all.'

One year later, in March 2018, having defeated former Conservative cabinet minister Gavin Barwell by 5,652 votes to take Croydon Central – Barwell was subsequently appointed as Theresa May's Chief of Staff in Downing Street – Jones attended an event commemorating twenty-year-old Kelva Smith. He had been stabbed to death in her constituency. On arrival at Smith's family home, Jones realized he had been one of the young men she'd spoken to on the campaign trail. The moment reinforced Jones's growing motivation to fight against rising youth violence.

'Knife crime was coming up as an issue on the doorstep even more than it was an issue in the national press. Setting up the APPG was a substantive thing I said I would do. So I spent most of the summer in 2017 going round meeting groups, organizations and people to find out what was going on in Croydon; what the issues were; the problems and solutions. At that time, it was sort of in the media because of the rise, but it wasn't getting the attention politically.'

Around the same time, Vicky Foxcroft, the Labour MP for Lewisham and Deptford, established the Youth Violence Commission (YVC): a network of politicians, academic researchers, community leaders and experts bound by the recognition that tackling youth violence is the responsibility of everyone in society.

'Vicky and I would stand up in Parliament, whenever we could, and ask: "What about knife crime?" We would say: "People are dying, people are dying, people are dying." And we'd get a wishy-washy response, in the knowledge that there wasn't enough focus on the issue from a media perspective to force the government to act.'

Brexit was not only hovering like a discursive dark cloud over the political machine. It was also completely drowning out the government's willingness to intervene in pressing social issues. The distraction of Brexit-induced unease only deepened the impact of budget cuts on things such as schooling, youth services and social care. This all-pervading presence would be replaced in 2020 with the British government's failures to contain the Covid-19 pandemic – an at once shocking yet predictable disaster I will return to in the Epilogue.

'Everyone's bandwidth was taken up with Brexit, and there was no room in the papers to talk about anything else. But the *most* frustrating thing for me was that Brexit was viewed as an excuse by the government not to act on a vast array of things, when they could have acted. Everybody kept saying Brexit was taking up everything, but it wasn't taking up parliamentary time. The perception is that it was. But they could have acted,' said Jones.

As Shadow Minister for Housing, she witnessed the same appropriation of Brexit as a diversionary tactic by government representatives shirking responsibility.

'In meetings, ministers would say: "When Brexit is sorted, housing will be our number-one priority; when Brexit is done, we can focus on this and that." But there was no reason why they couldn't focus on those things at the same time. Yes, Brexit took up a lot of the Prime Minister's time. But putting some extra funding in to reverse police cuts, for example, doesn't.

You just say, here's the money, let's do this. Brexit became an excuse for why the government hadn't acted.'

Jones, a former civil servant, is clear about the failures of the Labour Party to win the ideological battle across the 2010s, and maligns the damage that has peppered British life under austerity as a result.

'After the financial crash in 2008 we lost the argument that the way to grow the economy back was to invest in things and build infrastructure so that people have good jobs and good education. And the Tories won the argument, that the best way to recover was to cut everything.' In hindsight, in light of the public health crisis that would arrive with coronavirus, the long-standing victory of the Conservative argument for austerity and a dismantled safety net – a position that the Labour opposition would be defeated by across three general elections – barely lasted a month under the fresh, overpowering demands of the 2020s. 'There is no "state and us". It's not about whether you have a big or small state. It's about understanding that the state *is* us deciding that if we pool our resources, we can do something better. If we club together and pay our taxes, we can fix problems.'

Jones joined the Labour Party in 1992 after watching Peter Lilley, the Secretary of State for Social Security under John Major's government, give his infamous Conservative Party Conference speech announcing his intention of 'closing down the something-for-nothing society' and attacking people relying on the state as 'spongers, descending like locusts, demanding benefits with menaces'. Lilley created a 'little list of benefit offenders', spoken in rhyme, which included 'ladies who get pregnant just to jump the housing queue'.

At the time, Jones was nineteen – and pregnant. 'Bogus asylum seekers and teenage mums who wanted council houses were who everyone was blaming for society's ills. For me, it was, why are you labelling me a problem? I'm not a problem, I'm a solution. I may need a bit of help, but I'm not a bad person and I'm not the cause. You shouldn't be panicking about me.'

On turning her attention to knife crime in 2017, Jones detected a similar start point: those in power blamed individuals involved in violence rather than the clear dysfunction of their social circumstances, and the failings of institutions to ameliorate them.

'When we first started asking questions in the chamber, the answer was always: "We need to come down really hard on these criminal gangs, we need to lock people up more." It was a moral panic that these are terrible people and we need to get them away from us.'

She remembers meeting Jhemar and Demetri for the first time at the APPG roundtable. 'I remember Jhemar talking about how he'd see hundreds of violent images in a single day. That really struck me. I hadn't appreciated the speed at which this stuff was getting around. So, when he talked about his brother dying and the fact he lived on an estate where these things were all normal, that violence was everywhere around him, and the idea that he would be in his home, where you should be safe, yet you could still be bombarded with all this violent content . . . it was shocking. Obviously, Jhemar's situation I remember in particular because it was so raw. Him explaining that to the meeting had a *huge* impact on the people in the room. As a politician, you don't really understand the problem until you talk to young people and you see how they are receiving that problem.'

Alongside the YVC – for whom, in summer 2018, I attended a similar roundtable discussion event – the APPG shone a light upon the impact of wider societal trends on the lives of vulnerable young people. Further APPG roundtable discussions were held on topics from school exclusions to 'county lines' drug operations and to the role of the NHS. Jones noticed the conversation starting to shift towards a more sympathetic approach.

The biggest insight she gained from chairing the APPG was learning how preventable the life circumstances of perpetrators and victims of violence are. She highlighted one study, conducted by Croydon's safeguarding board, which found that from sixty cases of serious violence involving vulnerable children and young people in 2018, half of them had been known to social services before the age of five. All of the ones who'd been convicted of offences had been excluded from school. Three-quarters had experienced the absence of a father; one quarter the absence of a mother. In another study, by St Giles Trust, about drug-distribution operations running from London to Kent, Jones noted that '100 per cent of those kids had been excluded from school. It just goes to show how vulnerable a whole cohort of people are, whether they've been in care, they've got problems at home or they've been excluded. There is a definite pathway, and it is extraordinary how, time after time, cases show this. You can see the pattern.' Indeed, in November 2018 the Greater London Authority published data from that year showing that two out of three 13–18-year-old young offenders in the capital came from families that had broken down, 50 per cent of persistent offenders had themselves been victims of abuse and 90 per cent had been excluded from school at some point. One in every two young people in custody had spent time in the care system.

Campaigning bodies such as the APPG and the YVC serve to nudge attitudes away from the common tendency of seeing violence as inevitable or something that can only be solved by increasing the powers of law enforcement. The efforts of campaigners like Jones, Foxcroft and others fighting this fight in Parliament have often run contrary to government cycles that use big announcements and symbolic gestures to signal short-term progress. In reality, the broader underfunding of services continues to undermine hopes for systemic change. It makes genuine public health impossible – as the tsunami of the corona-virus has since proven.

'What the government tends to do is recognize a problem that is cutting through in the media and they will say, we will put a pot of £x million into this, which sounds like a lot, but when you divide it up across local councils it amounts to nothing. And it never replaces what they've taken away,' said Jones. 'With the huge cuts to mental health provision, which I feel like everybody kind of gets now, the government is still nowhere near close to replacing the funding that used to be there. The thing that is undoubtedly true is that if we did certain interventions, we could reduce violence very dramatically. And the knowledge of that is deeply frustrating, and the more you know about it, the more you realize that if we intervened at a younger age . . . we could stop a lot of this stuff. As well as the preventative interventions we could be doing right now: in youth work, in schools, etc. The more you know, the more you know that the government could intervene and fix stuff.'

On the morning of Michael Jonas's funeral I got the train from Brixton to Penge East, before walking to Christ Church, Anerley. I saw from the map application on my phone that the church was right across the road from Betts Park, where Michael's makeshift shrine stood, surrounded by flowers and candlesticks. I took a seat at the back of the church. Beside me rested glossy purple-and-white booklets scattered across the pew whose printed front cover was filled with a pixelated portrait of a young man wearing thin braids. His lips were pouted slightly, above which a wispy moustache was developing. He was looking into the camera lens with a deep stare. I recognized it too well.

The previous week, Jhemar and his family had gone to a funeral parlour to choose the coffin. They had arranged photographs of Michael at different stages of his seventeen years around it, in preparation for the ceremony. Jhemar had mentioned that the images sparked memories. He told me how he and Michael used to ride along with their dad as he drove the 315 bus, playing hide-and-seek between the seats. He remembered the time when he whizzed down the hill near Michael's house in Penge on his bicycle and fell off, grazing his knee. For Jhemar, after the first stage of seeing the body bag at Betts Park on the night of his death, seeing the coffin that day had felt like the second stage of accepting what happened. The funeral represented the third and final stage.

Once the church was full the ceremony started. It included prayers from two pastors, Bible readings by family friends and songs of worship. Michael Senior, Jhemar's father, recalled in a speech that Betts Park had been where he'd taught Michael how to ride a bike. Jhemar performed a gospel song called 'I Am Under the Rock' on the drums, before standing up to speak.

'Since I was young I've imagined again and again going with Michael to buy his first car. Now that's not going to happen. It'll be me going to buy my own car, without him.'

Outside, the family climbed into cars to drive to the burial in Croydon. I walked the twenty minutes back to Penge East station to return to work for the afternoon – a decision I soon regretted.

At the burial, Jhemar stood looking over the coffin being lowered into the ground. He tried to imagine what Michael might have been thinking before he died. It helped him to feel close to his older brother.

Everyone started singing prayers but Jhemar didn't join in. It was real now. He was burying a whole bunch of emotions and memories. He wasn't just burying his brother. He was burying a part of himself.

10. Back to Basic

Criminal Justice

The first time Carl went to court, he was coming to the end of his first year of college. He was completing a BTEC Level 3 Sport and playing football. Most of the other students were shook of him. They weren't from ends; they were mostly from the suburbs. Carl knew that they probably thought he was gang-affiliated. They either acted scared or tried to beg it.

On weekdays Carl would finish college, catch the train back to Brixton and start shotting. Sometimes he would be out all night and go to college having not slept. He'd miss eating or he'd get some chicken and chips. He was smoking weed a lot. All he could think about was making money. He'd recently got a pound coin sign tattoo.

Now Carl was shotting hard food, so he was making more profits. He was fearless. He would threaten anyone else who tried shotting near him. A couple of times he'd scared off some of the olders who'd been there for years. They were big men but they could see how crazy and energetic Carl was. They weren't ready for the new generation.

Carl would buy an eighth of light and dark, £120 for both. Then he'd cut it up at a house in Brixton. The man who owned the house was called Kevin. Kevin let some people use his house as a base to prepare their food if he could get some for free. He let Carl inside because Carl was polite. Kevin would tell Carl all about his work and family. Kevin smoked crack, but he wasn't a typical cat. Most people wouldn't have suspected he was a drug addict. Carl would sit at Kevin's marble table and slice up pebs, wrapping them tight in cling film. Then he'd put some of them under his tongue. He'd practised doing this using Skittles, so that he could still talk with them in his mouth. He put other pebs in a plastic bag and wedged them between his bum cheeks. Then he would go out to move them.

The bando Carl went to was full of people who looked poor and hopeless. Some of them looked normal, like Kevin. Inside, Carl often thought about how his life was like a depressing movie. It stank of sweat and old food there. The cats moved like zombies. Carl was making money off them, because they were addicts, which made him feel bad. But shotting was the best way for him to make money while he figured out other ways. Then he'd leave this crazy life behind.

Sometimes Carl took trips up to Oxford Circus at night to sell light to drunk, posh people going into clubs and bars. They always looked scared of him, even though they were the ones who wanted to buy drugs from him; even though he was only sixteen and they were adults who had serious jobs and smart clothes.

Carl also had a job at Burger King. He chose the one in Victoria because he doubted anyone would try it there. He earned barely anything. It made him greasy and tired. But it was good because he could steal burgers and chips and apple pies to bring home for his family and friends. Sometimes he would go clubbing with his colleagues. Because he was the youngest he would get treated nicely.

To get to and from Victoria Carl bought a moped for £300. It allowed him to get from A to B quickly. The quicker he could travel around, the more time he had to make money, and the more time he could stay outside of his flat. He didn't want to be at home because it was stressful. He would get into arguments with his mum. Carl blamed his dad, and he felt like his mum didn't understand what it was like for him growing up without a man there to give him advice.

On one weekend, Carl went to a party. He was drinking and smoking and chatting to girls. At 2 a.m. the police turned up and people ran away. Carl went outside to grab his ped but the police stopped him, saying it was stolen. They arrested him and put him in their police car. Carl was annoyed because everyone saw him get arrested. Loads of people at the party had weapons on them. He didn't have his shank this time, or a strap, so he was lucky. But it was embarrassing because he was going down for something stupid and the others got away.

Carl had been taken to cells lots of times, so he was relaxed. But now he expected they would punish him more than usual because he'd been arrested a few times recently. The police knew his name. His face was bait. Police drove past him in the street and called at him. Some of them had been stopping him for years and Carl was cool with most of the police officers in Brixton. He used to get angry when they stopped him, but he'd learnt to handle them.

There was no space in Brixton police station, so the police drove Carl to Walworth. The cell was old and dirty. He was there until 4 a.m., then they took him back to Brixton. He was offered a solicitor, who came to meet him in the afternoon, and he was nice. Carl told the solicitor that he didn't know the ped was stolen and he already knew to say 'no comment' when he got questioned. He went home on bail.

A letter arrived a few days later summoning Carl to court. When the day came he got a lift to the magistrates' court with his mum, where they met his solicitor. In the lobby he saw one of his opps, who yelled at Carl across the corridor, but Carl knew better than to respond. He pretended like he didn't know him; it was so stupid to be moving bait like that in a court. Carl didn't want to embarrass himself in front of all the adults. He needed to act politely, like he did at church.

In the courtroom Carl saw that his mum looked scared. He was given a fine. Carl was happy that it didn't go further but he was annoyed because he'd saved money from all the work he'd been doing. He would have to start from scratch.

At the end of 2017 I accepted a new job as a youth worker in London prisons. I was excited to take the opportunity and therefore get the chance to learn about the criminal justice system from the inside. I was ready to leave Willow's exhausting academy regime. But given my established commitment to my students, accepting the new role wasn't easy. I said goodbye to Year 13 students I'd worked with for two years and the boys in my discussion groups in the lower school. As a leaving gift, to commemorate the nicknames she'd given us – her Fagin, me Oliver Twist – Monica bought me a copy of the Dickens novel in which these characters live, and had its opening page stamped by the Willow library. One card I received from a group of Year 8 students was especially funny, including the poetically slang-laden line of best wishes: 'Man like sir! Roll safe!'

My new workplace was a charity providing life coaching to young prisoners. During my five months of employment I worked at four prisons across the capital. They housed a range of Category or 'Cat' A (high security), to Cat B and C, for lower-risk prisoners (there is also Cat D, which denotes an open prison, where prisoners can come and go). My job was to go on to wings to engage eligible participants. I would knock on cell doors or find candidates during association time, 'sosh', when prisoners were unlocked to socialize. Most were keen because it was a rare opportunity to spend time outside of their cells. Contrary to what one might expect, it was easier than getting boys to commit to my sessions at Willow. The dearth of freedoms in the prison setting was so stark and the bar for positive engagement and self-belief was so low that whatever I had to offer seemed to take on a special significance. Having acclimatized to being treated as a problem their whole lives, I found that these young men, failed by society, perhaps abandoned by people around them, valued someone listening. I would estimate that over 80 per cent of the sixty or so prisoners I spoke to during my employment were actively looking for an opportunity to better themselves. They were almost all polite and thankful, if often visibly weighed upon by their living conditions.

The main logistical problem was keeping prisoners enrolled on the programme once it started. My colleague and I were responsible for liaising with prison staff and the life coaches to make sure that coaching workshops were organized properly, and that the participants attended them. Written down, this sounds relatively simple. It wasn't.

I spent a total of roughly forty days across five months physically inside of a prison, which, compared to officers, wing managers and other youth or social workers who have spent years working in one, amounts to relatively little. But, of course, forty days was still enough to gather some understanding about how prisons feel and work. More than half of this time was spent in training. I spent other days reading about the prison system and sparking conversations with prison staff in different buildings and departments. I met people who had dedicated many years of their lives to helping those who are incarcerated. I found that plenty of prison officers do their job for reasons that are rooted in authentic personal experience and social justice. Some were enrolled on the Unlocked scheme, which, like Teach First for teachers in state schools, fast-tracked graduates into prison officer roles. Others had been officers for decades, rising up the ranks, remaining energetic and proud, while some gave the impression that the job had stolen their soul.

I got a brief glimpse into rehabilitative programmes. There were services like conflict resolution, yoga, GCSE and university education, construction, music recording, creative writing, catering experience in the kitchens, and psychological or social services like trauma counselling and family support. The life-coaching programme I was employed to sell to prisoners was far from perfect. But when it worked like it was meant to do, I saw first-hand how it could help prisoners who took part.

It surprised me that for many people who end up in them prisons are the norm, not the exception. They provide some men with a level of security, compared to the potentially dysfunctional and isolated lives to which they would return. For those who had been in and out since they were young – an overwhelming proportion I met were inside for repeat offences; their criminal records often started when they were fourteen or fifteen for committing minor drug-dealing offences or possessing weapons – the regular meals, roof over their heads, heating and strict regimes provided an anchor in their lives.

My visits redrew and coloured in my preconceived notions of what prison life is actually like, away from the dramatic distortions of BBC documentaries, Hollywood films and newspaper headlines. They contributed towards my understanding of austerity's impact on vulnerable young people, and my intuitions about how societal and educational failure might translate into instances of violence, social exclusion and, ultimately, the removal of someone's freedom. Prison work showed me what the end of the road looked like.

For much of the time prisons are unremarkable. Staff inside are drinking tea and typing up paperwork in their office. You hear the clink of keys, the whoosh of a mop, the dreary murmur of conversation between officers patrolling the wing or the rumble of music playing from speakers. You smell the waft of cheap pasta water or burgers frying, like in a school canteen, or the sterile spray of disinfectant.

Other times, things are less mundane. Occasional screams from the cells of disturbed prisoners pierce the corridor silence. The alarm goes off when there is a fight and officers rush past.

In my training I learnt about prison safety: how to withdraw keys securely, how to avoid being groomed by prisoners, and where I was and was not allowed to go. I learnt about the high rates of radicalization taking place in British prisons – Islamic fundamentalism as well as far-right nationalism – and received lectures about elaborate escape and drug-smuggling plans that had been hatched. I was shown photos of the new models of mobile phones which were the size of a human thumb. Efforts of smugglers to fly drones over the yards to deliver illegal pack-ages, as well as the prison's efforts to prevent such advanced compromises in security, were relayed to me. I discovered the extortionate costs of misplacing keys: how, if one set is lost by an officer, it can cost the taxpayer hundreds of thousands of pounds to have the locks changed for the entire prison. I was strictly advised to never, under any circumstances, step inside a prisoner's cell, and was told corresponding horror stories about kidnappings and the various cases of abuse that had taken place when workers ignored this rule.

A few wings I spent time on were clean and the staff and inmates took pride in maintaining order. Officers would offer to help me find someone, or happily point me towards the source of some administrative information. Parts of other wings, especially at the older prisons, looked like they hadn't been decorated or even deeply cleaned in decades. Some were tricky to navigate because of the narrow corridors and sheer number of doors that had to be constantly locked and unlocked to reach distant cells. Officers could come across as purposefully unhelpful and moody, set in their ways and dragged down by the lethargy of their wing office. Some looked fresh-faced and intimidated by their surroundings; others wore weathered, wary expressions. On a couple of occasions I interacted with officers who appeared more interested in having banter with the prisoners or mocking me than helping me do my job. It was an atmosphere of extremes. To cope, it seemed that you had to double down on smiles and effort, or cynicism and laziness.

Clearer to me than anything was that the prison system – the home of society's least valuable, least deserving, most feared members – was at the bottom of austerity's pile of priorities. This lowly rank was predictable. In the desire to financialize and bring about 'value for money' at all ethical or social costs, prisons and prisoners were being discarded and trampled on by the public sector market, just like in schools, where the 'least valuable' young people were having their inclusion team, mental health support and youth service lifelines pulled. In other words, if those in power and the people who voted for them had little motivation to fund social services, schools and hospitals properly, they were going to have even less motivation to fund the prison system.

On many prison wings I sensed an atmosphere of pure apathy. Violence or verbal abuse resulted in cell doors being locked for everyone, a collective punishment called 'bang-up'. Litter and soiled clothes were scattered on the floor. In rubbly outer walkways rats picked at rotten apple cores and juice cartons dropped from cracked cell windows. Sudden, strong whiffs of cannabis smoke, stale food, urine and sweat came in and out of recognition.

I knew that drug-taking was a problem. But I did not know how embedded it could be. On my walks through some wings there was a constant, lingering smell of burning tobacco mixed in with other less obvious ones. It is no surprise that skunk was being smoked. But the more troubling substance was 'spice': the synthetic, addictive strain of cannabis that has for years preyed on prison and homeless populations across the UK. One officer told me a story of a nineteen-year-old young man with no history of drug consumption smoking a spice spliff and becoming permanently psychotic. He was found drinking from his toilet. Other stories filtered through about spice addicts jumping from one of the high-up corridors and breaking bones, or mistaking their cellmates for food and trying to bite them, or becoming convinced that worms were crawling in their veins.

On one occasion I spoke to a twenty-one-year-old who, judging by the tangy odour coming from his cell, had been smoking what I can only assume was spice. His eyes were rolling backwards into his eyelids. He was swaying from side to side. I quickly realized our conversation was futile. I asked the officer who'd located and opened the prisoner's cell door if everything was okay. The officer shrugged his shoulders while locking the door up and walking me to the next cell: 'He's a spice-head, mate.'

Fyodor Dostoevsky said that 'a society should be judged not by how it treats its outstanding citizens but by how it treats its criminals.' Based on this normative metric, I was witnessing how modern British society should be judged: pretty badly. Of course, I knew that the roots of criminal injustice's eagerness to brand certain people as automatic, disposable failures, and the treatment of public services like they belong to an old, irrelevant world, did not start or finish in prisons.

Compared to many other prosperous countries (not including the US, whose failing prison system is well-documented), prisons in England and Wales are in many ways horrific. In Norway, for example, radical reforms in the 1980s shifted the focus to genuine rehabilitation rather than punishment. Prisoners have been granted more physical space and wide-ranging meaningful activities, leading prisoner recidivism to fall from between 60 and 70 per cent to nearer 20 per cent – which is much lower than in the UK.

Spending on English and Welsh prisons rose steadily across the 2000s, then fell during the first five years of the Conservative government as cuts took their toll, dropping 20 per cent in real terms between 2010 and 2015. This resulted in a deep reduction of 27 per cent to staff numbers over the same period. Although both prison funding and new staff numbers had started to increase again by 2018, due to the government's celebrated recruitment drive, the net number of officers had not: the new and the old were leaving as fast as the new were joining at this time.

The sustained underfunding of prisons has been blamed for the outpouring of reports about worsening hygiene, control, rehabilitation and danger both for prisoners and staff. In his HM Chief Inspector of Prisons for England and Wales Annual Report for 2017–2018, former police officer Peter Clarke opened his introduction with the following: 'The year 2017–18 was a dramatic period in which HM Inspectorate of Prisons documented some of the most disturbing prison conditions we have ever seen – conditions which have no place in an advanced nation in the 21st century.' The report found that roughly half of the thirty-nine male prisons inspected had too few activity places for their populations. HMP Wormwood Scrubs in Acton, west London, where I also spent some time, gave Clarke particular concern: 'It seemed as if the problems there were intractable,' he wrote, 'and prisoners were suffering not only appalling conditions, but an almost complete lack of rehabilitative or resettlement activity.' Assaults in prisons rose from 15,000 in 2007 to 29,000 in 2017; incidents of self-harm increased from 23,000 to 44,000. These steep trends would continue for subsequent annual reports, all the way through the bleak Covid-19 lockdown of 2020.

Overall reoffending in the criminal justice system, including for community sentences and licence breaches for those punished without imprisonment, has long hovered between 27 and 31 per cent. But the reoffending rate for those released from prison is higher, having remained between 36 and 42 per cent since the mid-2000s. For those leaving prison after a sentence of less than 12 months, the reoffending rate in 2018 was 67 per cent. Large numbers of people are stuck in a revolving door.

The England and Wales prison population nearly doubled between the early 1990s and the mid-2010s – from roughly 45,000 to just shy of 90,000. There has been a simultaneous lengthening of sentences. This means we have more people being sent to prison for longer amounts of time. Over thirty years the average custodial sentence has increased from 16 months to 18.8 months. And the proportion of prisons considered overcrowded has long remained well over half: the Ministry of Justice published data in 2017 that deemed 68 per cent of prisons to exceed their 'certified normal accommodation' (CNA); other estimates that calculate overcrowding with greater scrutiny place this percentage as much higher. Overcrowding, which has ebbed and flowed alongside the general rise in prisoner numbers, is widely cited in research literature around the world as the main reason prisons become more violent and less psychologically bearable for their inhabitants. There is perhaps no purer evidence than this from which to mount the argument that austerity should itself be understood as a form of state violence, as Vickie Cooper, David Whyte and other thinkers posit, using the decimation of prisons as one example, in their 2017 book *The Violence of Austerity*.

Within this increase in the prison population there has been a consistent racial disproportionality among adults from ethnic minorities, especially those who are Black – this demographic also being most likely to be excluded from school (especially those with Caribbean heritage in London, compared to the rest of the country) and stopped and searched by police. Of the prison population, 27 per cent identifies as being from a minority ethnic group, although ethnic minorities represent only 13 per cent of the general population. Within this, Black young males are just under three times more likely to be arrested and Black adult males are just over three times more likely to be arrested than their white counterparts. The Lammy Review in 2017 found that 12 per cent of adult prisoners are Black, despite representing only 3 per cent of the general population. This number rises to 20 per cent of children who are in custody, with 51 per cent of the youth prison population identifying as BAME, despite comprising only 18 per cent of the 10–17-year-old population. The all-party law reform and human rights organization JUSTICE has established a working group to investigate this racial disproportionality in the youth justice system. They report that despite celebrated falls in the youth prison population since its peak, from 3,200 young people in 2002 to just 835 in 2018, almost all of this decline has been a drop in the number of white young people being held.

There were six different prisons ministers across the 2010s, and seven different justice secretaries. The lack of available consistency in decision-making and strategy, as a result of wider political instability, has made any attempts at impactful, sustained reform impossible. This has only been reinforced by the non-existent appetite for funding or improving the rehabilitative potential of prisons among the voting public.

Austerity is therefore not the sole reason for the prison system's inefficacy. But as with policing, it has simply made existing structures and realities within it worse. By criticizing central government cuts to prisons, I am not suggesting that more money should be funnelled into sustaining a system that locks up and punishes people, per se. I am pointing out that under the current dysfunctional landscape that our country operates with, the stranglehold of cuts – both directly to prisons and criminal justice, and indirectly because of their negative impact on the life chances of the most vulnerable people in society via the removal of other lifelines – creates a potent multiplier effect. On top of other services, if prisons were funded properly and designed to be genuinely rehabilitative, instead of largely punitive, it would mean that wider society would be safer, too. Those who come out after being incarcerated – roughly 60,000 people every year – would be able to move on with their lives without reoffending or putting the public at risk. This shift of modelling should not be viewed as alien, either: HMP Grendon in Aylesbury is a Category B prison which self-describes as 'therapeutic'. It grants prisoners who have opted to go there more freedom over how they spend their time, as well as group therapy and community living. The initial cost of a regime like this is more than that of locking people in a dirty cell, yet repeated studies at the prison have shown that it works: for those who stay longer than 18 months, reoffending is consistently lower than the average prison; in 2011 the BBC reported this to have dropped to as low as 20 per cent.

Zooming out, it would be preferable, over time, to transition towards being able to free up finances, time and energy from prisons and policing for funding an effective, caring state that does not feel the need to use violence, surveillance and incarceration to threaten its population into short-term conformism. Funding social services such as mental health provision would mean the average person who can't afford private services has access to support they deserve, while reducing the burden on the criminal justice system. There were unprecedented dips in the number of crimes being committed in England and Wales around the turn of the millennium, falling to the lowest since statistics were first published in 1857. Although it is hotly debated why this happened, many say New Labour's high funding of social welfare programmes was responsible.

The prison where I spent more time than any other was HMP Wandsworth. It is one of the biggest prisons in Western Europe. Built in 1851, the looming, weathered structure sits behind tall walls next to Wandsworth Common, between Putney, Clapham, Earlsfield and Tooting, in leafy south-west London. 'Wano' is often cited as Britain's most overcrowded prison; it is designed for 963 men, yet houses over 1,600. Cells built for one are used for two.

One Monday morning in March 2018 I arrived at the prison's entrance, showed my identification at reception and handed in my valuables. I drew keys, fastened a keychain to my leather belt and waited to enter through a timed door. I walked down an outdoor path, up some stairs, into the main building and down some indoor stairs to the bottom floor. All of this movement required the constant unlocking and locking of heavy metal doors.

I was based in a small, cluttered office where designated prison officers were responsible for monitoring intelligence about high-risk prisoners. The floor also contained the isolation rooms – segregation or 'seg' – where especially vulnerable or violent prisoners could be kept in solitary confinement. I could hear occasional muted screams and bangs echo down the wide corridor.

Inside the office, the gang affiliations of particular wings, separated because of territorial rivalries brought in from the outside world, were written on a whiteboard. It was strange seeing some of the numerical or geographically defined gang names I'd become familiar with from listening to drill music, or from conversations with young people in south London, scrutinized like this as intelligence. Some of it was detailed, but I spotted errors. It said that Harlem was based in Kensington, rather than

Kennington. The gang names for Brixton were several years out of date (although this probably represented the lasting allegiances of the adult prisoners inside). I have no doubt that the listings served an important function for staff. But if it was this easy to see holes in such information, how effectively could it be used on the wing?

Each prisoner was on 'basic', 'standard' or 'enhanced': three possible levels based on their behaviour and risk, which in turn determined how many privileges they were allowed. Like the performance data in schools, it was another ranking system: a way of organizing, punishing and incentivizing people. At the bottom existed grown-up versions of the failed, shamed and demonized young people of the UK's state schools. Those granted enhanced status could play PlayStation in their cell, keep their door open, get a job and enjoy long periods in the gym. Those on basic were British society's least free human beings.

'Basic regime is supposed to modify an individual's behaviour. It is a last-resort method on the wing. It is demeaning and mentally draining,' explained one older prisoner I spoke to, who has been in and out of the criminal justice system since he was a teenager. He has experienced basic regimes at multiple prisons and seen others put on basic for a wide range of offences: from failing a urine test for drugs or fighting with other prisoners to verbally abusing a prison officer. 'Let's say they put you on for twenty-eight days. They'll remove your TV and your radio, and they'll only let you out of your cell for thirty minutes per day so you have to clean your cell, have a shower and make a phone call all in that time, which is just never gonna happen. Then you're sat in your cell with nothing to do apart from think and read for over twenty-three hours every day. For people who don't have no one looking out for them on the outside, they're just alone and isolated.'

He described how it becomes obvious when you're at the receiving end of it that this system is designed to break people down so they have no choice but to conform. 'You survive on rations. A standard prisoner might spend £20 per week on food. On basic, they can cap it, say at £5, so even if you've got money coming into your account from your family outside, you're unable to feed yourself properly. It makes you dependent on the establishment to stay alive. Then they seek to modify your behaviour by increasing your dependency; the establishment expects you to depend on them. But for so many people it has the opposite of its desired effect. They get so frustrated and desperate, either they turn to robbing another man for his food or his burn, or they turn to gangs instead to get fed. That way they become indebted to the gangs. I've seen man who were in jail for minor transgressions, like driving while disqualified or fraud, end up on basic. They become an easy target for gangs to take advantage of. They do things for the gangs to get fed then they're indebted to them. By that point it's a downward spiral: you come out worse than you went in.'

In one instance, he remembers hearing one of his nearby wingmates who'd been put on basic screaming because the officers had forgotten to feed him that day and he'd not had enough money to buy himself food. So he tied his bed sheet around a can of tuna and swung it through his door for his wingmate to catch.

'It's not a reasonable way to deal with people. And when you've been inside long enough you start to see patterns. If I had to guess I'd say that 95 per cent of people I've seen self-harm in prison were on basic.' In one prison he was at for only twenty-one months, twelve people committed suicide. One of them was eleven years into a fourteen-year sentence. He got put on basic for a month and didn't last. 'He was normal one day then the next he opened his window, called out to everyone to say he couldn't take it any longer. We were all shouting at him, trying to get him to realize he only had three years left. But it was too late. He killed himself. If grown men like that are struggling to maintain themselves with such a regime, God knows how younger people cope with it.'

At Wandsworth I had a printed list of eligible names and cell numbers for the coaching programme. The prison officer in the intelligence office grabbed a biro and wrote the letters 'VR' next to one of them. 'This one's on "violence reduction",' he explained, smiling to try to put me at ease. 'He needs to be your priority.'

When I arrived at the wing the prisoners were locked in their cells. I knocked on each door and, through the small slit, held conversations with each eligible young man to get them onboard. Then I'd slide the necessary paperwork under the cell door for them to sign and return to me. Within an hour I had successfully enlisted seven of the eight men I spoke to.

It would be dishonest of me to say that the letters 'VR' didn't distract me. I left this prisoner until last. His cell was in the top far corner of the wing: three floors up.

'Hi, is Jason there? Have you got a couple of minutes?' I enquired after knocking on his door, stating the prisoner's name to differentiate him from whoever else was sharing his cell. I paused for a few seconds, then I opened the slit. I stepped forward towards the door. A pair of eyes inches from the other side were staring back at me.

'How's it going?'

No reply.

I was used to relaying my spiel. I maintained partial eye-contact as I spoke, selling the life-coaching programme as best I could. But as the rehearsed words came out of my mouth, I wondered whether there was any point trying. The letters 'VR' seemed to glare up at me from the sheet of paper in my hand.

'Nah, I'm good,' came Jason's unimpressed response.

I shut the slit. I walked down the staircases to the ground floor. As I was unlocking the big metal door, I stopped.

'You going through, mate, or what?' a prison officer behind me asked.

I apologized and retreated back into the wing, shutting the entrance properly. I was hesitating. My response had been to give up on Jason before I'd properly tried. I walked back up the stairs and gave it another go.

'Jason? I'm sorry for disturbing you again,' I said. Jason appeared. I wanted my new-found conviction to sound like I wasn't going to accept no for an answer. 'You're on "violence reduction" right now. Do you want to get off it?'

Silence. His eyes pulled away from view, retreating into the shadows. I waited. After a few more seconds he returned. He peered down at the paper in my hand.

'This can get me off basic!? Say no more. Sign me up,' came the reply. I bent down and slid an information slip under the cell door.

The systems, rules and linguistic tools used to sort and place value upon the lives of young men I was meeting in prison reminded me of working in secondary schools. Segregation rooms were the adult equivalent of school isolation rooms. The statuses of 'basic', 'standard' and 'advanced' reminded me of the different levels that ranked students in performance-data charts plastered on school corridor walls. The letters 'VR', serving to signify a special list of high-risk men with whom I ought to be prioritizing contact, had formed a nearly stymieing label – similar to when a flustered teacher might complain about particular boys being 'aggressive' or out of line, deepening their reputations as disruptors, often in a way that I found unhelpful.

Saying this is not to be naive. Clearly, to end up in an

isolation room at school or on the wing of a Category B prison, you will have made a mistake or moral wrongdoing – perhaps a very big one. But there was no doubt that in the tunnel of my ongoing line of work these rigged value systems and loaded, negative labels distorted my interactions with people I was trying to serve – and therefore my ability to serve them.

'The labels of danger and violence are just ideas, in the same way that what "poor behaviour" looks like in school is just an idea,' said sociologist Dr Karen Graham. 'These things are inevitably gendered, racialized, class-based. They're dependent on ideas about what a young working-class boy is or isn't; what a Black boy is or isn't. Quite often, it's not based on direct evidence of something that the person has done or is capable of doing. It's just all these ideas and discourses that have been passed down over generations.'

Graham has interviewed hundreds of incarcerated men. She grew up in Birmingham, in a community where a disproportionate number of people ended up in prison. She visited family members in prison as a small child. When Graham started teaching in a local prison, she was required to complete administrative tasks filing the educational histories of each prisoner. She spoke to prisoners about their life stories. She began to make sense of their collective memories and found an almost universal experience expressed in their answers: that of social exclusion at school from a young age. One man had recalled to Graham how, in primary school, he was forced to sit outside the principal's office in silence all day instead of going to lessons. On the occasions he was allowed outside at break, the teacher drew a square with chalk on the playground floor, which he couldn't leave.

'Apart from this being horrific, I was immediately taken to people being in prison and being let out to walk around a square yard. There were a number of really clear . . . not even metaphors, but direct, parallel experiences,' she said. And she heard many stories of this nature: prisoners being subjected to hard-line control methods since their earliest memories of interacting with figures of authority. She argues that the school system treats dissenters like the prison system does: as unworthy, disposable products of their own making, rather than of systemic failure and demonization.

'If you're a child, and you are continually told you are a problem, not just by words, but by actions, not just by teachers, but by your peers, some people will withdraw because they won't want to play or be with you. You go home and your parents reinforce what teachers are saying. It's quite difficult as a five-, six-, seven-year-old to see a different possible self to the one that is constantly being reinforced to you. It pushes you to the margins of what might be considered the mainstream in the classroom, which restricts your ability to behave differently, no matter what you might try to do. If you're sent outside classrooms, or you're in an isolation room from an early age, it doesn't give you the opportunity to be a model student, for instance. All the guys I spoke to in my doctoral research described this point at which they knew very well from their teachers that it wasn't about education any more. That was not the purpose of their relationship with teachers, or anybody. Their education was off the cards. So when those same children come into the criminal justice system, they have been prepared for what would be considered a very extreme environment for other people. It's a system of control and management. It starts in school and inevitably continues so that, if you do end up in prison, you are not surprised by what it's like. You fit into the various roles that are expected of you.'

She interviewed some men who'd attended the same school as her. They told stories of harsh maltreatment and loneliness. As an academically able student, Graham was branded and rewarded as 'gifted'. Her subjects had a more problematic and punitive relationship with the same school corridors.

'Unless you've actually been inside a prison, you really have no idea of what that experience is like. It's similar to these places on the margins of schools: the designated rooms with the word "isolation" on their door. These places are hidden from most students.'

Often, when I was speaking to prisoners who seemed like they'd spent hours or even days on end without any intellectual stimulation, I thought of boys like Carl who described their brains turning to mush and their anger mounting as a result of being expected to sit in silence all day. Once the mould of their reputation had been set, they'd not been listened to by overworked teachers incentivized to use the weaponry of bad behaviour points to punish their way towards a peaceful classroom.

'The purpose is not to correct the behaviour of these particular children. Instead it's about keeping everybody else in order. If we remove one child from a classroom, we know it's not doing that one child any good, but what it is doing is making everyone else behave. There are parallel things happening in prisons. The purpose of prison is partly the stick that makes everybody else go to work. In order for people to feel like there is an actual meritocracy, for qualifications to apparently be fair, for the idea of getting a top job to apparently be fair, we have to have some kind of system that sorts people in a way that looks fair. We have to convince everybody in society that the way we live is justified and okay; that the reason we have inequality is because some people are lazy and stupid or bad, and others are valuable. It's basically a way to legitimize the shitshow that we're living in.'

Unsurprisingly, a high proportion of men Graham spoke to were excluded. Over 40 per cent of prisoners in the UK are recorded to have been permanently excluded from school. Over 60 per cent were temporarily excluded. The number of people imprisoned who were excluded from school has long hovered at around these marks, compared to the less than 1 per cent of the greater population it actually happens to. Herein lies the most foundational trend of the school-to-prison pipeline. The British population now takes school exclusions as an uncontroversial prerequisite for maintaining order. But in a society that prides itself on being one of the most progressive and wealthy in the world, should this really be so?

'I had one case where I remember the pupil saying: "I feel like the school decided I am bad." And this type of thing really matters, because when you track it through, the number of people who are in prison who were excluded from school is incredibly high,' said Michael Etienne, a barrister based in London who specializes in defending families affected by school exclusions and representing individuals who have been detained by the state, such as prisoners at parole hearings. 'You also find that a lot of those people have undiagnosed learning difficulties or special educational needs [SEN] and if they had been properly identified in school they might not have been excluded. They might not have been set on the road that has led to them being in prison. Schools are in a difficult position, because the funding for SEN comes from local authorities, and local authorities' budgets have been cut. Parents often have to have a fight to get the provision their child needs. One of the common things you see in exclusion cases is kids being excluded for behaviour that is effectively the result of the fact that they are just not being properly supported at school in the first place.'

Permanent and fixed-term exclusions in secondary schools increased year-on-year after 2010. As more and more power was granted to independent headteachers and school boards, removing a child from school became part of managerialism, undertaken with relatively little consequence. Under austerity, overseeing the spill-out of increasing social and behavioural problems has

become harder. The decision-making required for how to neutralize disruption from a school year group has become more
weighted in favour of students who are able to achieve academic
results, head to university and toe the narrowing line of nine-
to-five professionalism. The same process has become weighted
against students who struggle most, even if these struggles are
rooted in circumstances that are out of their control. This goes
at least some way to explaining the broader context of why
Freddie, Carl and others were excluded across 2017.

Research conducted by the Department for Education
showed that 6,685 pupils were permanently excluded from English schools in 2015–2016. The majority of these exclusions took
place in the run-up to students' GCSEs. It marked a 40 per cent
increase from three years prior. Schoolchildren were expelled
on 7,900 occasions across the United Kingdom in 2017–2018, the
highest number since 2007–2008. This equates to over 40 pupils
per day. There has also been a rise of methods like 'managed
moves' and 'off-rolling' – both of which I've seen first-hand at
schools I've worked in. The former is a method of moving a student to another school with the permission of parents, either for
a prolonged period of time or indefinitely, without needing to
record having excluded them (formal exclusions look unfavour-
able during Ofsted reviews). The latter removes a pupil from the
school roll without using a permanent exclusion, when the
removal is primarily in the best interests of the school, rather
than the best interests of the pupil. This includes cases in which
schools have pressured a parent to remove their child from the
school roll. I have seen and heard of this being done to students
shortly before exam season so that their likely poor grades are
not counted but their name remains on the school register. In a
2019 YouGov poll of over 1,000 teachers, over half conceded
that the main reason schools use off-rolling is to manipulate
league tables; 82 per cent said they felt it was most likely to

happen to students with behavioural problems. Although these practices could, in theory, offer an alternative to permanent exclusion, they represent another way in which academies manipulate their metrics, brush problems under the carpet, maintain good PR and protect their brand value – just like any business competing in a market does.

The short-term costs of this for society – higher numbers of young people oversubscribed in Alternative Provision (AP) schools and PRUs, and a raised susceptibility to the dangerous influences of the unmonitored outside world, such as grooming from drug-dealing gangs – are huge. The long-term costs will be even bigger. When this expanded generation of young people who have been excluded from school grow up, they will be more likely to remain unwoven into the social fabric of society, yet they will simultaneously be even more reliant on state services. They will have experienced a childhood in which adults and systems were more interested in punishing them or pretending they don't matter as a way of handling their non-compliance. This is both morally problematic, because it demonstrates an unwillingness by the state to support those who are victims of their environments at a young age, and in economic terms will cost the taxpayer much more anyway. The Institute for Public Policy has estimated that each excluded child will cost the state £370,000 in extra education, benefits and criminal justice costs. The most vulnerable young people, facing judgemental pressures and lacking support networks from every angle, have lost out most. We will all pay the price.

'I see the school-to-prison pipeline at all its stages,' continued Etienne. 'It's a magnification of the same issues. There is a culture of discipline in schools that is encouraged at government level, to see discipline as something that ought to be enforced like it was the criminal law or the prison system. So you have a combination of zero-tolerance policies (which by definition are probably unlawful, given the range of considerations that are supposed to apply to exclusion decisions) on certain issues and a whole range of others that are applied almost as punitively. For example, there are lots of issues that keep coming up about the way in which hair is being policed, and the fact that Black kids are being excluded from school, effectively, because they have Black hair, in the name of racially and culturally loaded concepts of what is or isn't "tidy". In both of the cases I had where there had been knives involved, whatever the actual facts were, you get the same rhetoric that you see repeated in the press: this is something we need to take a zero-tolerance position on, and we have to protect everyone at all costs, so it doesn't matter about the consequences for individual pupils who get excluded.'

Etienne argued that this harshness feeds through from school exclusions all the way up to prisons. Ultimately, everyone loses out.

'You've got this increasing and persistent narrative that prison is too soft. But I think one of the real issues in prisons is the lack of rehabilitation programmes or the difficulty in accessing them. We don't seem to get traction on the idea that the best way to protect the public is not to lock prisoners up and leave them there until the end of their sentence; the best way to protect the public is to enable people to address whatever it is that has led to them committing offences. That of course is putting to one side the fact that most people are not in prison for violent offences. Some are on remand, so not convicted of anything. And most people shouldn't be in prison in the first place.'

According to the coaches at HMP Wandsworth, Jason stood out immediately as the most confident and motivated of his group in the first coaching session. When I arrived at the classroom at the end, he had his arms crossed while sitting casually on the desk, his feet dangling below, his gaze focused on each of the coaches. He mentioned how he wanted to make sure that when he left prison he could spend more time with his young son. When they finished talking he shook the coaches' hands and thanked them. He walked past me and stopped.

'Thank you for making me do this, bro,' he said, 'it's important. Let me know if you need any help getting more people on the wing to come.' He held out his hand for me to shake, before heading out of the room and walking down the corridor, sparking banter with the officer.

'Something clicked for him today,' one of the coaches said as we made our way towards the exit. As per my programme delivery instructions, I'd not told the coaches about Jason's 'VR' status so that they could work with all members of the room with as few preconceived judgements as possible. I'd taken the label seriously as a signal of potential risk for the session and leveraged it as a motivation to get Jason signed up. But now, for a few hours at least, a new set of expectations were made possible. Everyone involved – Jason, his fellow prisoners, the coaches, me, the prison staff, society – was better for it.

In June of 2018, new guidelines were published for judges in court sentencing people for knife-related offences.

'I certainly noticed a palpable difference in terms of sentencing,' said Elena Papamichael, a Solicitor–Advocate specializing in criminal defence and youth justice, who is also a Director of The 4Front Project, a member-led youth organization empowering young people and communities to fight for justice, peace and freedom. 'The court would say that there are strong policy reasons to pass immediate custodial sentences for knife-carrying. This led to many more young people being sent to prison who had never been in trouble before, never committed any violent offence. That to me is a knee-jerk response to a serious public-health issue as opposed to an evidence-led solution.'

Papamichael noted that across 2018, a shift started to take place. Knife-carrying as an offence was being punished more and more with a prison sentence, rather than with a community-based punishment, where prisoners work with probation officers. The Ministry of Justice found that in 2018, 21,484 knife and offensive weapon offences were recorded by the Criminal Justice System: the highest number of offences dealt with since 2009 (25,103). In March of 2018, 37 per cent of such offences resulted in an immediate custodial sentence and only 12 per cent in a caution, compared to 22 per cent and 27 per cent respectively in March 2009, meaning that fewer cautions and more prison sentences were being handed out than a decade before. An overwhelming majority, 72 per cent, of offences in early 2018 were for first-time offenders.

'Handing out more prison sentences misses the point that often young people who carry knives are fearing for their lives. They hear about all the deaths of teenagers killed in knife attacks on the news and they feel scared and want to protect themselves. They don't have faith that anyone else will protect them. It then also means more young people are being introduced to people involved in criminal activity in prison and young offenders' institutes, as well as the risk of being bullied and exploited in prison. There are also the psychological and economic effects of being incarcerated: losing your home, the breakdown of relationships, the inability to find employment after serving a prison sentence. So a much bigger portion of the population is being subjected to negative experiences. When they are released from prison they're often not in a position to live pro-socially, whether that is a result of the trauma and stigma of prison or because of the structural barriers to rejoining society once you have been to prison.'

Tactics sold to the public as a response to rising violence have been employed more and more. One of these is the Criminal Behaviour Order or CBO – a modern equivalent of the

Anti-Social Behaviour Order or ASBO. Upon conviction for any criminal offence, the police can apply to the court for a CBO to be imposed. There doesn't need to be a connection between the offence for which the person receives the conviction and the behaviour for which the CBO is made. They can include restrictions like stopping someone going into a certain borough, hanging out in groups or making music videos.

'Before that time, the only time I'd seen CBOs was for really prolific shoplifters and drug-dealing cases. After April 2018 I saw it for any type of case. You could in theory be convicted of shoplifting and then get a CBO preventing you from doing drill videos, even if it's got nothing to do with shoplifting. If you breach a CBO it is a criminal offence, thus it is massively, massively widening the criminal net,' said Papamichael.

Another tool used is a 'gang injunction', introduced in 2014. Gang injunctions, which are available for people as young as fourteen, don't attach to criminal convictions. They can be made against people who have never been in trouble before. Taking a similar form to a CBO, they can be placed on someone – disproportionately young, Black men, referred to as 'gang nominals' – without them ever having been convicted of a crime. All that needs proving is that 'on the balance of probabilities' someone has 'engaged in, encouraged or assisted' in gang-related violence or drug-dealing. Interim gang injunctions are often imposed *ex parte* ; the court hears the application by the police without the person who is going to be subjected to it knowing anything about it. A letter turns up at the door of someone deemed to be in a gang, announcing a set of terms they must abide by or risk facing imprisonment. There is an opportunity to challenge the injunction in court, but usually the interim injunction remains in place for months before the case is heard.

'With the gang injunctions and CBOs, many of the usual

safeguards present in the usual criminal justice system are absent. For example, they use hearsay evidence, which is not generally allowed in a criminal trial. You can have a police officer write up a witness statement saying that the person is associated with another person, or they can say "this person is part of this gang, and this gang is known for doing x, y and z". Comparable to the subtle but problematic use of the term "knife crime", the word "gang" is racialized because it is used almost exclusively to describe and police Black boys, when the Met's own figures show that only 27 per cent of those responsible for serious youth violence are Black.'

The 'gangs matrix' is yet another measure used to surveil the lives of poor, mostly Black teenage boys at disproportionate rates. It has been employed by the Met since 2012, after the 2011 London riots. But it has been condemned by Amnesty International for being institutionally racist: 78 per cent of boys on it are Black. In early 2020, the Met removed more than 370 names from the list of over 2,500 after years of criticism about it being discriminatory and findings that it had breached data protection laws. The matrix features a red, amber and green colour system to determine a person's risk to the public. The majority of prisoners are in the green category. A significant number are victims rather than perpetrators, placed on the database after a crime had been committed against them. But in turn this information could be used by the state to monitor them in ways that are problematic even for demonstrable criminals. There is no requirement from police to justify why they place someone's name on the matrix. Someone could be stopped and searched, have nothing offensive or illegal found on their person and then still be added to the matrix, simply because the police considered them to be in a violent area or because they are deemed to look suspicious.

'The police and the media bounce off each other, and that

feeds into the justice system in a very real way because if there are accusations of gang association, then that can increase a sentence. All it takes is for one police officer to say a person is gang affiliated and then it makes it less of a chance that they're going to get bail,' Papamichael continued. 'How can you argue *against* the claim that someone is in a gang? A client told me that police had come to his family home and tried to get them evicted, because he was purportedly in a gang. But the parents owned the house so the police were not successful in that instance. It's alarming because this is all on the basis of a database that no one is able to challenge. It's a total imbalance of power. It is common for police officers with no specialist expertise, qualifications or training to give evidence that someone is gang affiliated because of who they have been sighted with; because of the fact that they have been stopped and searched in a "gang area"; or because they have appeared in a music video. But usually there isn't any direct evidence that the people they have associated with are in a gang and so this makes it difficult to challenge for a lawyer. Furthermore, often the people they have been seen with are cousins, school friends and neighbours. They may lead entirely different lifestyles and make wholly different choices in their own lives than those who they know and may spend time with. A stop-and-search in a particular area can and does routinely result in an entry in the gang matrix, regardless of whether anything unlawful was found. What if that area happens to be where someone grew up or currently lives? How can a young Black man avoid being seen as a gang member if it is no longer reliant on proving involvement in criminal offences? Quickly, an entire community is criminalized. Artists may demonstrate an allegiance to a certain gang in music videos. But appearing in a video does not mean that the person necessarily subscribes to the lyrics any more than an actor who plays a role holds the values of the character he plays. All the young people from the area may be invited to be involved in the shooting of a video and it can be exciting and fun. It does not follow that a person has ever done anything illegal in their life. I've had situations where the police officer has even written that the person is making a gun finger in the video as evidence that they are in a gang. But they tell me that they're just gesticulating because they are rapping. This also brings to light another point which is the fact that there is a real cultural blindness, too.'

In early 2018, CBOs, gang injunctions and the gangs matrix started being used in response to the rising popularity of drill music.

'I represented a prominent drill artist who was convicted of a driving offence. The police applied for a CBO and used his music videos to prove he is a gang member. The use of music videos as evidence of gang affiliation is more prevalent now than it used to be . . . it was usually reserved for very serious cases, like murders,' concluded Papamichael. 'The police are now spending precious resources and time funded by the public purse on scouring YouTube videos.'

Across 2018 UK drill music started being openly blamed in mainstream media headlines for the spike in youth violence. Within weeks of my article in the *Guardian* arguing that the music ought to be harnessed as a force for constructive change, Met Police Commissioner Cressida Dick denounced social media culture. She soon did the same to drill. Columnists fancied themselves as experts overnight. Within days of one another, the *Telegraph* and the *Spectator* repurposed my analysis of lyrics, almost verbatim, applying it to suit their own shallow agenda, from my article in the American music blog *Pigeons & Planes*. But the *Spectator* wrongly copied the word 'shank' (knife) as 'skank' (a dance usually associated with Caribbean-origin music, such as reggae or grime) not once, but twice. The *Guardian* posted the wrong photograph of popular Tottenham driller Abra Cadabra. Drill rappers were formally labelled 'terrorists' after legislation used for terror suspects was repackaged to convict people making music videos. 'Knife thugs to be treated like jihadis,' read one headline in the *Sun*.

YouTube removed thirty drill videos in May as a step to communicate to higher powers that they were doing what they could to help (despite leaving up the tens of thousands of unpoliced violent clips that didn't have any music attached to them). The police announced that since 2015 they had been developing a database of over 1,600 music videos which they used to gather intelligence and convict people with. I tried to imagine caricatures of how it worked behind the scenes: a rookie police officer, swivelling on a chair in an understaffed police station, playing keyboard roulette with videos considered to fall under the vague 'drill' banner. But I knew that one click of a button at the censor's end would send a draconian message to young people of colour seeking a way of expressing themselves. A 'no' to drill was a 'no' to the inconvenient truth being brought to the fore by poor, young, Black men from the UK's biggest cities.

Censorship would be practically ineffective at making the music inaccessible to young, determined fans, anyway. When a drill video was removed by YouTube, within minutes it would be re-uploaded multiple times. Deleted videos were gossiped about like collectors' items. Videos might even be shared *more* intensely because of their blacklisted status and helped to spawn an even greater presence in the digital underground. Banning drill made it infamous and more marketable.

Authority figures do not seem to have learnt that manic censorship has this effect, ultimately speeding up the wider exposure of the cultural voice it seeks to muzzle. This was the same for attempts to block makers of US gangster rap, partygoers in the

British rave scene across the 1980s and 1990s, and pirate radio assemblers and fans in grime's earliest days in the 2000s. Artists would simply adapt and strengthen in their ability to broadcast their art. The same has been true in attempts to suppress provocative literature. Penguin were taken to trial in 1960 for alleged obscenity in D. H. Lawrence's novel *Lady Chatterley's Lover*. After winning the case, the publisher sold over three million copies, inspiring a paradigm shift in the literary world. Writers suddenly had the breadth of freedom to publish explicit material that never would have been possible before.

Nonetheless, CBOs and gang injunctions were given to some of the most prominent drillers. Members of Zone 2 in Peckham, OFB from Tottenham and 410 in Brixton – including Skengdo and AM – were all issued with legal restrictions on their freedoms. Their prosecutors used the conviction of some groups to issue a three-year CBO detailing a list of rules, including having their music checked by police before its release and a ban on any lyrics mentioning death, injury or postcodes. It was correct that guilty young men were arrested for breaking the law and signalling intent to cause harm to others. But the simplistic, collapsed attachment of their criminality to the music had a distorting effect. Soon, in the artificial logic of the media internet's algorithm, all stabbers were drill rappers, and vice versa. Violent crimes – not just in London, but overseas in European cities, and even as far away as Sydney, where drill was popular among oppressed indigenous Australians – were unquestionably linked to music.

Those in charge at the websites of news publications figured out they could boost their articles' search engine optimization (SEO) rankings by placing the word 'drill' in their headlines. This marketing strategy was reminiscent of drill's original inception in Chicago. If you were a budding drill rapper across 2012, recording a 'diss track' and writing this category alongside your enemy's name in the title of your YouTube music video upload (e.g. 'Chief Keef diss') meant you could more easily piggy-back off their fame and provoke them to generate a response. The same thing was happening among newspapers in the UK in 2018; journalists who'd never heard of the music until they felt strong-armed to write about it were climbing on top of one another to prove who could denounce or support it the loud-est. It became a self-fulfilling prophecy. Even if an arrest or incident of violence had nothing to do with music, drill's name would be shoehorned into a headline or article. Everyone was guilty of this practice, from the BBC to the *Daily Mail*.

This fascination was even reflected in the fashion world. Nike were criticized after their release of a £69 balaclava in collabora-tion with designer Matthew Williams. The piece was clearly inspired by the DIY, all-black aesthetic employed in drill videos. Its advert showed a young man donning the branded balaclava with accompanying shoulder straps. It was discontinued.

'Hi, is Mo there?' I enquired at one cell door after knocking on it loudly. I waited for a few seconds before I opened the slit. I could see a bunk bed to the right. One man was lying on the top bunk. Another was sitting up on the bottom bunk, rubbing his eyes like he'd just woken from a nap. He stood up, walked over to the door and peered through the slit at me.

'Yeah, that's me,' he replied groggily.

'Hi, my name's Ciaran. I'm a youth worker from –'

'Yo! I know you!' came a loud, excitable voice. I could see Mo's cellmate sit up on the top bunk. He lowered his book, swung his legs round and hopped off, rushing over to the door. I recognized him immediately. He was a young man I'd seen once or twice at Jacob Sawyer but we'd never spoken properly before. 'You're from Sawyer, I swear!?' he quizzed. 'Why you here!?' He said his name was Abdoul. I smiled with familiarity.

'Can you get Tony to send my reference, please?' he asked.

'I'll see what I can do, but I can't promise anything,' I replied.

'What's that?' he asked about the sheet of paper in my hand.

'It's for my programme. I'll see if I can include you on the next one, if you're interested?' I replied.

'That'd be calm,' Abdoul said, smiling. He thanked me, turned round, walked across the cell and hopped back on to his top bunk.

When I returned the following week, having spoken to Tony about getting Abdoul's reference completed, looking to sign him up to life coaching, he was no longer Mo's cellmate. I never saw him again.

11. If I Could Tell You About Drillings
Youth Services

The chain around the metal doors at Jacob Sawyer remained padlocked for three weeks after the Nine Night at the end of July 2018. With the centre closed, there was one less safe haven for young people at a time when it was needed more than ever.

Throughout August 2018, London's Jekyll-and-Hyde character was mirrored in media headlines. Papers celebrated the smashed temperature record yet made urgent calls about climate-change forecasts. Journalists migrated from stabbing to stabbing. Stories about social dysfunction and human loss require patience, financial investment and diverse editorial teams. But none of these things have a stable tenancy in modern journalism. As a result, yet more objects of blame emerged, speaking volumes about the city's distracted, broken condition.

Low policing numbers was one of them. The *Guardian* reported that Camberwell police station was open for a total of three hours across August 2018. During this time, only two police officers and one community support officer were responsible for the whole of the Camberwell Green ward, which has a population of over 15,000. On Friday 17 August there was a quadruple stabbing on the Elmington Estate. The scarcity of law enforcement in such a violence hotspot signalled how hollowed out the police had become.

'They weren't perfect, far from it. But at least police used to have a presence in the area,' Tony bemoaned in one of our catchups over the phone while Jacob Sawyer's doors remained closed.

Despite his long-held cynicism towards many aspects of the police, he had nonetheless always maintained in our conversations that he saw his task of managing community safety as more achievable when there were local police who had built relationships with local people. 'When there's no police these young people can get away with what they like; there's nobody around to make them think twice. It's not the only answer but it certainly helps.'

In his Spring Statement in March 2018, Chancellor Philip Hammond had promised an extra £100 million to the police to combat violence. Given the historical structural trends, clunky racist injustices and draconian direction of policing practice in the UK, even more so in London, it was impossible to have any faith this money would be put towards a more compassionate, community-based, trauma-informed force. And because of the sustained neglect of other services, it implied yet again that using a stick, not a carrot, was the preferred strategy of the government. There was also a lack of clarity on the matter: Theresa May and the Conservative Home Secretary, Amber Rudd MP, denied that cuts to police were having any impact on youth violence, despite a report from the Home Office suggesting otherwise.

Rudd later resigned after being unable to explain away her overseeing of the 'Windrush scandal', in which people brought to the UK from the Caribbean as children were being wrongly detained and deported. It is reported to have happened illegally to at least 83 individuals; a further 50,000 people had been expected to prove their citizenship or face a denial of rights or deportation. Breadwinners of families in the 1950s had filled the health and social care professions on invitation from a post-war British government seeking to rebuild the country using the help of the empire's recently freed former colonies. Over sixty years later, the scandal reflected an inherent xenophobia filtering down from the highest level of political decision-making – sparked by Theresa May's 'hostile environment policy' from 2013. Black British Caribbeans were yet again being written out of national history; subjects of faraway control being used one century and disposed of the next.

As 2018's hot summer turned to autumn, London's mayor Sadiq Khan announced the establishment of a £45 million 'Young Londoners Fund' for community projects preventing crime across the capital, and the inception of London's first ever Violence Reduction Unit (VRU). The VRU's responsibility was to enact a 'public health approach' to stemming violence. This would, in theory, involve seeing violence as a symptom of social breakdown. The VRU would be funded by City Hall and central government to work closely with initiatives across the capital in a number of fields – education, healthcare, social services, police, youth services. It would aim to treat the capital's violence epidemic as a specific problem that required both bespoke efforts from borough to borough, as well as a city-wide coordination of best practice. Its creation was a step in a progressive direction, showing that arguments made by the APPG on Knife Crime and the Youth Violence Commission were translating into some tangible policy changes.

But with the fatiguing backdrop of an unresolved Brexit vote, blame games from the right-wing press were too easy to rig. On top of the moral panic about drill, headline attention was also placed on 'middle-class cocaine users'. This was based on the idea that the UK's soaring cocaine demand was bolstering a competing market and thus causing violent feuds between dealers. But it was inaccurate, given that research suggests the cocaine market is relatively non-violent and non-exploitative compared to the crack and heroin markets, which tend to lean on poor young people. The explosion of 'county lines' operations, in which networks of exploited young drug dealers were travelling to poor, rural or coastal towns across the country to sell their product, was also highlighted. But all of these phenomena were ultimately symptoms of poverty and social breakdown, not root causes of violence.

Between April 2017 and April 2018 serious youth violence had gone up 9.6 per cent. Knife offences were up 18.3 per cent. By August, 2018's murders had overtaken the total number across the whole of 2014. In London, the eighty-eighth murder of the year took place on 1 August when twenty-three-year-old Siddique Kamara was stabbed to death on Warham Street in Camberwell. He was otherwise known as Incognito, a leading figure in the drill collective Moscow17. Of course, his death gave further ammunition to those blaming music for the violence (although he was stabbed while trying to rob someone of their wristwatch). One week before the end of August, the Met launched their hundredth murder investigation.

As an island of stability amidst choppy, chaotic seas, the job of Jacob Sawyer Community Centre to provide a safe space for local young people in Brixton had never been more important.

Demetri woke up earlier than usual. During the rest of the holidays he had been staying up late and sleeping past midday. Not today. He turned on his computer and logged on to UCAS. He usually didn't care much about results but he had butterflies in his stomach. Not all of his exams went as well as he'd wanted them to. The idea of attending university still seemed like a dream that he couldn't quite believe.

The web page showed that he'd been accepted into Goldsmiths, University of London – his insurance choice – to study Criminology. He was pleased that he could stay in London and live at home. He could continue earning money working in the same retail job while he completed his degree. He felt a rush of achievement.

He got dressed and walked to school to pick up his A-level results. After opening the brown envelope he tucked the results sheet back inside. Holding it in his hand made him confident. Some of the others in his year group were looking happy because they got their required grades. Others were crying. Demetri spoke to someone in his Psychology class who hadn't got their grades. They were going through 'clearing' on UCAS. He was glad that he didn't ever need to do that. He wanted to head home to tell his parents the good news, and then out again to celebrate.

On his walk home Demetri thought about the last few years. He'd patterned up in Year 11 and now life was moving in the right direction. He planned to take a gap year because he wanted a break from education. He knew that at university there would be less structure so he'd have to be more disciplined. He needed some time to learn to be independent and keep stacking bread. He was ready for the real world.

'It's gonna take someone dying inside a place like this for them to wake up and take this seriously,' Tony explained when I visited him after Jacob Sawyer reopened, three weeks after the Nine Night. The building was empty. Tony was slumped into his chair. His usual spark was dampened.

One of Tony's new strategies for maximizing safety after re-opening was to keep the older generation of young men separate from the younger boys when they spent time inside the building. The olders were now required to book a fixed time slot to visit for key work or employment help. This freed up evenings for the under-eighteens. But while this strategy made sense as a way of minimizing risk – because those who were more directly implicated in local territorial feuds would not implicate their younger community members – it contained intense ethical complexities. He knew that the olders were in grave danger. Making it harder for them to hang out at the centre reduced the likelihood of trouble finding its way inside, but it left them more exposed on the roads.

'It's easy to sit here and tell them not to come inside in the evenings. It's easy for the police and the council to tell me that we need to look at policies and rules and outcomes. But policies take time to write, and time to enforce. I don't have that sort of time. Right now, it's about keeping people alive, Ciaran! We're not there when these boys are being run down with knives at night or when they can't leave their front door to get their family some milk because someone's waiting for them on the other side.'

Austerity-induced social dysfunction was becoming clear not only on this micro-level for teenagers and for community workers like Tony. According to him, the chaos extended from the macro-level, too – from global trends and national politics.

'You know all this Brexit populism in the air? From Nigel Farage and Boris? All that nationalism and xenophobia makes young people in areas like this feel like they don't belong. With Grenfell and now all this Windrush stuff, it sends a message: *you are not wanted*. Then there is all this gentrification in Brixton. There is judgement everywhere. If you're a poor, ethnic minority kid around here, and you're seeing all this wealth come in, and all these people who look different to you, and they look at you like you're a piece of shit on their shoe, of course it's gonna drive you mad. You're craving money all the time. Maybe you've got a nice phone and a television at home. But can your family pay for the electricity meter? Are you having three meals a day? When you're avoiding violence, that is tiring work. These boys should be sleeping eight, nine hours every night. But most of them barely sleep at all. They are go, go, go, all the time. Some of them can't catch the bus or go to the gym like normal people because they are in survival mode. All the media does is demonize them and call them thugs, but nobody's helping them properly. So what do people expect?'

Tony was clear on the disasters that were piling up before him and the lack of urgent empathy from those holding the purse strings of public funding to make places susceptible to violence safer. While always qualifying his rants with admissions about the imperfections of Jacob Sawyer's service – 'we've not figured it out yet, but we'll get there' – he recognized that there was a tall task ahead.

'First it's about challenging these young men, chipping away at their consciousness. We can talk about what it means to be a man; how it is okay to feel fear or embarrassment or shame without retaliating. The older boys are already in the river, and this is about stopping them from going over the edge of the waterfall. Then we stop the ones who are thirteen or fourteen climbing into the river in the first place. But that's difficult to do when we've been closed over the summer holidays.'

Tony often maligned the faltering trends of contemporary youth services as a structural limitation to the work he and others wanted to do. For over twenty-five years he'd seen how the funding tap from the government had been turned on and off. This wavering support stifled community engagement. Efforts to combat complex social issues had not been sustainably funded.

Various third-sector and charitable organizations are now required to compete in a marketplace for shrinking pots of money to survive. In the context of reduced central government funding it is the sector norm. As opposed to public services being resourced properly by the taxpayer, a landscape exists in which charities trying to plug the gaps rely on concepts like 'corporate social responsibility' ('CSR') pots from big companies. Large amounts of money can be gained at speed and often with highly impactful results. This funding can and does do a huge amount of good in the world; it pays the wages of people who save lives and challenge injustice. But the incentives driving social impact in such unbalanced relationships can collapse into disguised marketing ploys rather than genuine attempts to make deep, systemic change.

Portraits of children dressed in the uniforms of local academy schools are placed on pamphlets and stacked in corporate waiting areas on clear glass tables next to luxury fashion and new property magazines. Entire floors, from Canary Wharf to Farringdon to Westminster, are dedicated to the funding of social impact, when another floor in the same base will have auditors calculating how to avoid tax. I have seen time and time again from the inside how some prominent providers of funding design opportunities to support small social enterprises, charities or public services like schools and youth centres so that such an arrangement becomes a cynical marketing exercise under the guise of participating in a moral good. I have sat in offices offering skyline views while reporting back to CSR representatives of big investment banks and Magic Circle law firms, and been made to feel grateful that I, a mere charity worker, am even allowed inside. I've been policed by security guards for not wearing a suit at the entrance and scolded over the phone for making tiny adjustments to my programme delivery that go against the small print of funding contracts.

I am not suggesting that private funding schemes for social causes serve no purpose. But I would question the premise of *needing* private money to prop up vulnerable people. For anyone trying to keep society's members bound by a social contract it is, on a fundamental level, flawed – and it creates a sector dependency that has only become more entrenched under austerity. The more we believe that profit-making companies are our only saviour, the more power they can assume, and the more the government is let off the hook. As a result, contracts worth millions of public pounds for what ought to be state-run services are now habitually dished out by government ministers to leaders of big business without scrutiny or open competition from other providers. This cronyism would come to be labelled Britain's 'chumocracy' throughout the 2020 Covid-19 crisis, when it was discovered that many extortionately costed jobs relating to attempts to combat the coronavirus, such as the provision of PPE face masks, had been awarded directly to unqualified business people by members of the Conservative government – many of whom were granted such deals simply because they were personal contacts and family friends.

A priority in CSR arrangements often becomes the optical value gained for the funder, rather than doing what is best for the beneficiaries of the 185,000 charities across England and Wales: poor young people in overwhelmed state schools, the homeless, the underfed, those recovering from domestic abuse. This paradigm shift has led to an industrial-scale movement towards treating charity work, and therefore practices such as youth work, social care and education, as businesses. But these are flexible practices that must, by their very nature, go unsmoothly. They can take time to yield fruit. The more that 'responsible' or 'ethical' capitalism has been pushed as a proxy with which to justify inequality – an acceptable replacement to the state – the more front-line services have had to rely on sucking up to dollar-eyed suits and branding teams.

Tony was critical of the conditional nature of modern funding streams and the way they restricted what was possible on the ground. He wasn't interested in quick wins. He'd preached to me that while urgently arming the younger generation with the tools they needed to become employed was important, for the traumatized perpetrators and victims of violence, something much more fundamental was necessary. According to him, a youth club should be a place where young people who had nowhere else to go could relax; where staff should not need to feel overburdened with performative box-ticking. In 2018, a place like Jacob Sawyer was primarily needed for keeping young people alive and looked after, in the moment.

'It's all about bums on seats now. Back in the day, youth work was a thriving game. Unfortunately, a lot of people began to see it as airy-fairy stuff. And while knife crime was going on outside they were all like, why is this still happening? But I don't think anyone made the correlation properly between social deprivation and crime. Back then youth work was a type of escapism. It should be providing a place where a young person feels safe; where they can go on trips, build relationships and be shown opportunities. Now, to do youth work you have to be so multilayered. You've got to be a cook, a cleaner, a mum, a dad, a caseworker, a policeman, a mentor, a teacher. And that's always been there, but it's never been as hard as it is now, because there is no money. And young people have become a lot more complicated. With iPhones and technology, and the instant gratification we crave in society, people don't want to wait around. It's been too easy under austerity to cut youth services. But the government is reaping what it sowed. This work ain't a "come-in-today-and-change-your-life-tomorrow" kind of thing. This is a less formal setting, where you plant seeds in young people's heads and you watch them grow and blossom and mature. Now everything's pushed by numbers; everybody wants numbers: this number of young people in a couple of workshops during this month, that amount of qualifications or jobs in this year. And I get it, you have to prove you're having impact. You have to get the right data. But it's difficult to quantify the work we do sometimes, when it takes years to see the results: when you've built a relationship with a kid over two years and they open up to you about why they carry a knife; or you've finally got them to feel safe somewhere. That's the real work. Everyone's getting together and saying, "These kids need somewhere to go." But what else are they going to do, apart from sit on their estate and make trouble, if there is no service available?'

Tania de St Croix, a youth worker and lecturer in the Sociology of Youth and Childhood at King's College London, echoed

Tony's sentiments: 'Young people, especially in London, live in more cramped accommodation and have less disposable income than ever before. With the academization of state schools, which has emphasized discipline and punishment, there is less trust in teachers. A gap therefore exists for youth workers to fill, as adults who children *choose* to go to for personal, non-hierarchical support. Youth services really are at a crunch time.'

Between 2011 and 2019, cuts removed 46 per cent of London's youth service budgets. Over a hundred youth centres closed and hundreds of youth worker jobs were removed altogether. By the end of the decade, at least £35 million less per year was being spent on the city's youth services compared to pre-austerity levels. Action for Children found that funding available per child and young person for all children's services, apart from education, fell from £813 million in 2011 to £553 million in 2017 to 2018 across England and Wales. Unison reported that more than 1,000 children's centres and 760 youth centres have closed across the country. The YMCA found that overall funding to youth services had been cut in real terms by 70 per cent since 2011. Places like Gateshead, Nottingham and Norfolk suffered cuts of more than 90 per cent. Like schools, the NHS and mental health services, as well as rehabilitation in prisons, state-funded support for the most vulnerable young people has been phased out. It is against this backdrop that Jacob Sawyer has survived.

Of course, the creeping land-grab of property developers seeking central groundspace near to Brixton's desirable town centre has meant that gentrification only adds to the pressure on Jacob Sawyer's future. In 2018 a stalled regeneration proposal for the area included a plan to rebuild the centre and use the current land for new private homes. 'There is an assumption that young people need stuff to be bright and brand new. But there is a space for the old-school youth club which has been in the community for generations. That brings something special,' de

St Croix noted. She believed, like Tony, that the fundamental thing is simply having a basic space so young people can feel a sense of co-ownership and community around it, and lamented the endless losses of well-established youth clubs due to local authority closures. 'You're never going to get those buildings back to public ownership. That loss extends to the loss of an older generation of experienced youth workers, too, who aren't being valued as mentors or replaced when they burn out. Some people have put a lifetime into their communities.' On hearing her words, I couldn't help but think of veterans like Tony, and others like him who were holding on in academy schools, such as Monica. In twenty-first-century London their incomparable spirit and experience could be lost if transitions into a new social era continue to be managed by the insensitive market hand. But we cannot afford to lose their seasoned wisdom.

'Youth services won't fix the whole problem, but they will be part of the solution,' Tony continued. 'It's about how we perceive and want to treat young people in society. Every young person, aged seven, deserves to have an adventure playground. They deserve to climb on a climbing frame and swing on a rope. Because that's a key stage of life; when you're learning, taking risks. I always say to people: the kids that use youth clubs are not well-to-do kids, even in rural places, outside London. Why would a wealthy kid need to come here? They're comfortable at home. Kids that come to places like this, it's their escapism from everything else they've got going on in their household, in their school. The community centre is a place where they can be free for a bit.'

On exiting my meeting with Tony at Jacob Sawyer I noticed a young man with his hood up walking up the road towards me. When he got closer, I saw it was Carl. I'd not seen him for a while. He was taller. His hair was grown out. Despite the sun, he was wearing a black puffer jacket. He looked pained and exhausted – stuck in limbo, between boy and man.

'Carl! How are you!?' I asked as we neared.

'I'm okay, I got college and that starting again soon,' Carl replied in mumbles. He'd recently turned seventeen.

'Have you been keeping safe?'

'Yeah, kinda . . .'

'It would be good to catch up with you properly sometime.'

'Definitely,' Carl nodded, smiling for the first time. I asked if we could exchange phone numbers and organize a time to meet. Carl obliged. Then he headed over to the staff office windows to speak to Tony.

Carl kept telling himself that he was going to try harder, now that he was in his final year of college. He was still starting every game in football, playing at left midfield. He was fitter than most of the other players. But he wasn't doing any college work. He was paying other students to do it.

His coaches always looked at him funny. Carl thought it was probably because he had a cap on his tooth. They didn't take him seriously; when things were stolen from the changing room, they always blamed him. It reminded Carl of school, when the teachers picked on him. One of the coaches had seen him handling wads of cash in the changing room. He called Carl aside and told him to fix up. Carl ignored him. What did he know about Carl's life?

Carl had quit his job at Burger King. He had a new ped. He was making all his money from the roads. His family saw him as a lost kid. But he was growing into a big man now. He was dealing with big man things.

Carl met his friend Malachi at the train station. Malachi had a big pack and offered to split it with Carl. Carl liked the trips to cunch. If he worked hard, he could make more money than he would in Brixton. There were more customers. But he had to be more careful because the countryside feds were more suspicious of boys like Carl than London feds.

When Carl and Malachi arrived, they walked out of the station and up the road to the bando. They knocked on the door. Malachi gave the man who owned the house a crack rock so the boys could use it as a base for the weekend. It was stinking inside from all the unwashed people who gathered there. The carpets hadn't seen a hoover for months. The bins were overflowing. The bathroom was filthy. There was a smelly dog running around. There were women who were old enough to be Carl's mum or grandma. They were using syringes. They weren't looking after their bodies. Their arms were scarred. They were lost. Every so often they would start fighting each other about something stupid. Sometimes Carl had to step in to stop them hurting one another. To distract himself, Carl sat at the kitchen table facing the wall, scrolling down his phone on Snapchat and Instagram.

On this trip, Carl realized he didn't like how harsh Malachi was with all the cats. Malachi would hit and threaten them. He knew he had all the power and he had no respect. But Carl still had respect for his elders. He still prayed when he could and he believed in treating people right. There was no point in punishing people for the sake of it. Despite everything, Carl was trying to keep a grip on his morals. Malachi took it too far.

They spent three days without showering, brushing their teeth or changing clothes. Carl didn't sleep at all. They ate chicken and chips and pizza from the fast-food takeaway. Carl went out looking for new shots when there was no more bread to be made from the house. They smoked zoots and loads of cigarettes. They made £350.

On Sunday night the man who owned the dog offered to drive them back to Brixton. His car was much nicer than the house. Some cats had good jobs and money, but they still needed drugs. They were still miserable with their lives. Carl knew that his life could be good if he had a proper job. He could afford a nice car and he wouldn't go to any bando.

Carl and Malachi sat in silence in the back of the car with the smelly dog wedged between them.

As 2018 neared its end, evenings at Jacob Sawyer were quieter than earlier in the year. It was going to take a while to move on from London's worst summer of violence in years. By the end of the year there had been 130 homicides in the city, the most in a decade, within which the largest demographic group killed was men under the age of twenty-four. The majority of murders were stabbings.

My presence at Jacob Sawyer had become more ad hoc as I poured more time into my journalism and other freelance youth-working roles. Tony became preoccupied with fortifying the centre after the summer madness. But I still tried to dedicate at least two hours every week to visiting the centre.

Whenever I visited I still always spoke to Tony first. He had by now welcomed me deeper into his world view. He advised me on my career. He helped me to refine articles I was writing about austerity and youth violence. He enjoyed the chance to voice his assessment of society's failings and ideas for solutions. It was around this time that I came up with the idea of writing a book about my youth work in south London, and I told Tony about it. With his permission, I started to take notes whenever we talked so that I could capture his experiences and advice.

'You need to think about how your writing might affect your youth work. Can you balance both?' he'd ask probingly. 'You've got to keep your feet on the ground, mate. It doesn't matter which newspaper you're writing for. There ain't no such thing as an expert. And if there is, you ain't one of them.' Tony helped me to see my blind spots. We'd become so close that I'd started to view him like my wise uncle (in the Indian sense, a non-blood-related but respected elder). In turn, I think he saw me as a curious nephew he couldn't get rid of.

I'd dropped Carl a text and received no reply. Days later he rang me, agreeing to meet at Jacob Sawyer. I showed up, waited for half an hour, then headed home. No show. He messaged me later apologizing. We arranged to meet the following week. But the same thing happened again. I knew to conceive of this tug of war as a prerequisite for engaging Carl on a one-to-one basis. I was committed to helping him.

'Keep showing him that you'll be there when he needs you to be. This is all part of the test,' Tony advised me. 'I told you when you started: the aim ain't just about coming into their lives for six months. It's to become someone they can always rely on. Someone they can ring when they're in trouble. Five years down the line, when they graduate from uni, *you're* the one they text saying thanks. When they're getting married, they want *you* to be there. That's when the work really shows. Be patient.'

On the third attempt to meet, Carl turned up, and on time. The centre was empty and peaceful. Carl was in the same outfit of thick clothes as when we met the previous month, but he acted differently. He was energetic, talkative and open. He reminded me of his younger self. His prior despondency had morphed into a determination to make use of our meeting. Carl was on a mission to be heard. Words poured out.

'It's mad right now!' Carl conceded, collapsing his arms on the desk. 'My life is like a movie!'

Carl's candour startled me. It was a bold way of entering our meeting. I embraced his enthusiasm. Why was Carl's life like a movie? What did he want 'out' of? I would only get the fullest answers to these questions over the course of the next two years.

Since going to country, Carl spent most of the time hanging out at the bando in Lewisham. It was an easy shot. Even though it was grim inside, recently Carl had been staying over on the sofa and then catching a cab home before taking the train down to college. It was the dirtiest trap house he'd been to. Carl didn't care because he needed the money.

Whenever he did go home Carl's mum kept telling him that her church friends were praying for him. Now when he went with her to Sunday service the pastor was on to him. Carl knew the church people were trying to be helpful, but they were judging him. They didn't know how it felt to have no dad at home, and police and opps to deal with all the time. Carl felt he had no adult who would listen to him. Everyone was telling Carl what they thought he should be doing, but none of them knew what he was going through. Even getting to church was a slip because he had to pass the opp block. Carl couldn't go anywhere without being stressed. At least in the bando he could smoke and make money with other boys like him. They understood him. They were like family.

When Carl arrived at the bando, he walked up the stairs. He had eighteen pebs in his mouth, tucked beneath his tongue. After a few minutes some addicts came in through the door. Carl approached one of his usual shots. Carl knew most of the cats liked him more than the other trappers because he was always nice to them. Sometimes this man stole clothes from JD Sports to give to Carl instead of paying him for drugs.

'Police!' the cat mouthed to Carl, glaring at him.

Carl swallowed the pebs. They went down in one go.

The front door downstairs burst open. Thuds of approaching footsteps pounded up the stairwell. Police burst through the door and tackled Carl to the floor. Two officers climbed on top of him. One of them was pushing Carl's back. The other was grabbing his neck. The officer squeezed his throat. He was trying to stop the pebs going down but it was too late.

'It was only Skittles!' Carl yelled in gasps.

'For fuck's sake!' the officer moaned. They were angry that they didn't find any evidence. They let Carl go.

He hoped the cling film would hold.

He was annoyed that he'd taken another L – £180!

He knew he couldn't keep living like this.

In October 2018 Carl began opening up more. We started meeting every fortnight at Jacob Sawyer. In contrast to the first of our meetings, Carl usually looked drained of energy now, like he wasn't sleeping many hours. He talked about instances of violence he'd witnessed, times he'd been arrested, and admitted to being around lots of drug-dealing. He resented the money-hungry mentality that drove boys like him to do it. He told me more about his family troubles. He said he felt alone.

'Nobody cares about me,' he explained, gazing across the table. 'Nobody listens to me. Why do you think boys like me are involved in all this mad stuff? Risking our lives for the block. Nobody else cares about us, that's why. I have to help myself. I have to do crazy things to stay alive. The more I do them, the less crazy they become. You understand?'

I could see that he was being critical about how far he'd gone into a criminal lifestyle. His emotional intelligence and braveness in opening up was astounding. Something about Jacob Sawyer, something about our rapport after all those sessions in prior years, had laid a foundation for me helping him. I believe to this day that my whole time volunteering at Jacob Sawyer up until that moment had been preparing me for the task of being there for Carl when he needed it most. He gave me permission to use any relevant or concerning information he told me to help Tony come up with a plan for supporting his transition away from the roads.

By December 2018, Carl and I had met five times. Two weeks before Christmas, in our last meeting of the year, he expressed his desire to apply to university. His coach at college had told him that he'd be able to get a football scholarship to study Sports Coaching. I helped Carl write his personal statement. The practice of talking about his passions and achievements, typing them out in a Word document, seemed to boost his self-belief. His confidence zoomed upwards. We were carving in stone Carl's determination for a better future. When we finished the statement he wore a wide smile, and his eyes came to life. The introduction of the personal statement went as follows:

> Throughout my life, playing football, and being coached to play football, has played an extremely important role. In Brixton, South London, where I live, there is a large amount of pressure on boys and young men growing up. The discipline required while playing competitive sport, and the encouragement I have received from the coaches, has inspired me to pursue my own career as a sports coach. I believe by learning the skills of coaching at undergraduate level, this will be an achievable end-goal: one that will allow me to give back to my community and inspire future generations.

As Carl walked up the high street he noticed two Range Rovers parked outside one of the cafes. A group of people dressed in designer clothing were standing around talking. Carl was interested in what they were up to; how they'd got the money to pay for these nice things. One of the men called him over. Carl recognized him to be an older gang member from around Brixton who used to look all lost and bummy. Now he was smart.

'Bro, your name holds weight around here, right?' the man said, recognizing Carl from the few times they'd met in previous years. Carl smiled and nodded. He was gassed that the man knew who he was. The man invited Carl inside for some ice cream. The pair talked about what Carl was up to. The man said he used to be on the roads, too. He knew what it felt to be trapped with nobody helping. He said he was from a church called SPAC Nation where they could help Carl to earn legal money.

Carl listened attentively. He had heard about SPAC and how they were helping boys like him. He'd recently started realizing that more people were trying to help him. It made him feel better about himself. People looked out for him more when he opened up to them about his feelings and experiences. He'd started visiting Jacob Sawyer again and talking to staff there. Carl also spoke to people from a company called Spiral. He'd started visiting Carney's in Battersea once a week to do boxing circuits. He'd got a conditional offer to study at university, and a football scholarship to help pay.

Now this person from SPAC was buying Carl food and offering him a new life. Carl was ready. What did he have to lose? He wanted to start afresh. The man told Carl he'd come and pick him up that evening from his block in one of the cars. He told him to pack a bag.

Carl went home. That evening a Range Rover drove him down to Beckenham, in the suburbs of south-east London. Carl's new home was a six-bedroom mansion with a big garden, where other boys like him lived, too.

12. Flowers Through Concrete
Public Health

Demetri caught the 133 bus from Elephant & Castle and got off on Brixton Road. I'd invited him to come with me to see Tony at Jacob Sawyer for the first time. I asked him to meet me first so we could walk there together. The heaters were on full blast when Tony buzzed us in, leaving a smell of metal in the air. Jacob Sawyer had reopened for the new year after Christmas. The building was empty apart from Tony, a couple of youth workers and a couple of young people lounging on the chairs in the main hall. Staff were still working to regain the trust of local families after the summer.

'The famous Demetri! I've heard a lot about you, sir!' Tony exclaimed. 'What are you up to at the moment?'

Demetri explained that he was spending his gap year relaxing. But I knew he was being humble. He was becoming remarkably productive. He would take the bus to and from Lewisham to work as a shop assistant in retail most days, saving as much money as possible. He'd already looked over his degree reading list and made a note of which modules, books and papers caught his eye. He had also been invited back to Willow to mentor a boy in Year 11. The pair would meet in an empty classroom and Demetri would come up with different critical discussion exercises they could do together.

'Last week we talked about the Butterfly Effect – about how one small action can lead to bare other things. I found a diagram online and printed it off. I wanted my man to think about how, if he avoids answering back to teachers, it will save him a lot of trouble. I'm trying to get him to think differently.'

Three months earlier, I'd interviewed Demetri about people trying to understand and prevent violence. 'I don't feel like people are innately bad. I feel like they act as a result of the situation they are in, and to understand the situation people are in, you have to understand society,' Demetri had said. 'That's why I need to study Sociology.' In November, he'd been interviewed in the *Observer* about the same topic. I'd shown Tony and he'd become intrigued to meet the budding young advocate.

The three of us talked in the staff office for an hour and a half. Tony pressed Demetri like he did me, delivering his questions with his home blend of comedy and intellectual interrogation. Demetri replied with his signature cool confidence. Tony asked Demetri what kept him motivated; what he did to stay out of trouble. They spoke about hailing from Jamaican households, and the impact of religion on their lives.

As we got up to leave Tony shook Demetri's hand. 'You're welcome back here any time.' He looked impressed. 'Where did you find this one? He's gonna go far!' he chuckled to me.

We passed some older boys on our way out. They eyed Demetri. He eyed them back. A couple of them nodded at me and I bid them a good evening. I walked Demetri back to the bus stop. Having tried to persuade him to watch *The Wire* more times than I could count over the years, I'd finally remembered to bring the first season on DVD for him to borrow.

'I know it's going to seem old-fashioned to you, but trust me,' I told him, and he nodded politely.

'My man's proper wise, still,' Demetri said about Tony. The next time the two of them crossed paths would be under very different circumstances.

★

Politicians and parliamentary aides retrospectively describe the first quarter of 2019 as the 'Brexit Wars'. 'Every day it was like we were in the trenches, going over the top to slug it out. You'd be up early, work until ten p.m., then you'd go home, sleep and wake up to go at it again in the morning,' said one MP's researcher. Yet with Theresa May failing to gain support for her deal, it wasn't even clear whether Brexit was going to happen.

It was during this time, late one afternoon in January 2019, that I entered Portcullis House, the large building next to the Houses of Parliament which houses MPs' offices and committee rooms. I waited in the seating area in the main hall, by a row of decorative plants and indoor trees, underneath the grand glass roof. I'd been invited by the APPG on Knife Crime to attend a closed briefing with a Home Office minister, one week before the APPG held a debate in Westminster Hall.

This private, one-hour briefing was an invaluable opportunity for the APPG to ask a government representative questions. Briefings like this only occurred every two to three months. It was a rare chance to see a minister held to account directly on the issue of youth violence. I took a seat at the back of the small committee room. Sarah Jones, a handful of other MPs and Lords, and the Home Office minister took their seats around the large table. Jones introduced the briefing and the minister asked for questions.

One MP raised his hand to suggest that the rise in illicit drug sales was a reason for increased violence. A discussion started, then after a couple of minutes the division bell suddenly rang. MPs had eight minutes to get to the chamber to vote. A television screen read 'Merchant Shipping Law', denoting the vote's subject. After fifteen minutes most but not all contributors had returned. Nearly half the allotted hour of time for the briefing had elapsed. The minister asked for questions again.

'Should we blunt the ends of knives?' asked one MP, performing a downward stabbing motion with his arm.

It sounded like an insensitive joke but I knew it wasn't. The query stemmed from a suggestion circulating among some surgeons and in the media that sharp-tipped knives were mostly unnecessary in the home and should therefore be made less sharp and harder to get hold of. Because a higher rate of stabbings committed with pointed, longer kitchen knives resulted in fatalities, and are harder to treat, the types available should become a focus in policy debates, went the argument. Some commentators had suggested that owners of kitchen knives could have the knives' sharpness ground down by police.

But the idea ignored the complex reasons for why violence happens among teenagers. Young people in the real world – not the sherry-soaked imaginations of society's old and wealthy – are able to order knives to their door at the click of a button. Thousands of websites sell long 'Rambo' knives and serrated, multicoloured 'zombie' knives, designed to be difficult to withdraw from flesh. In other words, if you really want to get hold of a knife, you can, no matter what age you are, and no matter how many kitchen knives might be blunted in your mum's drawer or the local shop. Knives are so low-tech that any ban on them or attempt to blunt them would be extremely easy to bypass for those who feel the normalized need to carry one in secret to protect their lives.

In raising this, I am not suggesting that we should leave the form and economics of knives unpoliced. I am arguing that concerns over these factors are both secondary to the trauma, fear and exclusion of young people, and unrealistic in the grand scheme of things. Such a narrow fetishization of the household instrument was an emblem of how distracted the conversation had become from focusing on the structural failures of the state to care for its citizens, or how unsafe and alone young people were feeling.

'Surely we cannot deprive talented chefs the freedom to have high-quality equipment?' the minister replied. I saw her aide taking rigorous notes and wondered what he was writing.

'What about "drill music"?' another politician asked.

The previous week Skengdo and AM, who were by now international rap stars, had been handed a suspended nine-month prison sentence for performing 'Attempted 1.0': a catchy, haunting UK drill track whose lyrics refer to alleged clashes that had taken place between the pair's Brixton crew, 410, and local rival groups of Harlem Spartans and Moscow17. Videos of the performance were shared by fans on Snapchat and uploaded on to YouTube. On discovering one of the clips, the Met police found the pair guilty of breaching terms of a gang injunction they'd been issued the year before, stopping them from entering Kennington's SE11 postcode and, crucially, performing or broadcasting songs containing references to rival rappers or crews, or recounting 'intrusions on to any other gang or group's perceived territory'.

'When the injunction came through, we read it and realized they were saying that they would potentially send us to jail,' AM told me over the phone. 'It was like . . . woah! When did you guys have time to draft up these documents? It's not just a thing where they stopped us on the road and said "stop doing this". It was premeditated. They gathered together these documents, got it approved and took us to court. It didn't seem real. We didn't really believe they were allowed to do that to people.' Neither twenty-one-year-old rapper even had a criminal record.

I'd been invited to the concert they were being penalized for, at Koko, a music venue in Camden, north-west London. In the midst of the hall's euphoria they made everyone take part in a minute's silence, 'for the brothers who couldn't make it'. It forced the overwhelmingly teenage, ostensibly quite middle-class audience to stop their mosh-pitting and Snapchatting to reflect upon the normalization of violence and imprisonment that drill artists overcome to become successful entertainers. A communal catharsis was brought to the room. Of course, none of this part was reported in the press. Later, the haunting instrumental for 'Attempted 1.0' dropped. AM's deep voice boomed. I can say with certainty that although it drove the crowd wild with excitement, the mere performance of it, in itself, let alone its existence as an uploaded video, did not encourage or cause actual 'gang-related violence' as the police claimed. It documented violence, sure. It represented violence and replicated in song the social relations and common vernacular associated with violence. It communicated the unfortunate realities of violence to a keen audience. But claiming it did anything more was detached speculation.

Sarah Jones pointed out that more than ninety videos had been deleted by YouTube across 2018. She explained that the APPG were working with social media companies to develop ways of monitoring unsafe digital content.

'I certainly wouldn't want my child listening to it!' the minister scoffed.

To launch the meeting's final act, Sarah Jones instructed everyone in the room to refer to the text on the front of a briefing sheet we'd been given. It had details of an amendment to the Offensive Weapons Bill. The government was rolling out a 'Knife Crime Prevention Order', or KCPO, which would be announced the following morning. Much like gang injunctions, CBOs and other tools the police use to limit the freedoms of alleged criminals, the KCPO would impose requirements and restrictions on a person's freedoms, like who they could spend time with and where. It could last between six months and two years, with a breach being punishable with up to two years' imprisonment. It could be applied for anyone aged twelve or over who was 'suspected' of having been in possession of a knife two or more times. In other words, it was clearly targeted at children. The measure's prescriptive, punitive detail was dystopian. The government had let slip yet more evidence of their ideological belief in blaming young individuals for their own disenfranchisement. Human rights and criminal defence lawyers took to Twitter to denounce the KCPO as harsh and pointless.

The briefing sheet expressed the APPG's support, in principle, for the prohibition of young people using the internet to facilitate or encourage violence. This would mean that those proven to be using the internet to achieve violent ends – which, to be clear, is an extremely difficult motivation to prove beyond reasonable doubt – could be banned from using the internet. It was a strict measure, but it was one that at least rested upon a recognition that the internet is a powerful tool whose use should not be a free-for-all, especially for people who are not mature nor stable enough to use it responsibly. I'd come to view social media like a car: it is a technology that is powerful and useful but potentially dangerous. Its autonomous use should require training to demonstrate ability and maturity. If not, people who are incapable of using it safely are most likely to use it irresponsibly; to provoke and be provoked. They are most likely to hurt and get hurt when digital interactions spill into real life as violence. A law therefore limiting young people's demonstrably harmful access to social media technology – rather than, say, their freedom to make music – made sense.

The APPG agreed that restrictions on internet use among young people were a reasonable measure. But the briefing sheet expressed concern 'that the Government's approach is heavy-handed, fails to address the root causes of young people carrying weapons, and is likely to further criminalize and marginalize vulnerable young people'. It argued that 'a two-year maximum prison sentence for a breach of the order is a severe punishment for a young person, and will have lifelong consequences . . . we should not be imposing punitive orders on children as young as twelve'.

Jones referred to the KCPO. The minister listened. Here was the golden opportunity to press the powers that be. But the division bell sounded again and MPs at the table stood up to head to the voting chamber.

Despite the importance of the issue at hand – there had been 285 murders using a knife or sharp instrument across 2018 nationwide, the highest number since the Home Office Homicide Index began in 1946 – the briefing had barely lasted thirty-five minutes. Westminster's ethics were numb and confused, its resources misallocated. Campaigners such as those affiliated with the APPG and the YVC may have been achieving some successes in forcing government ministers to act – London's Violence Reduction Unit was weeks away from opening and the Home Office had launched an 'Early Intervention Youth Fund' for charities combating violence to apply for – but responses to the crisis were largely disparate and knee-jerk, the pots of money inadequate and uncoordinated. Now, the rushed, clunky systems of parliamentary democracy, weighed down by the Brexit Wars, had brushed a potential moment of accountability aside.

Jhemar was enjoying his half-term break from college in Kingston-upon-Thames, where he'd chosen to enrol so that he was far away from Penge. He was heading back to Brixton from his girlfriend's house. He boarded the P5 in Elephant & Castle to ride its winding route through the ends. He sat at the back. There was condensation on the windows. He was writing lyrics on his phone's note-taking app, rhyming them in his head to the instrumentals playing from YouTube into his headphones. He couldn't wait to get home to eat his mum's food.

The bus turned right off Walworth Road, passing Brandon Estate's tall blocks, then Kennington Park, then Myatt's Fields. It headed through Loughborough Junction and came to a stop. The opening doors made Jhemar glance up from his phone. He peered through the misty window at some flashing blue lights. He noticed police tape outside Jacob Sawyer. He went to his contacts list, scrolling down to 'C'.

'Bro, it's looking *peak* at Jacob Sawyer!' Jhemar explained, his voice taut.

'What do you mean?'

'There's hella feds!'

'Where are you?'

'I'm on the P5, on my way home. You should ring Tony.'

I was in bed with a cold. I'd intended to go to Jacob Sawyer to do outreach in preparation for relaunching a weekly group discussion programme. But to avoid passing on my illness, I'd stayed at home. After hanging up Jhemar's call I rang Tony.

'Hi, Ciaran,' he said, picking up.

'Tony, did something happen at Jacob Sawyer?'

'Yeah. There was a murder.'

'Inside?'

'Yeah, mate. They ran in and killed him.'

'Are you okay?'

'I'm a bit shaken up. I'm on my way to the police station. You take care of yourself. We'll chat soon.'

I jumped out of bed, put on some clothes and trainers, and grabbed my keys. I walked to the community centre through the empty streets. My mind was racing. I was trying to visualize what might have happened. I wondered whether Carl or other boys I knew had been there.

When I arrived at the centre, police tape was tied from lamp post to lamp post. A couple of female officers were standing with their hands behind their backs. Two men dressed in blue overalls and face masks were carrying equipment from a large van into the football cage round the back of the community centre – the SOCO team collecting forensic evidence.

I stood still for five minutes, staring ahead. I was paralysed: by my inability to do anything useful and the deluge of dreadful thoughts pouring down my mind's windscreen. As I walked home, thinking about the number of lives that had been frozen in time on the cursed, icy road beneath my Nikes, my phone started buzzing with messages.

One evening in February 2019, two eighteen-year-olds chased a group of boys into the entrance of Jacob Sawyer Community Centre. Before anyone could stop them, they attacked a visitor who was standing by the table tennis table in the main room before fleeing. The incident was captured on CCTV.

When the ambulance arrived, the young man, who was in his early twenties, was suffering from deep stab wounds. He died within an hour. He had been visiting the centre with a friend – in the wrong place at the wrong time.

That night, the centre had been bustling with people. A football tournament was taking place for 5–8-year-olds with coaches from a local team. Mothers and toddlers had been there watching. Helen Hayes MP and Mahamed Hashi, a local councillor and co-founder of Brixton Soup Kitchen, arrived within minutes with chicken and chips for children stranded inside the crime scene. A swinging door had been the only thing separating them from the terror of the main room.

'Hi, Ciaran,' Tony said when I picked up his phone call, one week later. His tone was stern. 'What were you doing on ITV News last week?'

I'd woken up the morning after the murder knowing very few details, but I got up and returned to the community centre for the second time in twelve hours. I was on autopilot, seeking anyone with a relationship to the centre – Tony, staff, young people – with whom I could make sense of the chaotic situation. Caught off guard – feeling guilty that I'd not been there the night before, lost in a daze of figuring out how to help – I agreed to speak to ITV London News. Journalists had been hanging around by the police tape, trying to get someone from the centre to go on camera and be interviewed. I decided it was important for me to steer the media's narrative in a constructive direction. Knowing how the centre's reputation had been affected the previous summer, I sought to defend Jacob Sawyer in the public eye. I hadn't anticipated how my decision to do this was inappropriate.

'When I saw your face I couldn't believe it,' Tony scolded me. 'Why didn't you speak to me first? Some of the mandem didn't like seeing you up there. I've spoken to them. I explained you were just trying to help. But it pissed them off. It looked to them like you were using what happened to get your face out there. You know what I mean?'

'I'm sorry. I hadn't thought of it like that.'

'Nah, you didn't think,' he replied. 'Also, I'd rather you don't write anything about this right now. It's all too fresh. We're trying to batten down the hatches. I'm not saying it can't happen in the future. But until I let you know, it's off the table.'

I'd pitched an article to the *Guardian* arguing for why it was essential Jacob Sawyer stayed open. Like when I'd agreed to go on ITV, I was trying to use my journalism to advocate for the benefit of keeping the centre alive. The article was ready for online publication. I'd rung Tony about it in the preceding days, but had no luck getting through, so I emailed it to him instead. He'd called just in time. It was a second mistake.

Tony had long warned me not to let my youth work and writing compromise one another. But during a moment in which I should have prioritized my relationships at the centre, pausing to respect the tsunami of shock and trauma flooding through Brixton, I'd allowed my writing mind to take charge. I apologized to Tony again. We said the only solemn goodbyes of our friendship.

Over the following weeks, fuller details of the murder broke. The dovetailing politics of blame and recovery spread through Lambeth, via community meetings, email chains, social media shares and media reports. Families and friends mourned. Jacob Sawyer's board and staff figured out how to keep the centre's pulse pumping. The two guilty teenagers, who'd ridden off from the crime scene in a car before attempting to torch it, were found and charged.

I'd stumbled in my role as a community volunteer and, in doing so, learnt when not to speak or write – when simply to think and do. I'd identified a firmer set of ethical boundaries. I'd realized how to reconcile my limits as a youth worker and a journalist, and the dangers of spreading myself too thinly across these roles. I'd reached another life and career juncture along-side people I had come to consider as family; those who were experiencing loss in a way I'd never had to confront before. Like British society waking up to its man-made violence epidemic, and Tony being given no choice but to rethink Jacob Sawyer's future, I knew that I needed to move on with a renewed per-spective; a tighter, more targeted, more patient speed.

After hanging up the call with Tony, I made the decision that I would be most useful going forward, to everyone – Jacob Sawyer's staff and young people, as well as myself – if I stopped and recharged for a few months. I disengaged my brain from thinking about the centre. In any case, I had other responsibilities to attend to. I was writing more journalism to pay my rent. I was delivering regular bouts of youth, education and consult-ancy work for different charities: from those intervening in schools to improve student engagement, to those facilitating music-making on housing estates and those training the next generation of political leaders.

But locally, in Brixton, with Tony's unbreakable guidance – he continued working round the clock, sitting in his office metres from where forensic ink was still marked on the floor – I focused on accompanying Carl into the return leg of his hero's journey.

Brixton youth worker Ben Kahn – who first enrolled Jhemar as a primary school student at IntoUniversity back in 2011 – was watching football at a bar on the Walworth Road. Once the game ended, at a little after 9 p.m., he left with his friends. He spotted Carl and another young man getting stopped and searched on the street. Having worked with Carl before at Jacob Sawyer and at Spiral, a careers education social enterprise which works across Lambeth, he was concerned. He approached the officers and asked what the problem was.

'They explained that the boy who Carl was with was on the gangs matrix, so they'd stopped them because of that. I asked Carl if I could stick around. He said yes. He looked appreciative of my help,' Kahn said. 'They weren't going to let him go and wanted to take both of them to the station.'

The officers took Carl into a small storage cupboard to strip-search him. They made him pull down his trousers and bend over. 'It was three big white men, me and Carl. It was eye-opening, because although I've been a youth worker for over ten years, I've never seen that sort of thing happen first-hand. But what's scary is that for Carl it was totally normalized, being dehumanized and degraded like that. He acted like it was stand-ard. But it really shook me up. Also, it was obvious that the police were pandering towards me because I was a so-called well-spoken, white youth worker. I felt there was a tone change when it emerged that I knew Carl and would be sticking around. The tone initially appeared quite accusatory, but once I was involved, they were intentionally clear about the process and why they "had to" do what they were doing. It definitely felt that they were as much talking to me as they were to Carl, which I found quite strange and unfair. They knew I was watching them. When they didn't find anything they said, "Have a nice day," and we left.'

Rory Bradshaw – with whom I first started volunteering at Jacob Sawyer – was getting ready for an adult boxing session at Carney's community centre in Battersea. Having qualified as a Geography teacher and taken over as Lead Youth Worker at the centre, he was in charge of the evening's activities. Teenagers were hanging around in the dining room, queuing up for their food before eating it on the benches. Rory glanced over the boxing gym and did a double-take, recognizing one of the young men. It was Carl. His hair was long. He was wearing a puffer jacket. He looked scruffy.

'How's it going, Carl!?' Rory said, holding out his hand to greet him. 'Remember me?'

'Oh, hi! Yeah, I do, you know, you used to do those sessions with us at Sawyer!' Carl replied. 'I'm good, thank you, just here trying to work on my fitness for football and that.'

Carl had been going to Carney's since he was younger, just like he'd visited Jacob Sawyer. Rory pointed to a photograph of Carl hanging up on the wall, which showed him when he was fourteen. 'I thought I recognized you up there,' he said.

Carl explained that he originally visited because his auntie lived in Battersea. She used to attend fitness sessions at Carney's and was into her training. She'd encouraged Carl to go but she had since passed away. Carl said she'd always inspired him to take physical fitness seriously.

Carl would continue to attend the same boxing sessions every week. Rory would speak to him and check in on his well-being.

Since starting to work at Carney's, Rory had always

wondered why there were flowers planted in yellow hard hats out the front of the building. He would later find out that they were there to remember Carl's auntie, who'd worked at Battersea Power Station.

During a meeting at Jacob Sawyer, those of us working from different angles with Carl came up with a strategy for keeping an eye on him. We'd heard that he'd gone to live in a SPAC Nation house in the suburbs of south London. SPAC was a church working across the city. They were known to own many large properties where they would house groups of young people looking to escape life on the roads. They would hold outreach meals, drive plush cars around town and organize events in corporate venues to preach to large audiences.

SPAC were clearly successful at enticing boys like Carl from across the country to live in their mansions, out in suburbs like Surbiton, Norwood and Beckenham. But there were lots of questions to be answered about their methods. Where did all their money come from? What right or formal authority did they have to be housing so many vulnerable young people?

SPAC even had their own UK drill group, Hope Dealers, who had garnered millions of views rapping over drill beats but with evangelized lyrics: replacing weapons with Bibles, drugs with Christian principles, and so on. The church appeared in news segments across most major publications and television news channels. Documentaries were made by BBC and Vice. It was impressive but worryingly elusive; apparently positive, negative, popular and bizarre all at once. Ultimately, I was primarily glad to hear that Carl was safe and sound. More information would become known to everyone about the corrupt goings on at SPAC in subsequent months, but the organization had undeniably helped him to get away from what I knew were extreme circumstances in Brixton.

The first time I visited Carl at his SPAC house I travelled with Joel Balkwill, Ben Kahn's Spiral colleague, on the bus. We walked through quiet, residential streets. When we rang the doorbell a young man slightly older than Carl opened the door, welcoming us inside. The rooms were fitted with high-end furniture, but the interior design was plain and sterile. There were three cream sofas in the living room and a clear glass table that hadn't been cleared in the dining area. The rooms were stripped to their bare bones; a blank slate on which people could scribe their life stories afresh. Bibles lay resting on arms of chairs and windowsills.

Joel and I had brought Carl some food and a drink from Morley's chicken shop, a local favourite of many young people, based exclusively but plentifully across south London. We sat outside in the garden, placing our chairs on the uncut grass. A tiny tricycle lay at an angle by the wooden fence. Birds tweeted in the greening trees. Carl spoke calmly compared to our conversations in Jacob Sawyer. He was washed. He'd removed his heavy winter coat. He spoke about Brixton like it was an alternate dimension, a place in his distant past, not somewhere he'd been cutting up drugs and fearing for his life months before.

'Out here, I don't worry about nothing. I just have to wake up early to pray and go to services,' Carl explained. 'They've got me bringing in some of the mandem, too. The more people I bring, the more they like it. There are some other Brixton boys living in a house round the corner.' As a popular young man, Carl was capable of recruiting people for the church. He would later estimate to me that he brought over thirty other young people to SPAC over his four months of living with them. In return, they paid off one of his outstanding police fines. They started to kit him out with new designer clothes; when we met, he was wearing new Dsquared2 jeans and a Moschino T-shirt. 'They're getting me a job in trading so I don't have to shot no more. They told me they'll pay for my driving lessons and let me drive the Range when I pass my test.'

On the one hand, something clearly wasn't right. So many aspects of the SPAC's apparent model of community service were unaccounted for. Carl had packed his bag and left home for good in a random man's car. He was now living with other young people like him – those from places as far away as Birmingham, Beckton and Ilford. He explained that he had his own single bed upstairs, but in one room I'd caught a glimpse of a suite of electric recliner chairs lined up in a row with blankets draped over them, where other boys slept. Carl said he had older pastors who oversaw the house's routine, but I wondered whether they were qualified to have such influence over so many traumatized young people who'd left their original family homes.

By offering Carl money, new clothes, driving lessons and a pending job doing online currency trading, SPAC Nation were using him as a way to recruit more young people from Brixton. The church was targeting influential boys like Carl to gain access to others who were being lost to the system, and thus expand their reach. While Carl explained his weekly pattern – he was still going to college but, instead of heading back to Brixton, he returned to this house, where he would be fed, read the Bible and sleep at an appropriate time – I was struggling to figure out how the set-up was so brazen in its operation.

In the months after this visit, media stories broke about the church's questionable activity. Following a deep investigation by the *Huffington Post*, SPAC were reportedly forcing young people to take out bank loans and then never paying them back. Yet police would decline launching an investigation into the church's practices. SPAC's elusive leader, Pastor Tobi, would still be invited to the Conservative Party Conference in October 2019, where he sat in the second row as the recently crowned Boris Johnson briefed his cheering audience. The Tories even fielded Jayde Edwards, one of SPAC's pastors, in a council by-election in November. Their presence ran all the way up the political food chain.

On the other hand, I could not deny that SPAC had played a containment role in Carl's journey. By removing him from Brixton, they had given him a lifeline. This, combined with the alchemy of different services like Jacob Sawyer, Spiral, Carney's and youth worker Winston Goode from Juvenis, a charity which specializes in working with vulnerable young people (Winston is also a Partner of Chief Inspector Jack Rowlands's custody intervention programme, Divert), was giving him space to navigate these crucial months of his adolescence safely. He had mentors in the house who were helping him. He found it therapeutic to talk about his problems and gain relatable advice from pastors with similar life experiences.

Carl explained that his mum had been upset with him for leaving. It initially placed their relationship under further strain. But over time even she saw his demeanour changing for the better. It was difficult to argue with the present fact that Carl felt much more at peace at SPAC, away from the extreme dangers of his prior lifestyle. I kept thinking to myself that Carl was unrecognizable compared to the shaky young man I'd reconnected with over the previous autumn.

Over the coming weeks Carl became more attentive at college, although he still struggled with completing his BTEC work. He received help from Ben at Spiral with his CV. When he could he still went to Carney's for boxing sessions, where he would talk to Rory. We all fed back to one another and Tony at Jacob Sawyer on Carl's progress.

'For kids like Carl, Jacob Sawyer and Carney's have proven the importance of having a safe space,' Rory said. 'Boys like him have grown up in an environment where they will do what they want to do. But at the point at which they want to change, and

have had enough, when the support is long-term and uncondi-
tional, that is the reason they feel able to come back. A trusting
relationship with that young person has been earned. The open-
door policy of a youth club, which does not give up on or exclude
any young person but works with them through their ups and
downs, is what's needed. You build a relationship over a long
period of time and intensify support when the young person
needs it most and provide them with opportunities when they are
in a place to take them. Change is never a smooth curve and
maybe it never will be. But the fact that I'd met Carl years earlier
at Sawyer and he'd been to Carney's before meant he felt able to
accept support and to engage in the opportunities offered to him.'

Ben Kahn echoed Rory's sentiments: 'Carl is a prime example
of what happens when lots of people invest in a young person. But
even with all the tools we were able to offer, his charm, academic
success and desire to change things, it still took all of us and him
living at SPAC ages to get anywhere. It just goes to show that
youth work is hard and time-consuming and difficult and expensive. But when it works, we can support young people to take
control of their own lives and make positive changes. That is why
the sector is fucked, because everyone is looking for quick fixes and
numbers. But things don't change for young people like Carl by
doing things quickly or as a one-off. There is a massive mismatch
in what funders think works and what it *actually* takes to help young
people to make positive changes in their lives. For young people
like Carl, loads of things have to click together for them to believe
that they matter and can have a positive future. Because they've
been screwed over for so many years, it's going to take some serious
investment for us as a society to deal with the problems we've created and ignored. It's easy to blame a young person, tell them their
situation is due to poor choices they made – a lot easier than dig-
ging into the real reasons why young people struggle, the issues
forced upon them by society. That way we can justify why it is

okay for someone like Carl to walk down the street fearing for his life, but unimaginable for someone like me.'

Kahn also noted the difference between supporting someone like Jhemar compared to other, more lost boys. The difference was that Jhemar had always had people in place to be there when it mattered most. 'Jhemar grew up with support and aspirations. He had big dreams from a young age. He was told he could achieve them.'

I wanted to organize for Carl and Jhemar to meet, so after discussing the idea with Tony and ensuring it was safe to do so, we convened at Brixton tube station on a weekend. We were going on a trip to the theatre. I'd spent the previous few weeks helping an urban music theatre company called HighRise to develop a production about the relationship between violence and UK drill music. I'd invited Demetri and Jhemar along to the workshops I was taking part in so that they could help to develop a show that unpacked the lives behind the masks and balaclavas. It was performed as part of the Sick of the Fringe festival at The Place theatre in Euston, central London.

The scenes that Jhemar, Demetri and I helped to create played out on stage. One involved a comic, rhymed interpretation of the APPG briefing I'd attended, including a comic mockery of knife-blunting as a viable solution to violence. Another showed a school student happily playing with cards at a desk while being bullied by masked avatars; eventually he loses his temper and erupts in a rage.

In the final scene, a young actor called Ore Shoderu delivered a tense monologue describing travelling to a park to discover that his older brother had been stabbed to death. He spoke on resisting the temptation to take revenge. He conceded that he felt it was important to talk about his feelings with his mentor and his parents. Audience members were moved to tears.

After a standing ovation, Jhemar rushed off to find Ore and debrief having witnessed his own story being performed. Carl and I headed through to the drinks reception, where he expressed how much he could relate to the show. He took a selfie clip of himself in the theatre's VIP seating area.

In the spring of 2019, Lib Peck left her role as Lambeth Council Leader to lead the Mayor of London's Violence Reduction Unit (VRU) at City Hall.

'The energy behind it was: what we've been doing to tackle violence hasn't been working,' she said. 'The underpinning principle of the VRU is a partnership approach, bringing in the big public sector organizations – the NHS, Metropolitan Police, education and local authorities – together, but also making the point that unless you work with young people, unless you work with communities and put them at the heart of solutions, then we are not going to succeed . . . I am absolutely passionate about reducing violence and improving safety. But I'm also passionate about changing some of these organizations I have experience of, which too often become too distant from the communities and people they are there to serve. They don't analyse the needs of the people they serve and they can lose the knack of listening.'

The public health approach had finally entered the common vernacular. Lib Peck had been noticing that conversations about serious youth violence at the top level of policy did seem to be moving more in a direction of compassion and collaboration. The London VRU was established in the capital as the first major building block.

'There was something in the air around then: a negative shift, in that violence was centre stage, but also a positive shift. I think people had realized that it was important what opportunities young people are given, it was important they were in school, it was important the way they were interacting with the police, and that achieving that was going to take a long period of time. It was important that the school environment was inclusive for all children and young people, and each child was supported to achieve and learn.'

Seventeen VRUs in other cities and violence hotspots across England and Wales were also launched, collectively receiving £70 million of initial Home Office funding. The Youth Violence Commission would estimate that over the next ten years the total cost of running these VRUs would amount to £350 million – a minuscule amount compared to the calculated £11 billion that violence has cost the taxpayer since 2008, and the estimated further £10 billion that it will cost over the next decade if rates continue. In other words, treating the spread of its disease early makes both moral and financial sense.

The public health approach has been successfully implemented in cities such as Chicago, Boston and Glasgow, albeit in very different contexts and with varying interpretations. Chicago's murder rate has halved in thirty years – there were 929 murders in 1991, and 492 in 2019 – but it remains one of the most infamously violent cities in America. Boston implemented 'Operation Ceasefire' in the mid-1990s, focusing on targeted policing and enabling peacemaking conversations between relatively small, warring groups of men. It famously saw a 50 per cent drop in violent crime over two years. And the VRU in Glasgow, and efforts to curb violence across Scotland more generally, have significantly reduced violence over the last two decades. A United Nations report conducted between 1991 and 2000 found that, excluding murder, Scots were almost three times more likely to become victims of assault than Americans. Glasgow was labelled murder capital of Europe in 2005, and fifteen young people were killed there with knives from 2006 to 2011. In contrast, from April 2011 to April 2016, none were, showing a huge amount of progress had been made. But with a population of just over half a million, it is much smaller than London's nine million people. Glasgow's experience cannot be easily shoehorned into the English capital.

Dr Keir Irwin-Rogers, a lecturer in Criminology at the Open University and academic partner to the Youth Violence Commission, argued that one of the main benefits of applying a public health approach to London 'is that people are encouraged to step away from seeing violence as something that can be addressed solely through a criminal justice and enforcement approach'. However, he provided the caveat that there is a risk of the approach becoming dilute and ineffective at creating systemic change if there is an imbalance between how it is treated by people in political power compared to workers on the front line. 'A holistic public health approach will require a significant and lasting commitment to change at all levels if it is to be effective – of course, it requires front-line practitioners and local communities to mobilize and adapt their ways of working, but equally it depends on those efforts being supported by people and institutions who can influence and drive change at a societal level.'

As she took over the VRU, one of Peck's key aims was to bottle the spirit of how communities come together in the aftermath of a fatally violent incident. 'A lot of the most powerful impressions that were made on me as a leader have been the result of some of those tragedies; looking at the energy behind individuals who turn an entirely negative and horrible experience into something very positive.'

She recalled one incident in the last few months of her Lambeth leadership. 'There was the horror of that on an estate that I knew had been trying to change. I saw how hard everyone was working, and the repercussions for everyone's emotional state after it happened.' But months later, when she returned to the same community as the VRU's leader, she saw how people had used what had happened to drive change. 'A hugely horrible, defining moment had energized the community. I think that is a really powerful phenomenon. It often occurs. I've seen it in plenty of places across London. It is those moments which make you stop and think and see initiatives that come together after an incident as the way forward.'

Jacob Sawyer would remain shut to young members of the public until the end of 2019's summer. The main room's ruined old floor was stripped and replaced with new, speckled linoleum surfacing. Tony worked with the board to form a plan of action for how the space could eventually reopen. A new system for securing the centre, and a strategy for building community presence again, would come into being. There had fortunately been enough support across Lambeth – from politicians, community leaders and local residents – for it to stay open.

The intensity of 2019's first half, and my proximity to the damage and healing that had taken place in my community, inspired me to start writing more deeply about London life from angles that had not been covered in the press. In April I'd started a regular online column for *British GQ* called 'All City', with the remit of reporting on stories from the city's fringes.

The most enlightening and transformative article I wrote as part of this effort was about the perspectives of women and girls on youth violence. Almost all of my journalism over the five years in which events in this book took place has clearly been dominated by male voices. On the one hand this has been inevitable as someone working on and writing about issues disproportionately affecting boys and young men: overpolicing, school exclusions, youth violence, incarceration, UK rap and drill music. On the other, however, I knew it had created a blind spot. What had I missed? Just because young men are the disproportionate perpetrators and victims of violence, was it just, or even useful, that male perspectives and experiences are always those analysed? As I have seen time and again, young women – often young Black women – are the ones who first respond to instances of male violence. Yet the role that women play in potentially solving youth violence has been woefully undervalued. What impact was this having?

'I was about to give up, to be honest. But across 2019, after what happened, we got stronger,' said Ebinehita Iyere, Founder of Milk & Honey, an expressive safe space for girls and young women in Lambeth affected by violence. Participants come together and heal through therapeutic and trauma-informed youth-work practice, peer-to-peer mentoring and group creative activities. 'Suddenly, girls needed support, because the schools around Jacob Sawyer didn't know what to do with them. When violence happens, boys retract, but girls try to be present. They wanted to go to Jacob Sawyer and lay flowers and be in that space. Boys stay away and plot. But for girls, it's a case of: I want to *feel* this person. I need to *feel* this loss and experience this grief.'

Iyere – who is also a therapeutic diversion practitioner for Juvenis, working with Winston Goode – founded Milk & Honey in 2016, following the death of a young person she knew. Her initiative to mobilize around the deaths of community members echoed Lib Peck's observations about some of the most effective learnings and initiatives against violence being those that emanate from great loss and pain, like a vibrant flower growing through smashed concrete.

'There is something about when a young person dies that triggers us as youth workers to either become numb or keep going. So this time, I didn't want to keep going without taking on the learning,' Iyere explained. She had long felt that a woman-led organization was needed to contribute towards wholesome public health and fill the gap of specialist services for young, Black and brown women affected by violence. She was determined to frame women and girls not just as victims of exploitation or abuse, but as community protectors.

'My nickname used to be "counsellor of the block",' Iyere said, proud that her teenage nickname had been reflected in the trajectory of her adult work. Born and raised between Lambeth and Southwark, she was a teenager during the spike of violence in 2007 and 2008. She lost at least two male friends per year to violence, and more to the criminal justice system. Her best friend was killed in 2014. But she was never supported to process her emotions or to understand the hypervigilance she developed afterwards. She started studying therapeutic practice to convert her own life experience into Milk & Honey.

'For every boy who has been affected by violence, there are ten females – sisters, mums, aunties, cousins, girlfriends, friends – who were behind him trying to keep him off the road, or sending him "good morning" texts, or keeping him clothed and fed. Instead of grieving, girls have to wear this armour and protect boys. Girls put out the flowers, girls organize the funerals or memorial services, girls are on the phone to the boys at night when they can't sleep and they're crying because they're so traumatized and they don't want to speak to the mandem about it. In other words, girls are spending more time mobilizing for others than healing themselves. And there is often no service that picks that up unless girls come out and say they've been exploited.'

Iyere would work with several boys and girls affected by violent incidents dotted across 2018 and 2019 in Lambeth. This included primary school children who had been at Jacob Sawyer on the night of the murder and teenagers whose entire social networks were shaken in the aftermath.

'It happened in a place that was supposed to be safe. So the ripple effect of that for people who were there and those who were not there was: this place is not safe. But there is another layer for the siblings, the friends, the families in the community who may have been already going through so much loss and bereavement over the years. Jacob Sawyer was their safe space. And the thing with Jacob Sawyer is, it's far from perfect, but when you step inside you know that you're in a youth-led space, whether it's the yells of people playing football on the pitch, or young men lifting weights in the gym, or some little kids arguing about who's going to get the last bit of food in the kitchen, or the laughter of staff members in the office. Growing up, it always represented that sense of safety. It was that place where you could go and, no matter what, you'd be okay, because there were people there to talk to.'

After the spring of 2019, Iyere was able to gain more momentum behind Milk & Honey as a local initiative and a model to be replicated in other parts of the capital and beyond. She would later be invited to become part of the Violence Reduction Unit Partnership Reference Group under Lib Peck. In 2020 she would be awarded the Young Leaders with Impact Award by the London Community Foundation in recognition of her work advocating for the experiences of young women and girls.

'Unfortunately, Milk & Honey has had to come out of these tragic incidents. But it's meant that going forward we can be there to support the most unheard and most unseen. I'm able to learn both with and for them. The story I want to tell is not one of victimization but of how trauma can be turned into power if it is supported in the right sort of way.'

As spring 2019 transitioned into the summer it felt, for me at least, that the darkest days had come and gone. The same was not true for the broader context of serious youth violence, which continued to head in a bleak direction. By December 2019, 45,627 knife offences would be recorded, 8 per cent higher than 2018, and the highest since records of this nature began in 2010. The homicide rate in London had increased by more than 50 per cent since 2014.

But Demetri would soon be heading to university. He'd first been inspired by the death of someone on his estate and the fall of friends to the habit of knife-carrying. Jhemar's proximity to violence in Brixton and his loss of Michael had led him to advocate for the power of mentoring to solve social exclusion among young people. Carl still had a long way to go but his emotional scars were finally receiving treatment and beginning to heal. He was a true beneficiary of a multi-agency public health approach towards saving young men at risk of violence. He had displayed unimaginable resilience and good faith.

The murder at Jacob Sawyer had galvanized the sense that something had to change. It was a microcosm of community feelings across the city. I came to see what happened as a double-sided coin. On one side was the external context of overwhelming societal breakdown, unavoidable from a service management perspective. The chaotic forces of youth territorialism had, in one moment, grown to be too big, too sharp. I saw Jacob Sawyer among London's serious youth violence epidemic as a tiny island in the middle of a sea storm. Tony had been shouting about the storm's blatant, towering form to anyone who would listen, from visiting police officers after the summer of 2018, to me when I sat in his office to receive his urgent lectures. But even if people were listening, his warnings were ultimately in vain.

Of course, the island metaphor falls short on realizing that sea storms are products of the natural world. They happen no matter what decisions we make. They are not avoidable. Youth violence – abuse, neglect, selfishness – is avoidable. Love and hate, pride and paranoia, are strong feelings, but they can be controlled. Protection and safety can be maximized.

This was the other side of the coin. Internally, within its compromised sanctuary – the only thing in this grand equation it might have control over – Jacob Sawyer should have done better for people under its roof. Whether or not murder could have been prevented is impossible to know. But in the context of London in 2019, a time of national disarray and local restlessness, the security system ought to have been tighter.

It would be naive to suggest that much had changed for the better, as a city and a nation, since 2015. High rates of violence inside and outside of major cities up and down the country had persisted. Brexit remained unresolved. Public services faced a disaster. Doubt and division pumped through society. Public health was waning – even if this shortcoming was being acknowledged more than ever before. Meanwhile austerity remained, perfectly normalized, its original architects-in-office unfussed by the crumbling foundations of their project. Former chancellor George Osborne had become editor of the *Evening Standard* newspaper in March 2017. Appearing on *Newsnight* in October 2018, he defended his decision to inflict austerity on the country and his pledge to cut £12 billion from welfare budgets (while permitting various tax breaks for the rich and protecting state pensions). Speaking to BBC Radio 4's *Today* programme two months later, he denied that 'a lack of money' was a contributing factor towards rising homelessness, after being asked about figures showing child homelessness to have increased by 70 per cent since 2010. Meanwhile, David Cameron retired to his £26,000 garden shed office to write his memoirs, in which he not only defended his time in government, but expressed regret that austerity didn't go far enough:

> My assessment is that we probably didn't cut enough. We could have done more, even more quickly . . . to get Britain back in the black and then get the economy moving. Those who were opposed to austerity were going to be opposed – and pretty hysterically – to whatever we did.

Ultimately, however, a new, brighter, more unified future had become possible. Despite years of cyclical failures, some semblance of progress in the discourse, and in broader attitudes towards young people trapped in lifestyles of criminality and trauma, was detectable. Witnessing those I'd worked closest with progress and win, against all odds, made me see that there could be light at the end of any dark tunnel. I felt more prepared to put learnings, mistakes and triumphs to a greater use. The insights I'd gathered on the ground – from Willow to Jacob Sawyer, from Her Majesty's prisons to the debating chambers of Parliament – would need capturing, melding and upscaling.

The young people whose lives had been cut short in the time since I'd moved to south London could never be forgotten. On the contrary, they would spur my determination to continue working with and mentoring young people suffering from systemic disadvantage. And I'd watched the lives of my three core mentees transform before me. I'd learnt from Tony's faith and unwillingness to give up. It was time to celebrate the spirit and wisdom of these heroes.

Conclusion: Rework How the Road Works

The second time Jhemar and Demetri met at Parliament they made their way alone, meeting me outside Committee Room 16. We went inside to take front-row seats for another event chaired by the APPG on Knife Crime, a collaboration with the APPG on Youth Affairs, about the role of youth services in preventing violence.

Coinciding with the event was the publication of new figures showing that parts of the country in which the worst cuts had been made to youth services were also where the biggest spikes in knife offences had taken place. Councils had cut real-terms spending on youth services by 40 per cent over the previous three years. There had been a 68 per cent increase in knife offences recorded by police in England and Wales over a similar period (from 25,516 in the year ending March 2014 to 42,790 in the year ending September 2018). But, crucially, the top four worst-hit local authorities in terms of cuts to youth services were City of Wolverhampton (91 per cent), City of Westminster (91 per cent), Cambridgeshire County Council (88 per cent) and Wokingham Borough Council (81 per cent). Police forces serving these areas had in turn reported the highest knife crime increases. Since 2013/14 there had been an 87 per cent increase in knife crime offences according to West Midlands Police, a 47 per cent rise in London according to the Met, a 95 per cent increase for Cambridgeshire Police and a 99 per cent increase for Thames Valley Police.

Arguments about the need to reverse cuts to youth services could now be made with substantive evidence. The news of the findings was reported in newspapers, but the front pages were given over to the announcement of the birth of Prince Harry and Meghan Markle's son, Archie Harrison Mountbatten-Windsor, the day before.

Politicians, youth sector leaders, front-line workers and groups of teenagers were dotted around the committee room. One of the six panel seats in the middle, arranged in a horseshoe, was empty. The name-card revealed that it was meant for Tony. Sure enough, within a few seconds of the room quietening and Sarah Jones giving an introduction, a tall oak door in the corner opened. Tony slid in, wearing a grey long-sleeved shirt over grey jeans. He crept carefully through the crowds of people who'd failed to get a chair. He passed Jhemar, Demetri and me, and looked up, his eyes sparkling with fond familiarity, his fist held out so we could spud him. He took his seat with glances and nods around the panel.

Jones announced three questions that would structure the session.

In response to the first – 'What do young people want from youth services?' – a video of the south-east London singer Ray BLK was played on a television screen. She explained the importance of having a youth club in which to spend time as a teenager. She was followed by Sephora Ochou, the Parliamentary Ambassador for the British Youth Council, who made the case for having safe spaces for young people to spend time away from potentially stressful home and school environments.

In response to the second question – 'What does effective youth work look like?' – Leigh Middleton, CEO of the National Youth Agency, talked about the lack of properly trained youth workers. Mervyn Kaye, CEO of Youth First, an independent youth service for the London borough of Lewisham, explained the value of a voluntary relationship that a young person can form with a trusted youth worker. He lamented that so many youth workers quit their jobs because the pay was insufficient to live in a city as expensive as London. He recommended offering

competitive salaries to attract people to the profession, and recommended paying youth workers more.

In response to the third question – 'What role do youth services have?' – Dr Michael Whelan, a senior lecturer in Childhood
and Youth Studies at Coventry University, advocated for a
detached, street-based model for engaging with hard-to-reach
teenagers – what criminologist Craig Pinkney calls 'on-road'
youth work. This involves youth workers engaging with young
people in their communities, literally on the roads, away from
formal services, in more chaotic, less controlled settings than in
a classroom or youth club. It is a response to the reality that in
contemporary Britain, with fewer safe spaces for young people,
there is an urgent need to enter places where social exclusion
and violence is most likely to manifest.

Tony closed the expert speeches.

'If you're a young person and every day you wake up and you
think you're at the bottom of the pile, and you live in a society
which is violent and which tells you not to worry about anyone
else, but to just focus on yourself, it's going to take a lot to get
you to change your lifestyle. So this work has to be innovative.
It's not going to be for everyone, but it needs people who are
prepared to do a 24/7 job; who are going to stick around for
more than the two years it takes to really get to know someone;
who will take a call in the middle of the night for a young person. And that means paying youth workers properly, making
youth work feel like a high-standard profession, getting rid of
egos and professional snobbery. And it's not just about getting
ex-gang members in to do work. It's also about having other
ingredients to bake the cake; other people and professions who
can expose young people to new things.'

When the briefing finished, Jhemar, Demetri and I embraced
Tony, then made our way through Parliament to the exit.

'Ciaran, I beg we go munch some curry! We haven't been in

time!?' Jhemar looked at me with desperate excitement. He nudged Demetri for support, knowing he'd caught me in my weak spot.

'Today was different,' explained Demetri as we took our seats at Dawaat in Tooting after catching the tube down. 'Seeing man like Tony doing bits was hard, too, still. Things like today did give me confidence that progress is poss—'

'Oi, bro, what's that ting we got last time? That plate of meat that sizzles?' Jhemar suddenly enquired.

'A tandoori mixed grill?' I replied.

'Fam, you don't understand, it's peng!' Jhemar exclaimed to Demetri, who sat frowning, one eyebrow raised in a scold for the interruption. But by the time we'd finished, Jhemar and I had successfully inducted him, too, into my lifelong ritual of feasting on Punjabi food at milestones of achievement.

The week Carl moved back to Brixton I bumped into him while walking home from Jacob Sawyer. He looked like any person who has just finished college and turned eighteen should look: youthfully energetic, hungry to take on the world, endearingly self-conscious.

'I'm living with my mum again, which is okay, you know. I do things to show her I'm making an effort. I help with things around the home. I clean the flat and pay for groceries,' he explained. He'd started working for a hospitality agency, which would place him at different events across London to plate-wait. He'd lived in Beckenham for just shy of four months before moving out of the SPAC house, but he remained in contact with mentors at the church.

We kept in touch over the phone, speaking every other week to catch up. He called me a few times when he had an argument with his mum or brother, and we would talk it through to come up with a plan for how to resolve it. I kept Tony up to date on our meetings and conversations, and liaised with Ben and Rory about their interactions with him at Spiral and Carney's. In the autumn Carl and I met for tea several times at the Black Cultural Archives cafe. He would tell me more details about his prior life on the roads. He opened up more about the violence he'd seen and his resentment towards adults in his life. His relationship with his dad had improved since Carl had made an effort to contact him, but he said he still found it hard to trust him. I tried to give Carl space to talk through his ongoing battle with transitioning back into living in Brixton while avoiding temptation and harm.

When I later told him I was writing a book about my youth work, featuring Jhemar, Demetri and Tony, Carl said he was keen to fill its pages with tales of his recovery. Like the others, he seemed to find it therapeutic to make sense of his experiences and then have them written down and read out loud back to him; to be listened to. 'If I can help other boys like me, then I don't mind,' he reasoned. So at the start of 2020 we began planning how to weave his story into these pages.

Carl was insistent that he would never carry a knife again. He was fascinated with marking out this line in the ethical sand. It was a symbol of having crossed the threshold from the depths of the unknown back into the ordinary. 'I don't care if a paigon tries it,' he said. 'I'm tired of carrying a shank. I'm tired of being arrested.' Occasionally Carl would carry the plastic end to his mum's hoover in his jacket pocket so that he could use it as a weapon to defend himself if he got attacked, but also so that he couldn't be accused of carrying anything illegal if he was stopped and searched. Once, when I walked with him down Brixton high street, he stayed as close as possible to the shopfronts on our left so that, as he explained, 'If I buck one of my opps I can run inside to safety, or grab a mop or something to fight back.'

Carl estimated that he'd been in roughly ten situations that could have killed him in his life – from being lunged at with long knives to being rushed by groups of opps, and even shot at. He kept a log of them in dated photos and videos on his Snapchat account. Occasionally he'd show them to me and shake his head in disbelief. 'These remind me how far I've come,' he said. 'I shouldn't be alive. Yet here I am. So I know that God is watching over me.' He spoke more and more about religion as an organizing framework. He was going to church again with his mum, where he'd been given books about Christian ethics, which he'd started to read every morning.

But it was physical exercise that took up most of Carl's time. By the end of 2019 he was sneaking into the local gym every day to train, and he still visited Carney's in Battersea for adult boxing sessions. Rory organized for Carl to start a gym instructor course. At the end of 2019 he joined a local athletics club and signed up to a 5km Park Run in Crystal Palace, in south London, where hundreds of people would gather to take part in a timed race. At the sound of the starting pistol Carl ran as fast as he could. People were cheering him on, even though they didn't know him. After he crossed the finish line he caught the bus home. On his journey he received an email notifying him that he'd come 15th out of 500 people – the fastest teenager.

When Carl got home he told his mum the news. She recalled how she used to run when she was growing up, with her sister, Carl's auntie, the one who'd been a regular at Carney's. Carl's mum told him that the two of them used to win all their races as teenagers. She told Carl that his auntie would be proud of him and that running was in their Kenyan blood. They started to dream of him training to compete in the Olympics one day.

In June 2019 I attended an exhibition by Russian artist Andrei Molodkin at the palatial Saatchi Gallery in Sloane Square, central London. Molodkin had worked with Skengdo & AM to create a sculpture spelling out their lyrics in block capitals while filling them with human blood donated by visitors. It was a provocative comment on state censorship.

'It shows that we're levelling up. Before, they never would have had us in a place like this, no chance!' Skengdo told me after we greeted one another in the gallery entrance.

'I feel privileged to be here and to be a part of history,' said AM. 'Drill is heavily misunderstood. This shows people actively taking a step to try and understand it a bit more.'

One week later, the pair were invited by Labour MP Diane Abbott to talk beside UK rap stars Krept & Konan in Parliament about musical censorship and the need to invest properly in London's disadvantaged communities. The genre of UK drill and its artists still faced widespread demonization. But its most successful proponents had come a long way.

Around this time I co-founded a charity called RoadWorks with my friend Mehryar 'Reveal' Golestani, a veteran UK hip-hop MC and ethnomusicologist. RoadWorks was our attempt to fuse together many of the practical learnings gathered in the stories of this book: working directly with at-risk teenagers on their terms, battling systemic disadvantage in education and criminal justice, harnessing technological change, exploring home-grown rap and the music industry to empower and upskill young fans.

Over the summer holidays of 2019, we delivered a week-long music education course with a twist. It was made of three strands. One strand was academic: we used discussions about London music culture to explore formal subjects like History, Sociology, Philosophy and Politics. The second strand would provide participants with transferable career skills like marketing, artist management and performance, with guest visits from industry experts. For the third strand we took a trip to the Digital Holdings in Lewisham, the studio otherwise known as

'Switzerland' due to its reputation for being a safe space for rappers, run by Brixton veteran and UK music industry mogul Corey Johnson. We spent two afternoons there while the boys wrote tracks – Jhemar, Demetri and various students I'd worked with at Willow attended. After they recorded a RoadWorks anthem at the studio – a social commentary on coping with the harsh realities of south London – we organized a professional music video shoot. They donned high-vis jackets and hard hats and climbed on a small cherry picker parked in a construction site to film in the pouring rain.

Demetri rapped the song's first verse:

> Protect what you love, do it with a kitchen.
> Guvs do it too, using the system.

Jhemar rapped the chorus:

> Talk about the roads
> You ain't really from the roads
> So how you gonna know how the road works?
> More than diversions, road blocks
> Really tryna rework how the road works
> Too many have to deal with the road hurt
> And the realest know that the road burns
> All them man know is hold work
> Ask them man, they'll tell you that road earns.

Weeks before Jhemar started his second year at sixth-form college, he and I attended a residential weekend led by a charity called Through Unity. The organization specialized in supporting people who had lost family members to homicide. It consisted of group coaching discussions combined with team-building activities like climbing and archery, set in the grounds of an old country estate, Woodrow High House, a seventeenth-century manor in the Chilterns. It gave Jhemar a chance to connect with other people who'd experienced fatal loss with similar abruptness, away from the noise of London.

A few weeks later he was asked to perform at a show by Franklyn Addo, a youth worker, writer and rapper. Franklyn and I had worked together at The Access Project, after which he went on to work in hospitals for Redthread, caseworking young victims of violence. He'd also attended discussion sessions with boys at Willow and Jacob Sawyer. Franklyn was performing songs from his new *Archives* EP in Hoxton, east London.

After being invited up on stage, Jhemar gave a speech: 'When I reflect on how everything took place, it's weird, because you know how they say everything happens for a reason? I wouldn't say what happened, happened for a reason. But it might have been a bit purposeful.' He thanked his parents, who were standing in the audience with his younger brother, Jerome, for raising him right. Then he reflected on the first time we met. 'It's mad because it's, like, even when I first met Ciaran, I was still at secondary school, I wasn't really in on the whole trusting teachers ting! But, obviously, the way he came about it, I didn't take it like that. So he's like a brother to me now, you get it? We used to have this book called the "Book of Wisdom", and every time we met each other we'd write down some metaphors and just, like, go into lyrics and break them down. We'd figure out the correct words and stuff. And it helped me a lot.'

In that moment I realized that mentoring Jhemar had allowed me to discover what I was good at and passionate about; to learn the value of volunteering and the relationships that can be forged through it. He'd helped me to apply academic interests to social endeavours. Without Jhemar's charm, openness and collaborative spirit, this book would not exist. The benefits of our rapport were, like all good mentoring dialogues, reciprocal.

'There is always hope to do better for other people. That's why I started mentoring people myself,' Jhemar continued. 'Really and truly, people don't recognize the power of conversation. And if you are looking to get involved in youth work then please do, because I'm telling you, having a mentor was a life-changer to man! It was mad! When I reflect on things, it's like, woah! What could I have been doing now? I may not even be here now, you get it? So please do speak to the young people around you. Trust me, you can make a difference.'

On 2 November 2019, as fireworks exploded in the windy night sky above, I joined Jhemar's extended family at a memorial event for Michael in Betts Park. We gathered near the shrine of flowers and candles standing in the middle of the grass, where a painted white wooden stick remained hammered into the soil, supporting a sign offering a £20,000 reward for information about Michael's death (for which, at the time of writing, nobody has been convicted).

Michael Senior brought a microphone and sound system. As he spoke, the speaker's bass boomed across the park. His voice could be heard by the people living on its fringes – those belonging to the same local community as Michael when he'd been alive, as well as some of his alleged killers.

'We have an environment we have to keep safe for people. The thing about this now is that when tragic things like this happen in the community, for us to keep the community safe, we have to take action. If you share information about Michael's death it doesn't make you a snitch. It shows you are someone who is concerned about people's well-being, concerned about people in the community and concerned about being a respectful person. We keep hoping that one day we will get a victory in some way. The victory is there to be won. It's coming. Everything takes time. But it's coming. Only then will the work stop. Until I die, I won't give up.'

On the morning before the launch of RoadWorks, Demetri had been at 10 Downing Street delivering a letter making recommendations for how to curb youth violence. He'd been invited by Sarah Jones.

'Today I hope the Prime Minister sees the letter and stops throwing money at things that are ineffective,' he told Sky News, live on national television. 'I feel like the government's been doing the same thing from day dot, and it's obviously not working. They can see it's not working . . . I think they need to relook at it and start afresh.'

Two months later, he started university at Goldsmiths. He found the new environment refreshingly free compared to Willow. He knew the school had served him well, but he was glad to have left.

At Willow, Monica continued to work tirelessly for her students, as she had done for the best part of two decades. She invited me in to deliver careers workshops a couple of times, where I was able to catch up with some of the boys I'd worked with in my discussion groups. Many of the 150-or-so young people I worked with across London for The Access Project went on to study at competitive universities. Some have graduated and entered the world of work; others have returned to TAP or their secondary schools to mentor younger students.

One of Demetri's modules at Goldsmiths was called 'Modern Knowledge, Modern Power'. The course description said it was focused on the 'sociological imagination'; the 'relations between individuals and groups in modern industrial societies' and the study 'of classical and contemporary accounts of social power, identity and inequality'.

In one seminar about 'cultural capital' – the social assets held by a person which allow them to navigate between groups, classes and cultures – the lecturer played a video from YouTube. Demetri recognized it to be from *The Wire*. It showed the character of Bunny, an ex-cop who'd been running extra sessions for young people at an inner-city Baltimore high school, taking three of his students for dinner at a plush steak house. There is no doubt that watching this scene as an undergraduate student myself in 2009 must have planted the seed for the idea of taking Jacob Sawyer boys on a trip to The Botanist years later.

When the clip finished, the tutor asked if anyone knew where it was taken from. Nobody else did, so Demetri raised his hand to answer.

Jacob Sawyer Community Centre reopened for local young people in September 2019, one month before one of the young men who had committed the murder inside the centre was found guilty and sentenced to a minimum of eighteen years in prison. Its entrance was fitted with two bulletproof glass doors. A new regime of safety had now become enforced. Attendance records for all visitors, young and old, were taken more strictly without fail. New registration forms were distributed and strictly collected. Procedures for opening and closing became tighter.

Tony received consultancy support to help him focus on managing the service, rather than being its front line. He started meeting with local charitable partners who could help breathe fresh life into the centre's historic, revitalized space. I relaunched my weekly evening discussion group for under-sixteens at the start of the academic year in September 2019. The new cohort were just like Carl and his friends had been years before: excitable, unruly, but creative and wise beyond their years. After our sessions the boys would head to record bars in the music studio or out to the football pitch at the back to play a pick-up game.

I'd get asked to go in goal, which, given the approaching wintry months, I wasn't particularly pleased about.

Towards the end of the year Tony suffered multiple heart attacks. He survived, just. He'd nearly given his life to Jacob Sawyer. He was hospitalized for several months. Losing his guiding presence at the centre and his voice at the end of a phone line during this time affected me deeply. It became yet another wake-up call for me to slow down. 'Don't burn out, son,' he'd always told me in our catch-ups, warning me against trying to do too many things at once, 'because if that happens, you'll be no good to anyone.'

Over the course of this book, invisible forces have been at play for forgotten teenagers in the English capital city: the pain and trauma of an unstable home; the short-term temptation of making quick money; the survivalism of trying to live to the end of the day without carrying a knife, coming into contact with opps or seeking revenge for past humiliations; the rational distractions of gaining validation and influence online; the resonant tug of hyperlocal music culture; the shameful awareness of being publicly labelled a failure, and more. These have pushed and pulled the most disenfranchised boys and young men away from the comforts of normality. Meanwhile, the state has not only failed to intervene, but has actively dismantled the systems of support that might, if they were funded and respected properly, give everyone a fair start in life. This story has been a tale of two cities, in which I have tried to show how inequality, not only between different classes and races but within precise demographics, makes following the rules easier for some and harder for others.

In Chapters 1–3, I introduced you to Jhemar, Tony, Carl and Demetri alongside my arrival in south London, where most of my interactions with these characters have taken place, between Brixton and Elephant & Castle.

In Chapters 4–11, while moving in and out of the developing lives of these four heroes and my evolving career, I have profiled contemporary life in London. I have ultimately tried to prove how systemically harmed young people are being overwhelmed by forces that are beyond their individual control. Some of these forces are new and insidious; they exist in computer-data systems, glossy advertising campaigns and violent Snapchat videos. But in the way they reinforce socio-economic inequality, their fundamentals are as old, dense and creaky as this ancient city and the global empire it once commanded.

Chapter 4 looked at the heavy-handed institutional racism of the Metropolitan Police, and argued that while officers on the front line have a tough gig, the mismanagement of this service and its resources has made it more difficult to develop meaningful community relations.

Chapter 5 showed how the British education system is serving some young people well but failing others who do not fit its marketized model. I argued that academy schools need to be doing more to remember the complex lives of students their performance data represent, before it is too late. They can do this by providing more opportunities to talk, collaborate and feel a sense of belonging to those at risk of harm.

In Chapter 6 I tracked how the takeover of social media technology has impacted young people and generated resulting shifts in cultural expression. I suggested that we need to be developing robust digital solutions to child disenfranchisement, including providing avenues for the most excluded teenagers to thrive and receive constructive validation. I also argued that poor behaviour in schools should be taken much more seriously as a signal of unmet needs and that this insight ought to be absorbed into inclusion initiatives, rather than schools turning to permanent exclusion as a stick to enforce conformity.

Chapter 7 showed how, without efforts by those moving into regenerating areas in cities to forge better community relationships, gentrification is displacing and devaluing long-standing communities. What should be 'affordable' housing has become too expensive, and instead of caving to profiteering developers, councils ought to be advocating more for their citizens.

In Chapter 8 I argued that 'knife crime' as a term has become loaded, simplistic and racially prejudiced, reflecting how the strained British media landscape has driven a wedge between the complex realities of violence on the ground and how it is reported in the news. Storytelling about young victims and perpetrators ought to be nuanced and responsible, seeking compassionate progress, not clicks.

By highlighting the full extent of austerity politics over the 2010s in Chapter 9, I showed how the state has failed poor young people. But by exposing young people to environments they perceive as elitist, for example by taking them to advocate in Parliament, I proved that barriers can be broken down and genuine policy change achieved.

Chapter 10 showed how the criminal justice system is trapping particular groups of vulnerable, excluded young people, and then failing to rehabilitate them. I argued that prisons, and other attempts to limit the freedoms of young people, are used too much to stem what is ultimately a series of public health failures. What's more, I maintained that creative expression in the form of music genres such as UK drill music is not to blame for youth violence – it is a reflection of and distraction from deeper, messier issues, and an extension of uncontrolled technological and social change.

Having profiled Jacob Sawyer as a crucial space for local young people in Brixton, I argued in Chapter 11 that the closing down of youth services since 2010 has had a catastrophic impact on the safety of public life in the capital and beyond, and reduced our capacity to learn from the experience and wisdom of professionals like Tony. As a result of the dismantling of central government funding, a culture of relying on private funding has sunk into the third sector, letting the state off the hook for failing to look after its citizens.

Chapter 12 presented a public health approach towards combating youth violence as a practical, trauma-informed philosophy in which all areas of civic life and state support are considered as essential and cooperative. To help the individual, the collective need to be responsible.

Throughout *Cut Short*, I have aimed to capture instances of *loss* – loss of life, faith, security and common ground – and analysed the impact on people and society. But through the interwoven journeys of the four heroes, I have tried to prove that loss can be learnt from, overcome and converted into *hope*.

Jhemar converted his pain into action and found creativity in his raps. Carl's survival instinct kept him alive; now it fuels his athleticism. Demetri's daringness to question what is right and wrong led him into competitive undergraduate study. May their journeys present a blueprint for what is possible. And may Tony's seasoned authority, passion and humility – ingredients forged by the unforgiving heat of inner-city pressure – be bottled here and stored on shelves for ever.

In February 2020, Jacob Sawyer held a 'Celebration of Life' event. Young and old attended to show their respects and signal support for a new era. Hearty plates of Caribbean food were served; young children had their faces painted in bright colours; locals set up small stalls selling soap, taking printable portrait photographs and advertising charitable services.

'It was the turning point to bring back hope,' said Pastor

Lorraine Jones, a local community leader. Pastor Jones founded Dwaynamics, a boxing gym tucked in the brick arches of Loughborough Junction's overground train line, after the murder of her beloved son Dwayne in 2014: 'It showed that the heart of the community spirit was not destroyed. It was like we held a blazing torch in the air.'

Pastor Jones led a memorial walk through the streets. I joined her small group, which included Miranda and Amanda Elie – the mother and auntie of Jerrell, who had been killed shortly before I moved into the area in 2015 – as we passed different spots on the local pavements to say prayers.

When we arrived back at the centre, chairs were set up in the sports hall so that visitors could take their seats for a small ceremony. A saxophonist performed. Helen Hayes MP gave a speech. Two young men performed a rap. Another spoke to the room about the importance of Jacob Sawyer in his life. 'Jacob is where we go to feel safe,' he said.

From my first visit to the centre I'd committed to bringing value to my new community. By engaging with hundreds of community members, I'd gained a strong sense of how interconnectivity and belonging can be nurtured in life-changing ways.

My volunteering and youth work experience in south London is my way of creating evidence that progress in this apparently mad, furious city is possible. British society is deeply unequal. It has been and remains run by and for the few, not the many. And from what I can tell, people seem to know this. Yet instead of looking outward into the world to get through catastrophes together, the decimation of public services and Brexit have proven that we would rather trust Eton-educated, Bullingdon Club card-carrying career politicians to lead us into social breakdown and isolation on the world stage. But even if everyone recognizes these bizarre symbols of moral failure, crises of bumbling masculinity and marketeering illusion, do we all *feel* them? Are we moved enough to get out of our armchairs and act? I don't think so. Not yet, or we wouldn't be here.

Young people are losing their lives at unprecedented rates. But it doesn't need to be this way. We can make society fairer and we can all gain from opening ourselves up to people from our different tribes. In fact, to battle the polarization facing the United Kingdom and the rest of the world as we enter the 2020s, to have any chance of surviving, we have to. Despite the forces of neoliberal individualism, despite the accepted truth that people – not their circumstances or the powerful who design them – are to blame, despite the threats posed by ongoing catastrophes like the Covid pandemic or climate change, a small switch in attitudes is where we could start to make a difference.

Maybe you feel like you are already doing enough to make society, as well as your place in it, better off. Maybe you fall into the category of someone who is at a disadvantage and needs the input of those who enjoy privileges. I appreciate you coming on this journey with me. Seeing as you're still here, let me ask you some questions.

Are you in a position to help someone less fortunate than you – someone poorer, younger, less confident, less mobile, physically and socially – without expecting something financial in return? Have you dreamt of achieving social and moral progress but let it remain a dream, after becoming distracted or convincing yourself it isn't possible? Are you tempted by volunteering for a local cause? Do you seek a greater connection with people that internet technology alone cannot fulfil? If your answer is yes to any of these questions, why not take a bold leap of faith? What is stopping you? Seek to remove what is stopping you: build a pot of savings, start exercising, read a new genre of book, talk to a stranger on the street, rediscover what drives you fundamentally. Then leap.

Start with something small. Walk into your local community centre, youth club, old people's home, homeless shelter or food bank. Do so with an open mind. Drop your defences. See what happens.

Epilogue

I was roughly halfway through writing the first draft of *Cut Short* when, on Thursday 12 March 2020, Prime Minister Boris Johnson addressed the nation via live television broadcast to speak on the Covid-19 virus. He called it 'the worst public health crisis for a generation' and conceded that 'many more families are going to lose loved ones before their time'. He stressed the need to 'look out for each other and commit whole-heartedly to a full national effort'. Eleven days later, on Wednesday 23 March, with coronavirus cases and deaths rising, and fears for our strained National Health Service becoming more frantic, he announced a lockdown, plunging the British population into quarantine, arguably too late. Tens of people had been dying every day, but soon this number entered the hundreds. By April it was at four figures.

I'd spent half a decade trying to understand the rampant epidemic of serious youth violence in London, and now a different disease had arrived. Only this one, a pandemic, transcendental in scale and unfathomable in impact, was global. It ruled all: a discursive dictator commanding every corner of the human universe. Over the opening months of the new decade, the crisis prompted a state of emergency whose alarms were heard by everyone, from those reading newspaper headlines to those sharing and arguing in social media frenzies, and to others receiving erratic government guidelines disseminated over mass email, letter and text message. There could have been few people across the UK, indeed the world, who were not tuned in to the behemoth of the coronavirus. It felt like it had descended from another planet; a biological mothership floating in our collective imagination's blackening skies. We could never have seen it coming.

Or could we? This question bothered me deeply while I wrote these pages in lockdown.

Across 2020 the concept of public health that generations of front-line workers and campaigners against austerity have long sought to protect took centre-stage. But only because it had to. When Boris Johnson – and by extension his Conservative government and the wider parliamentary political system – suddenly spoke those two words in every speech, 'public health', it was by necessity, not choice. Representatives from Public Health England stood on the podiums beside Johnson and Matt Hancock, the exhausted, baggy-eyed Health Secretary who'd inherited a poisoned chalice. Johnson even caught the virus and went to hospital. He was rumoured to have nearly died. *This* is what it took. These panicked, in-the-moment signals made our guardians suddenly care about the masses. They needed us – bus drivers like Jhemar's dad, carers like Jhemar's mum, NHS receptionists like Carl's mum, teachers like Monica, school nurses like my mum, doctors like my dad – to save lives. A continuum of research papers, expert witnesses, front-line worker testimonies, newspaper columns and debates over years about the health service being at 'breaking point', or schools being in crisis, or the care sector being woefully undervalued, had not been enough. Ed Miliband and Jeremy Corbyn were not enough. Poor children killing poor children has never been enough.

Nobody could have predicted a pandemic emanating from the food markets of Wuhan, China (although many scientists have long warned of a coronavirus). But in the treatment of British society's least valuable people since 2010, and long before, there had been symbols, statistics, languages, sounds and trends that *could* have predicted that our proud, wealthy country is not

functioning properly. The system is rigged. For teenagers who
have come to see it as normal that people in their communities
are murdered, the 'public health crisis for a generation' has *been*
happening. It's all very well applying a 'public health approach'
towards the decades-old problem of knife and gun violence.
Clearly, as I explained in Chapter 12, I believe in this framing.
But our government has been allowed to do as they please under
the guise of old-boy decency and market efficiency, and thus
has already destroyed the institutions we needed to achieve
public health. If it was a 'national effort' after Covid-19 hit, then
why wasn't it a 'national effort' before?

Public health is not a possibility when the NHS has been
starved of money and its arms and legs have been snapped off and
shipped out to private companies who chase numbers, not heart
rates; pound signs, not acts of empathy. It is not a possibility
when the maintenance of social housing estates like Grenfell
Tower is overseen by people incentivized to save money first and
worry about human life second. It is not a possibility when public
services across the board have been deliberately shrunk and the
market's invisible hand has been given the robotic freedom to
grab at what it wants. It is not a possibility when socio-economic
inequality has been not only permitted but actively pursued as an
implicit policy position under neoliberal capitalism. It is not a
possibility when power, individualism and greed are values taught
in our schools above all else, encouraged in our advertisements
and incentivized in our conception of land ownership. Public
health is not possible if shared experience, collaboration and
community – a capacity for generating value whose currency is
attached to more than money, materialism and trauma-insensitive
data metrics – are all drowned out. In the rush to survive, under
starker conditions, public health becomes totally impossible.

Many commentators, including members of the Cabinet,
tried to argue throughout its takeover that the coronavirus

'doesn't discriminate'. But this was a treacherous attempt by those who benefit from the status quo to create faux solidarity and buy themselves the clean comfort of time. Their rationale is as shallow as someone saying that rain does not discriminate between those with and those without umbrellas in a storm. Yes, the natural world, be it disease or precipitation, is a neutral entity. It cannot be ascribed moral blame. But the human-made world is not neutral. Its architects can be ascribed moral blame. One's ability to stay dry and comfortable while standing in the rain is contingent on the availability of an umbrella. It is our access to security in the face of a storm, or lack thereof, that discriminates. Our access to social security is the responsibility of the state, and our collective participation in it. Umbrellas can be distributed, and shared.

On 25 May 2020, an African-American man called George Floyd was killed by police in the city of Minneapolis. A video clip depicting his murder, in which officer David Chauvin knelt on his neck for eight minutes and 46 seconds while his colleagues watched and Floyd pleaded, was circulated on social media. Within days, protests started in hundreds of cities across America, then the world. The tension created by the coronavirus – its disproportionate effect on ethnic minorities in the US and the UK, and the enhanced magnification and shareability of viral content due to lockdown – created fertile ground for mass outrage. George Floyd, alongside victims of other high-profile racist killings from earlier in the year, such as twenty-five-year-old Ahmaud Arbery in February and twenty-six-year-old Breonna Taylor in March, became global symbols of racial inequality and police brutality.

Protests across cities in England followed, organized by those who could relate to the American experiences of unjust policing and our governments' mutual mishandling of the virus (the US and UK had two of the highest cases-per-capita in the world). Protestors rejected two months of quarantine and social-distancing norms to march through Peckham, Brixton, Trafalgar Square and past Downing Street. They gathered in London's Hyde Park and Manchester's Parliament Square with placards and loudspeakers. Signs reading 'Black Lives Matter' were pinned to living-room windows and graffitied on white vans. Louder calls were made to defund the police. On 7 June, the statue of eighteenth-century slave trader Edward Colston in Bristol was toppled and thrown into the harbour's waters. The novel deadliness of the virus fell back into second place in the news for the first time in months, behind the timelessness of racism. Helicopters started to circle overhead in central London on a daily basis.

With people stuck in their homes, forty-three police forces across the United Kingdom would report an average fall of 18 per cent in crime between May and June. Although issues like domestic violence and cyber-crime were untouched, if not exacerbated, lockdown meant that London's streets became safer. Yet police use of stop-and-search zoomed upwards, especially against those suspected of drug possession. The Met carried out 30,608 stops in April and 43,000 stops in May 2020 compared to 21,000 and 20,981 stops during these months one year earlier (2019 had faced the first year-on-year increase in uses of the measure in a decade).

The clunky racism which plagues the police force's tactics – highlighted in Chapter 4 – was predictably borne out within this year's shift. Between March and May, Black men aged fifteen to twenty-four were stopped 21,950 times in London, a number which equates to roughly a third of this entire demographic's population (although some were likely stopped more than once). Of these searches, 80 per cent yielded no results. This meant that for someone who was young, Black, male and seeing out the lockdown from the confines of an inner-city social housing estate – as Jhemar, Carl and Demetri were all doing – they would not only have to remain indoors more than usual, in cramped conditions, but if they dared step outside, they would be more likely than at any other point over the last decade to be fruitlessly stopped and searched on suspicion of being in possession of drugs.

On 25 June, vans full of police officers were run out of Angell Town housing estate in Brixton by young residents after trying to intercept a block party (as they'd been doing in high-density housing areas across the city in an attempt to enforce social-distancing rules). Just over one week later, however, on Saturday 4 July, photos of Soho's trendy streets rammed with adult party-goers and bar drinkers circulated online. Police officers watched the crowds from raised platforms. As ever, the difference between the way people were being policed, and therefore granted or denied freedom, could too easily be delineated by class, geography, age and race.

Coinciding with lockdown in March, schools were ordered to remain closed for all students apart from the children of key workers. Until July pupils were either taught lessons remotely via the internet or homeschooled by their parents. The images of empty corridors and classrooms, and the necessity for teenagers to be spending even more of their time glued to a screen, became a bleak vision of what the robotic future of state education might look like: bulk-buy, cheap, virtual and insensitive to household circumstance. Students lost the routine of the school run, the opportunity to socialize with their peers and the encouragement to take part in regular exercise. The National Foundation for Education Research (NFER) found from polling 3,000 teachers that 98 per cent of them believed their students had not made much progress in their learning over lockdown. Vital developmental years of all young people – from the young in primary school to the old in sixth-form colleges – were stymied.

But the development of disadvantaged young people would be

hindered more than anyone. Some schools in the most deprived parts of the country reported that more than 50 per cent of their pupils did not have access to a computer, leaving them forced to complete work on their smartphones. The phrase 'digital poverty' entered common educational parlance. In May, the Institute of Fiscal Studies surveyed more than 4,000 families to find that by the end of the month children in wealthier families had received 1.5 weeks more learning than poorer children over lockdown. The NFER polled teachers at the start of the next academic year, in September 2020, finding them to estimate that their average student lost out on three months of learning due to the lockdown. This estimation rose to four or more months for students living in the poorest areas. Teachers deemed 44 per cent of all students to need intensive catch-up support. This proportion rose to 57 per cent in deprived areas. The Education Endowment Foundation predicted that the attempts to close the attainment gap between disadvantaged students and their wealthier peers made since 2011 – the progress that academy schools like Willow have managed to achieve for an entire generation of learners – would be reversed. By studying primary school children across the summer holidays of 2020, the median estimate was that the educational inequality gap between poor and rich children would widen by 36 per cent.

Predictions about school exclusions took a turn for the worse. A paper published by Oxford University's Excluded Lives Research team expressed fears that there would be a surge in exclusions on return to school as students who were already at risk were pushed still further away from the reach of limited mainstream educational staff bodies and resources.

> Over-represented groups include children and young people with Special Educational Needs and Disabilities (SEND), from particular ethnic backgrounds and those living in areas of high

deprivation [the report summarized]. Heightened anxiety, bereavement, poverty, disconnection from schooling and the digital divide have heightened the risk for children and young people who were already struggling with aspects of schooling and produced new unexpected categories of risk.

With challenges, however, came solutions. Tens of thousands of teachers found their own ways of adapting to the crisis and holding the attention of their students online. The National Tutoring Programme was later launched by the government so that for the 2020/2021 academic year, tutoring would be made available to state school students who had fallen behind. The Access Project's volunteer tutors delivered a total of 5,600 virtual tutorial hours, and the charity's team completed 1,003 check-ins and 96 group workshops about higher education (including 28 parents' evenings) remotely. They managed to get one of their funders to raise money to buy sixty Dell laptop computers, which were installed with Microsoft Office and couriered out to students. Willow Academy's leadership team lobbied their corporate contacts to do the same, as did plenty of schools across the country, signifying a key advantage to the model of being well-connected to big business when government support is lacking.

On Thursday 13 August, A-level results day, an algorithm used by Ofqual, the government's Office of Qualifications and Examinations Regulation, was estimated to have downgraded the results of 40 per cent of students across the country. Teenagers attending state schools, especially those with historically low grades, were downgraded most.

Islington-based eighteen-year-old student and writer Abubakar Finiin – who received four years of tutoring from The Access Project and six months of remote journalism mentoring from myself, as part of RoadWorks, throughout lockdown – was accepted by Oxford University to study Politics, Philosophy and Economics. But his grade for History had been a B, dropping him below his original offer. He'd never received anything lower than an A in the subject. In an article he wrote for *Vice*, Finiin spoke to one young woman who missed her offer of AAA to study at Oxford after she got ACC, having been predicted A*AA. Another student was predicted A*AAA but got BBDD and missed her chance to study Medicine at Imperial College London. All the while, students at wealthy independent schools saw their grades jump upwards at a higher year-on-year increase than ever before. Four days later the Education Secretary Gavin Williamson was forced to U-turn on the algorithm's use, allowing grades to be calculated by teacher predictions instead.

The deep embeddedness of social media predictably got deeper over the lockdown. Applications like Houseparty, allowing users to host a virtual party with their friends over their smartphones, spiked, with people seeking new ways to connect. In the thirty days between mid-March and mid-April the app was estimated to have received over 50 million sign-ups worldwide. Video conferencing call apps experienced a record number of 62 million downloads in March alone; by May, the popular workplace application Zoom had experienced a 535 per cent rise in downloads from January. Within weeks, getting things done over Zoom would become normal. Meanwhile, overall time spent on apps like Instagram, Snapchat, YouTube and TikTok, a short-form video-sharing platform proving especially popular among teenagers, all soared.

I learnt about the implications of the lockdown for social media use among young people via my mentoring, which I sustained remotely for RoadWorks, Jacob Sawyer and Spiral. On the one hand, I heard many anecdotes of teenagers spending more time on their phones or playing video games to an extent that would not have been possible under a normal school regime.

On the other hand, the adaptability of digital natives used to leading large chunks of their lives remotely meant that many teenagers appeared quite prepared for the prospect of staying indoors and online.

This willingness to adapt was reflected sonically in the bizarrely successful continuation of youth culture. The masked-up aesthetic of UK drill videos – what had been, in hindsight, the ultimate predictor of London's very own state of mask-wearing hypervigilance and contagion – remained an intimidating symbol of moral panic, but now because of the pandemic, not violent musical content. The self-determination and DIY infra-structure of Black British music meant videos still poured on to YouTube. Some artists had already recorded and filmed enough to drip-feed regular releases without having to worry about new restrictions. Others managed to organize video shoots which either stubbornly disregarded or cleverly abided by social-distancing rules. The video for UK drill stars Frosty, Bandokay and Double Lz's song 'Hate On Us', released on 23 April in the deep depths of lockdown, showed each MC taking separate selfie clips on their smartphones, which were stitched together to form a video that has since been watched millions of times.

My straddling of social networks gave me a split window into the unequal manifestation of the virus's impact in terms of housing. I stayed living in my flat in Brixton for the entirety of lockdown until it eased. But many of those I know, or know of, from secondary school, university and elsewhere – middle-class young professionals with stable jobs; the precise demographic, like myself, who have made affordable parts of central London our home over recent decades – were able to leave London for the outer city or the countryside. Many did so while enjoying state payments from Chancellor Rishi Sunak's 'furlough' scheme without having to work. Meanwhile, every young person and local community member I spoke to in the inner city lasted months in the population-dense boroughs. They often did this without any outdoor space to spend time in apart from public parks, which were policed heavily across April and May. Suddenly, dazzlingly desirable central postcodes lost their revered appeal. Nonetheless, property development continued. On 24 September 2020, the Elephant & Castle shopping centre shut its doors for the final time, with many of its traders left without anywhere to go – much like residents of the Heygate Estate once were. 'In a £1bn-plus project to develop a "new town centre", as part of developer Delancey's wider overhaul of the area,' wrote Dan Hancox in the *Guardian*, 'the shopping centre will be torn down and replaced with gleaming new retail units and malls, and high-end residential towers of up to 34 storeys – and scant affordable housing.'

In the year to March 2020, police recorded 46,000 knife offences, up 6 per cent from the previous year and 51 per cent higher than when this reporting began in 2011. Before lockdown, serious youth violence had been travelling on the same upward slant that began back in 2015. But over the month of May 2020, the *Guardian* reported that stab wounds among under-twenty-fives in London were down 69 per cent from the year before. Met Police Commissioner Cressida Dick told the press that it was a 'silver lining' of the pandemic. With most journalists unable to get out into communities to report on the shifts properly – not that the British print media lends itself to reporting on youth violence at the best of times – and youth services and hospitals preoccupied, the 'knife crime' narrative, after several years of dominating headlines, all but disappeared. It was harder than ever to tell what was actually happening on the roads.

'The coronavirus has widened the problems young people face,' said Franklyn Addo, who caseworked young people at a central London hospital throughout the spring and summer of 2020 – all remotely, from home. 'Under lockdown there has been more apathy among young people. More boredom. And lots of young people were coming to harm – not just from stabbings and shootings, but domestic violence and self-harming – we were all just less aware of it.' If a young person was admitted to hospital, Franklyn would support them via video calls. 'There has been a serious limit to the effectiveness of my work. When I'd be trying to contact other services, like social care, a lot of the time those workers would be at home, too. Or I wouldn't get through and it would just ring out. Young people are forgotten.'

I can sympathize with the professional relief that Dame Cressida Dick must have felt while contemplating the first month since she became Met Commissioner in which youth violence statistics had fallen. But I cannot take her 'silver lining' comment seriously. Those of us with authentic community connections to vulnerable young people knew that tragedy was still in shocking proximity to us all. Weeks before lockdown, one of Carl's friends, who I'd met previously at Jacob Sawyer, was shot in the leg and hospitalized. Weeks into lockdown, another young man, who Carl had befriended at SPAC Nation, was murdered. Two people he knew from another part of Brixton were given life sentences after being convicted of murder later in the summer. (Carl stuck to prayer and athletics.) Silver lining for who?

It would later be revealed that, had the government listened to calls from the World Health Organization to enforce a stricter lockdown earlier, thousands of British deaths and an immeasurable spill-out of stress, heartache and financial instability could have been prevented. Johnson missed emergency Cobra meetings. There weren't enough ventilators, masks, hospital beds. Repeated promises of mass quick-testing would remain unfulfilled well into the autumn. The idea of 'herd immunity' – letting people catch the virus and thus either die or become immune to it – was put into practice and was then scrapped. There were other U-turns: from removing the NHS surcharge for non-EU migrant workers,

to extending the free-school-meals scheme for low-income households throughout the summer holidays (only after Manchester
United and England footballer Marcus Rashford campaigned for
it), to whether students and teachers would be expected to wear
masks on their return to school in September.

The hypocrisy of ministers clapping for the NHS every
Thursday between 26 March and 28 May, having voted as a government to halt pay rises for junior doctors and nurses over the
previous decade, rang as loud as the claps themselves. Indeed,
the clapping ritual stopped days after Dominic Cummings,
Boris Johnson's right-hand man, was discovered to have broken
the lockdown rules he helped to create when he drove up to
Durham to visit family. After he appeared on a live television
broadcast refusing to apologize, it became clear that it was one
rule for the political class and another for everyone else.

It was widely claimed that austerity officially ended when
Chancellor Rishi Sunak made the first real-terms increase in
public spending for over a decade on 6 March 2020. But if the
government had enough money to pay the entire population
not to work and to stay in their homes under his 'furlough'
scheme, surely it could have paid for the public services whose
suffocation has led to the suffering and death of poor, vulnerable people all along? Surely investing properly in public
infrastructure could have prepared us? If there has been enough
money to grant local authorities to, say, house their homeless
populations in hotels, thus keeping the virus at bay – as several
local councils across the country did – why was there not enough
money to do something like this before? The 'magic money
tree' that Theresa May famously claimed did not exist in 2017,
while responding to a nurse complaining about her eight-year
pay freeze, seemed to sprout suddenly in 2020. In contrast to the
ignorable, arms-length disaster of teenagers killing one another,
of course – a problem that most of the population can be

persuaded has nothing to do with us – the coronavirus inspired a different course of action.

Based on figures from the Office for Budget Responsibility in September 2020, the Treasury's independent budget forecaster, spending on Covid-19 could see UK government borrowing reach £400 billion for the 2020/2021 financial year. In August 2020 alone the Conservative government borrowed a record £36 billion to help fund the furlough scheme, 'Eat Out to Help Out' (subsidies for restaurant, bar and cafe meals to encourage people to spend their money on food) and other measures, pushing overall UK government debt to over £2 trillion, which is more than the value of the entire UK economy. To put this into perspective, after years of failed attempts to lobby government to spend more on services affecting serious youth violence, in March 2020 campaigners such as the APPG on Knife Crime and Violence Reduction called on the government to invest 'a minimum of £1.57 billion in children and youth services in the budget and upcoming Spending Review'. That investment would be just 0.39 per cent of what the government would be set to borrow across the tax year in which Covid-19 hit, and 0.075 per cent of overall government debt. It is 4 per cent of what the government borrowed in August 2020 alone.

'Maybe through the coronavirus people will see how we fix problems,' said Sarah Jones MP, when we spoke over Zoom during the lockdown. 'The role that politicians play in that narrative as we come out of coronavirus will be unbelievably important because we could potentially steer people towards thinking that we could fix violence if we intervened in places. But the worry is that they won't because after the crisis there will be people saying we need to raise taxes to raise money for what's happened, and the government will go back to saying, we can't put money towards youth work because we need to put money into the hole we've created through resolving the coronavirus.'

People stuck in the trap of the criminal justice system had to deal with a double lockdown. And for those who had not yet been tried or sentenced there were a spread of repercussions. Criminal defence lawyers reported instances in which judges have passed more lenient sentences than usual: less time in custody or a non-custodial sentence, when ordinarily immediate custody would be imposed, in order to avoid yet more overcrowding in prisons. They also noted that, often with the encouragement of the judge, prosecutors have been more proactive in reviewing cases and discontinuing those where the public interest in proceeding isn't particularly strong, or where an alternative to criminal sanctions can be agreed between the parties.

But as the impact of lockdown sunk in, more trials were delayed, leaving many prisoners on remand – incarcerated without a conviction or sentence – for a time period that would not, under normal circumstances, be allowed. This means there were growing numbers of men and women stuck in prison without having been found guilty and without a timeline for when they were going to have a trial or be sentenced.

Prisoners in England and Wales were stuck under 'twenty-three-hour bang-up' over the lockdown. They had limited time to clean, exercise, do their laundry, go to healthcare or make calls – like someone being kept on a basic regime. Opportunities for education and visitors were cancelled. Prisoners used an application called Purple Visits to make secure video calls to their friends and family. One prisoner I spoke to was sent to a Category C prison in January, and he described how the conditions he lived under for at least half of the time after that meant he felt like he was living under Category A strictness, despite his good behaviour and 'enhanced' status.

Either prisoners spent long stretches of time in solitary confinement with no mental or social stimulation or they remained stuck in one of the many overcrowded prisons. The *New Statesman* reported that prison officers were fewer in numbers than usual, with up to a third self-isolating; suggestions to take the pressure off by releasing 4,000 low-risk prisoners in April were later scrapped (by comparison, Iran released 85,000 prisoners in May).

If the youth sector across the country had already been decimated by austerity, Covid-19 brought a hammer to its weakened foundations. Much like teachers, youth workers were forced to reconcile needing to check in on a growing number of vulnerable young people in precarious circumstances at home with the expectation that their jobs were under threat. In June 2020, London Youth published a report, 'Running on Reserves', about the impact of Covid-19 on London's youth sector. They found that 47 per cent of organizations in the capital who responded to their polling had furloughed their staff. They also found that funders had responded well to the crisis, providing 66 per cent of organizations with emergency funding and 34 per cent with unrestricted funding. But this was little consolation after a decade of drastic cuts to the sector. The report stated that 31 per cent of organizations expressed concern that they could be unable to operate by the end of 2020, while 73 per cent said that the mental health of their young people had been affected. Over half felt that their young people had not received necessary mental health support, nor were they living in a safe environment.

Jacob Sawyer, however, made it through the lockdown by providing remote counselling and casework check-in services to local young people. A number of new initiatives were launched, including Cook-to-Care in April, providing free, daily food for those in need across Lambeth. The organization distributed roughly 1,000 meals per week to local people over twenty weeks across the spring and summer of 2020, all of which were cooked in Jacob Sawyer's kitchen. Carl volunteered at Jacob Sawyer all summer long.

Reveal and I put our heads together for RoadWorks to create

a three-part educational video series called 'Drillosophy', a part-nership with popular YouTube channel Mixtape Madness. The episodes used UK rap and drill lyrics to explore philosophical themes: knowledge and perception in Episode 1 (which Skengdo, AM and Jhemar featured in), the catharsis of storytelling in Episode 2 (which Franklyn Addo featured in), and panopticon and surveillance in Episode 3 (which Demetri featured in). We created accompanying worksheets for parents and educators to use at home with young people. Our videos were watched tens of thousands of times all over the world.

In the middle of July I video-called Demetri to read him the last chapter of *Cut Short*. We'd not spoken in a while; he'd been quiet since the beginning of lockdown, even for his elusive standards, as he finished his first year of undergraduate work at Goldsmiths.

'How's it going? Any news?' I asked him when he picked up, like I always do.

'Yeah. You're not gonna believe this one, though, still . . .' he replied with a big, cheesy grin. For someone usually so serious, his expression suggested he had something important to share. I could never have imagined what was around the corner.

'Uh-oh, what is it? Is it good?'

'Yeah, fam. It's good.'

He flipped his phone camera from the front to the back, so that instead of showing his face, it broadcast what – or who – was in front of him.

A newborn baby boy was lying in his cot sleeping. He was less than two weeks old. Demetri had become a father during the pandemic. I will forever be baffled how he managed to keep it from me until then.

Glossary

back the shank – draw the knife

bait – well known, easily recognizable, obvious

bally – a balaclava

bando – also known as a 'trap house', where addicts and dealers gather to consume and sell illegal drugs

bare – very, or in other contexts, a lot of (e.g. 'bare people' is 'a lot of people')

beg it – desperately try to impress

buck – to bump into, to meet with

burn – tobacco

burst – to be shot

casing a place – preparing to rob somewhere

cat – a drug addict

certi – certified, authentic, cool

chef – to stab someone

county lines – describes the practice of travelling out of London to smaller towns or cities in order to distribute drugs

cunch – short for 'country', meaning the countryside or a smaller town or city outside of London, where drug dealers travel in order to distribute drugs; this practice has become known as 'county lines'

dark – heroin

deep it – to reflect on or deeply consider something

dip – to stab

doing bits – excelling

ends – one's local area

fed – a police officer

flicky – a flick knife

food – illegal drugs

g-checked – to be asked where you are from by a group of unfamiliar, suspicious people in an attempt at intimidation; to be confronted by someone in an intimidating way

gassed – excited or overconfident

GM – gang member

hella – a large amount of

L – a loss (e.g. of money or drugs)

lacking – to be outnumbered, unprotected, caught off-guard

light – crack cocaine

line – a mobile telephone number, typically contacted for business

mandem – a group of males

on crud – willing to commit crimes, such as engaging in acts of violence and/or drug-dealing

on ends – in one's local area

on my Js – on my own

opps – members of the opposition, or enemies, who often live in a rival part of London

pack – a quantity of drugs, usually a large amount that is ready to cut down and sell

paigon – an enemy, or just someone who antagonizes you

pattern – to fix up or sort oneself out, to organize

peak – bad or awful

pebs – small amounts of crack cocaine or heroin

pen – prison

peng – nice, beautiful

permed – to be permanently excluded from school

PRU – Pupil Referral Unit, where young people are sent after being excluded from and/or deemed unsuitable for mainstream education

score a point – to stab or shoot an enemy, thus improving one's position on the 'scoreboard', an imagined, vague ranking system of the most feared young men

shank – a knife

shook – to be scared or nervous

shotting – selling

shotting hard food – selling Class A drugs

slip – a risky or dangerous situation; the result of getting caught

strap – a gun

tapped – mentally unstable, unusual, eccentric

trap house – a place where addicts and dealers gather to consume and
  sell illegal drugs

undie – an undercover police officer

wagwan – what's going on (?)

whip – a car

Acknowledgements

Cut Short would not exist without the support of a vast, diverse community of people. Some helped me to realize, understand and write its story. Others helped me to refine my youth work practice, research methods, aims and arguments. Others lent me their time, ear and voice. Others kept me energized, smiling and moving forward. Many did all of these things, and more.

Thank you, Matt Turner, for planting the seed, and Connor Brown for nurturing it. Thank you, Chloe Davies, Rose Poole, Amelia Fairney and Poppy North, for helping me get this book into people's hands, and everyone else at Viking and Penguin who worked on it.

Thank you, Jesse James Solomon, for the epigraph. Thank you, Dave, Nas, Burial, 150, Jorja Smith, Mizormac, One Acen, Bis (RIP), Jesse James Solomon & Suspect, Jehst, Headie One & Skepta, Sav'O, Ray BLK and, last but not least, Rippa, for the chapter title inspirations. Thank you to the artists and thinkers mentioned in this book whose music and words I have mined for educational gold; whose ideas and artwork enabled me to make greater sense of my home city.

Thank you to everyone I spoke to in the process of thinking about and writing this book: Andre, Lucy Knell-Taylor, Lita Wallis, Ria Chatterjee, Ben Mace, Joel Balkwill, Ben Kahn, Miranda and Amanda Elie, Renford Carr, Luke Billingham, Gavin Hales, Jack Rowlands, Adam Elliot-Cooper, Caleb Femi, Tasnima Ahmed, Aneesha Hussain, Hema, Joshua Adeyemi, Tatiana Walker, Forrest Stuart, Craig Pinkney, Daniel Renwick, Jaja Soze, Corey Johnson, Skengdo, AM, TK & SK of

Finesse Foreva, Dan Ayim, Kwabz Ayim, Gary Younge, Sarah Jones MP, Tom Hughes, Karen Graham, Mafs, Naim, Elena Papamichael, Mike Etienne, Hannah Pittaway, Tania de St Croix, Keir Irwin-Rogers, Lib Peck, Ebinehita Iyere and Pastor Lorraine Jones.

Thank you to the organizations and individuals I have worked or connected with over the years who each played their role, big or small, in my personal development and the impact of the work completed in these pages: staff at the IntoUniversity Brixton Hill centre, The Access Project (Lucy Ball), the Spiral family, School Ground Sounds, Advocacy Academy, Redthread (John Poyton), Juvenis (Winston Goode), Milk & Honey, Young Urban Arts Foundation (Kerry O'Brien), the HighRise Theatre mandem, SoundSkool (Samuel Conley), Through Unity (uncles Bob Singha and Robin Lockhart), Franklin Scholars, Year Here, Divert, Carney's Community Centre and UK Youth.

Thank you, Ira Campbell, Daryl Cyprien, Patricia Cyprien, Margaret Pierre, Adam Rinarelli, Andrew Tulloch, Jojo Sureh, Emmanuel Imiure, Jonathan Saint Marie, Neville Thomas, Darren Duncan-Paig, Fabio Carvajal, Jessica Pero, Jacqueline Gomes-Neves, Solomon Smith, Mahamed Hashi, Conroy Grant, Haroon, Clemency Penn and Cyrus Gilbert-Rolfe.

Thank you, Monica, for biscuits, life lessons and my copy of *Oliver Twist*. Thank you to all the members of school staff for seeing value in me, holding me to account, providing belief, companionship and support, and doing the work you do, especially Maureen Malcolm-Douglas, Holly Rigby and Derya Maci.

Thank you to the young men and women I've worked with in different spaces – especially anyone on TAP and all of the original heroes. Please get in touch if you read this!

Thank you to everyone who has helped to pave the Road-Works way so far: Ore Shoderu the Icon, Henry Onilude, F.M. the Southside Shinobi, Abubakar Finiin, Hayden Magezi,

Milli-Rose Rubin, Edwina Omokaro, Casey Brown, Ishmatic Beats, Sound Connections, Livity, Social Switch Project, Youth Music and more. Thank you, Annie and T, for helping to launch a star.

Thank you, Tony, for your unmatched wisdom and strength; for always being there to talk to; for being honest, wise, supportive, critical and giving me a sense of responsibility and direction.

Thank you, Carl, for showing me what resilience, humility and hope really mean; for being patient and trusting; for motivating me; for underlining the values of respect and gratitude in all situations. Thank you for teaching me how to run faster, and not give up. Thank your mum for being there and praying for me.

Thank you, Jhemar, for making me laugh and showing me the purest form of hope. Thank you for helping me find purpose. Thank you for the bars rapped over Zoom and phone calls. Thank you, Michael, Patricia and Jerome, for making me feel part of the family; for the Christmas cards, phone call check-ins, Tupperware boxes of stew chicken and gifts from Jamaica.

Thank you, Demetri, for the hours put in mentoring, reading, writing, studying and thinking; for the old-soul spirit that can't be taught. Thank you for being the ultimate apprentice. Thank you, Xavion, for arriving in this world just in time to remind me what really matters — by the time you get to read this, your dad's mark will have been made. Thank you, Shauna and Joseph, for raising such a legend.

May Jerrell, Michael, Dayo and others mentioned in this book who lost their lives prematurely, rest in peace.

Thank you, Rory Bradshaw, for inspiring me to work with young people; Tristan Bejawn for that zen approach and photographic eye; Franklyn Addo for the calm and steady voice at the end of the phone; Reveal for problem-solving, hip-hop lectures and cups of tea; Jake Jones for the relentless commitment to my cause; Dan GG for visits, walks and talks; Benjy for wavy art; Ed for political conversations; Kartik for philosophical conversations; Suki for more philosophical conversations, and your generous spirit contributing to these pages; Koyejo for musical flavours, past, present and future, and hosting such a brave intervention; Jacob for teenage urban adventures; Rory C for a strategic ear; Mim for Tooting debriefs. Thank you, Husam, Arjun, Bobby, Fernando, Louis Dragon, Bezza, Jasmine, Ollie, Kumara and many others for love, laughter and loyalty. Rhys for the wheelbarrow. Cousin Joel for being the older brother I never had. Jaden and Ez for replenishing my energy. Koosha for the rooftop.

Thank you, editors, mentors and role models. Armand Attard for introducing me to JC. Matt Bamford-Bowes, Anoosh Chakelian, Chal Ravens and Tom Seymour for giving me a shot. Dan Hancox, Simon Wheatley and Sam Knight for setting a fine example. K Biswas and The Race Boat for solidarity. Jonathan Heaf for seeing the vision. Ceri Thomas for Chicago. George Mpanga, Akala, Zadie Smith, Hanif Kureishi, Nikesh Shukla, Riz Ahmed and David Simon, among many others, for laying vital blueprints.

Thank you to the Tiffin staff whose teaching will stay with me forever: Martin 'Coach' Williams for longevity; John Haskey for politics; Naomi Anson for sparking my deeper love of the English language, Jo Humphreys for reinforcing it. Thank you, Mike Otsuka, for introducing me to moral philosophy. Thank you, Peter Forbes, for helping me discover narrative non-fiction.

Thank you to my family for the love and support. Dad for playing me vinyls. Mum for reading to me. Sian and Naomi for your smiles. Grandma Thapar for prayer and chapati. Grandpa Thapar for cricket and leadership. Grandma Sheila for walks and kindness. Gramps for security. Aunties, uncles and cousins for protecting me. Asmaa and Fatima for being fans of my dreams. JP and Alex for giving me a place to escape to. Julie, Rodrigo, Lauren and everybody else for welcoming me.

Thank you, more than anyone on this planet, Yasmin. For reading, correcting, laughing, crying, dancing, singing, mirroring, loving, lockdowning, debating, creating and staying. Thank you for making me whole; for encouraging me at the depths and celebrating with me at the heights. Thank you for believing in me. Thank you for leading the way.

Index